Praise for *Show Me the Bodies: How We Let Grenfell Happen*

Winner of the Orwell Prize for Political Writing 2023

'*Show Me the Bodies* is a clear, moving and powerful account of Britain's worst fire since the Second World War... Never before, in years of reviewing books about buildings, has one brought me to tears. This one did.'

Rowan Moore, *Observer* Book of the Week

'*Show Me the Bodies* will never leave the mind of anyone who reads it. The tragedy is that those who should read it probably won't.'

Guardian

'A searing indictment of the construction industry and regulators... The book that follows reads like a prosecution, meticulous and fierce.'

The Times

'A jaw-dropping account of a callous system that swept individual conscience aside in favour of profit and politics. It is hard to convey how moving and enraging the book is – I urge you to read it for yourself. Because one thing almost all of us have been guilty of since the worst disaster in the UK this century is complacency.'

Evening Standard

'However painful the story of Grenfell is, it is one we must hear. Apps' powerful testament tells us how injustice was manifested and how lessons still fail to be learned.'

David Lammy

'Enormously important... A painstaking chronicle of an entirely avoidable tragedy, its aftermath and its causes.'

James O'Brien, LBC

'A harrowing account of the fire itself and a searing indictment of the society that allowed it to happen.'

Financial Times

Apps writes that Grenfell "tells us something about... the priority our political and economic system places on human life – especially when those lives are likely to be poor, immigrant and from ethnic minority backgrounds." He has done their stories justice with this urgent book.'

Prospect

'The best account of the tragedy and an unsparing indictment of the disregard for working-class lives that made it possible.'

Jacobin

Homesick

How Housing Broke London
and How to Fix It

PETER APPS

A Oneworld Book

First published by Oneworld Publications Ltd in 2025

Copyright © Peter Apps, 2025

The moral right of Peter Apps to be identified as the Author of this work has been asserted by him in accordance with the Copyright, Designs, and Patents Act 1988

All rights reserved
Copyright under Berne Convention
A CIP record for this title is available from the British Library

ISBN 978-1-83643-036-0
eISBN 978-1-83643-035-3

Typeset by Geethik Technologies
Printed and bound in Great Britain by Clays Ltd, Elcograf S.p.A.

No part of this publication may be reproduced, stored in a retrieval system, or transmitted, in any form or by any means, electronic, mechanical, photocopying, recording or otherwise, or used in any manner for the purpose of training artificial intelligence technologies or systems, without the prior permission of the publishers.

The authorised representative in the EEA is eucomply OÜ,
Pärnu mnt 139b–14, 11317 Tallinn, Estonia
(email: hello@eucompliancepartner.com / phone: +33757690241)

Oneworld Publications Ltd
10 Bloomsbury Street
London WC1B 3SR
England

Stay up to date with the latest books,
special offers, and exclusive content from
Oneworld with our newsletter

Sign up on our website
oneworld-publications.com

Contents

Introduction	1
Past	13
1980s	15
1990s	50
2000s	73
2010s	103
Present	145
Social housing	147
Private renting	157
Buying a home	171
Homelessness	179
Future	187
Exodus	189
Generation rent growing old	214
Housing in the Anthropocene	233
Another way	251
Acknowledgements	302
The Londoners	304
Notes	306
Index	338

*To Samuel, Benjamin and all the other children
who call London home*

Introduction

The detritus of London's gig economy is scattered around the living room: chunky, weatherproof coats with the branding of a popular food delivery app hang on the door and an e-bike is plugged into a charger. A high-vis vest is draped across the arm of the sofa, work boots next to it. A retail uniform is drying on a rack. This is the living space in typical working-class housing in the city.

One of the tenants clatters down the stairs and into the room, alarmed. 'What is going on here?' he asks, Indian accent, a thick black hoodie pulled over his head against the chill, glasses slightly foggy.

'It's just a property viewing,' says the agent. The tenant mutters something and returns to his room.

Outside in the backyard, one of the tenants has erected a makeshift weather shelter – timber battens and sheeting create a flimsy canopy which is lopsided following a recent storm. There are chairs laid out under it and a few scattered beer bottles and cigarette butts. I imagine the residents of the house unwinding here after a shift, sharing a moment before returning to their individual rooms.

The stairs lead us up to a landing – whitewashed walls, numbered doors with individual locks, fire exit signs and emergency lighting. I shudder as I note the wooden bannisters and narrow carpeted stairs. If a fire broke out, it would rip through this escape route in minutes. We reach a loft conversion, which provides two further rooms and a tiny bathroom, choking with the twin smells of mildew and bleach.

The agent shows me into the front bedroom. Bare floorboards, a double bed and a couple of flatpack wardrobes. Judged by eye, I'd say it's about 120 square feet. The bed takes up most of the floorspace. The room is too cold for me to want to take my hands out of my pockets, and if I stand close to the window my breath comes out in clouds. I notice new paint above, sloppily applied – the black mould it was supposed to cover up is still visible in the top corner.

'How much is the rent?' I ask the agent.

'£1,000 a month,' she says. 'But we might negotiate to £950, say.'

She tells me I will need to provide a month's rent in advance and a deposit of £1,000.

'You have a British passport?'

I nod.

'Good, that helps,' she says. 'We will just need three months of bank statements to make sure you can afford it.'

My work is flexible, I explain. I have money, but I might earn more in one month than the rest. Her eyes become a little steely.

'You need to be able to afford the rent. One day late and we charge fines every day until it is paid.'

I just nod, not seeing the point in mentioning that this is illegal under the Tenant Fees Act 2019. We leave the property together and she thanks me for coming, shutting up her keys in a key box next to the front door that gives her access to the property at any hour (also illegal).

I step outside and look around this cold, crisp December morning, with bright blue skies and a biting wind. The cars on the road are shedding their overnight frost, and a couple of people hurry past, swaddled in scarves, gloves and winter coats. Plastic Santa is aglow in one of the homes opposite.

It is an odd feeling standing here, like a dream.

This is the road I grew up on. My childhood home is four doors away on the other side of the street. Locked-away memories of my early years start to push their way forward.

It doesn't look that different. These are pokey, two-up two-down Victorian terrace homes, built for dock workers. For decades, most of them were privately let by the Scrutton family, a large East End family business which has been active in the property market here since the nineteenth century. After World War II, these neighbourhoods managed to escape the slum clearances which saw 85 per cent of this type of housing demolished in this area of London.[1]

As such, I find myself in a bit of a time capsule, the mazy streets, brick-built homes and front doors which open straight onto the road looking like the set of a period drama about the Blitz. The homes are closing in on 150 years old and are showing their age. Paint flakes from walls, chimneys have gone crooked and the yellow, black and orange bricks look like they would crumble at a touch.

There is more double glazing now than I remember, more white plastic front doors and more electric cars parked on the street. But otherwise, I may as well have stepped out of my home in the early 1990s, on my way to the primary school at the end of the road.

That familiarity is an illusion. The truth is that the thirty-six years that encompass my life so far have changed areas in London like this beyond any recognition. And the driver of that change has been housing.

In 1987, my dad came here seeking a home, just as I have today. His financial circumstances were similar to those I've just described: an income which is not terrible but a little uncertain. Some months he would do well, others he would need to scrape by a little. My dad left school at fourteen with no qualifications and an expectation that he would work in the docks. But he was able to pursue his talent for drawing to art college, and from there into studios in central London where he worked in advertising and publishing as a professional illustrator. By the time I came along, he was freelance – picking up work mostly from Christian book publishers, which kept our family afloat but came with the precarity of the odd dry period.

In 1987, that sort of financial position was enough to buy one of these houses. My parents secured a £26,000 loan from a building society and paid an interest-only mortgage, which amounted to a monthly cost of about £200. Adjusted for inflation, this would be £73,000 overall and £565 a month in today's money, which meant buying a home was something young families – nurses, teachers, post office clerks, bus drivers, mechanics, builders – could do. I grew up in a London where the children of all of these professions lived in homes their families owned, with gardens, their own bedrooms, living rooms and kitchens where they could enjoy family meals, birthday teas and the sense of security which is so foundational to a happy childhood. Even for those who could not afford to buy, there was abundant social housing and private sector tenancies that offered long-term security and rent control.

The result was a permanent community, stretching back to World War II and beyond. We lived next door to an octogenarian East End couple we called Lord and Lady Darlow. They had lived together in the house since before the Blitz. The dinner ladies at my primary school had homes down the street and I knew where most of the children from my class lived. We'd go to each other's houses after school or play on the green at the end of the road in the summer, buying Tangy Toms 10p crisps and cherry-flavoured 'twist and squeeze' drinks from the corner shop with pocket money.

It wasn't always a pleasant area. Anyone who lived there in the 1990s will remember the odd, thick and faintly putrid smell that wafted from the nearby Pura Foods factory, as it manufactured processed oils and fats for export around the world. There were whispers of organised crime and regular stories of murders and muggings. Our house was burgled when I was four, the intruders fleeing when my sister went downstairs to the toilet. Children at my school came in malnourished; more than half the class seemed to have asthma. There was a girl who was teased about her dirty clothes every time we got changed for PE and a little boy who lived a few doors away from us, who would be shut out in the back garden in his pants, even at night and in the rain, when his mother lost her temper.

But it was a place where a family could find a home. These old buildings, rickety, cold and draughty as they may have been, offered security and space for children to grow up as part of a community. Immigration was already widespread in London at this time but immigrants also had permanence – the opportunity to forge their own communities or to join pre-existing ones.

In just thirty-six years, this has vanished. Most of these homes are not owned by the people that live in them, but by a wide variety of landlords. And they do not offer a home to one family, but rooms to many. The current generation of low-income Londoners are squeezed for well over half their salaries to get a dingy room and offered no security beyond the end of a six-month tenancy. The result is that the community has gone: died or moved out to Essex, and it has been replaced by transience, unfamiliarity and atomisation.

This is no accident. We have deliberately changed the primary purpose of houses from providing a home for a family to providing an income-generating asset for an investor. Social homes have been sold off, private rents have been allowed to spiral, tenants' security has been stripped away and house prices have exploded beyond incomes. The year of my birth, 1988, saw the birth of a new London – the year in which a new Housing Act opened the door for a deregulated rental sector, with no control on rents and no long-term security for tenants. I was among the last generation of Londoners born into an affordable and secure city, and my lifetime has seen that security systematically dismantled.

On Avenons Road, homes now change hands for £450,000 each if you are buying outright – meaning you would need a household income of £100,000 to get a regular bank mortgage, or a very large cash deposit. Within a generation, homes which were available to low-income families are now unattainable for anyone but the top 5 per cent of earners.[2]

In 2023, I found a home identical to the one I grew up in down the same street. Marketed by Unwind Holidays, the inside has been entirely renovated: plush leather couches, gold and brown furnishings, exposed timber floors and a manicured fake lawn in the back garden. 'This beautifully furnished house is a perfect base for visiting London with fantastic transport links,' boasts the property description. 'Canning Town is a diverse and unique area to live. With huge redevelopment taking place, it really is a great place to be.'[3] At the time of writing, the property cost £489 for a single night. These profits have come at the cost of a generation's chance at finding a place to call home.

*

The idea of 'home' has been explored in writing, both academic and personal. It is one of those slippery concepts which we all innately understand but struggle to pin down.

Home seems to be more easily identified as a feeling rather than a building. One definition which has stayed with me comes from Alain de Botton. 'Home', he writes, 'is the place where we can stop being the various selves that society has demanded that we be. We can close the door, breathe out and simply exist. We need a home in the psychological sense as much as we need one in the physical: to compensate for a vulnerability... [at home] we can slowly resume contact with a more authentic self, who was there waiting in the wings for us to end our performance.'[4] At home, we can just be.

Perhaps survival is at the core of what our brains are seeking in a 'home'. We have evolved from being small, vulnerable creatures in a vast, hostile wilderness to the planet's dominant species through our ability to form collective societies. Our survival depends on belonging to a bigger system, and a home affords us ownership of that feeling. My country, my town, my village, my street, my house, my room. These attachments are so strong that we go into fight mode as soon as we're under threat, from a teenager slamming their bedroom door to a nation rallying an army against invasion.

But this feeling is under threat – we are in the midst of what some academics have branded a 'crisis of belonging'.[5] This is something that goes well beyond London. Across the world, our homes, our communities are being taken from us. Those most impacted are those who have literally been forced to leave their homes – the thirty-five million refugees globally, the highest number ever captured by modern statistical reporting.[6] Then there are people who have had to travel to provide for their families – the mass, forced global displacement driven by the inequality of currency values and minimum wage levels, which mean work pays far more in some economies than in others.

But even in Western countries, where people are rarely forced from their homes by war, famine or the need for a salary in US dollars, there is a creeping sense of homesickness – a sense that the world is transforming before our eyes, that we are increasingly adrift and that social bonds are fraying. It is a dangerous state of affairs. In the words of psychology professor

Geoff Cohen, a lack of belonging is 'associated with physical illness, early death, cardiovascular disease, and vulnerability'. 'One of the worst things our central nervous system can say to the rest of our body is "you are alone here",' he says.⁷

The mid-twentieth-century thinker Martin Heidegger, sometimes described as 'the homesick philosopher', wrote widely on the idea of home and its importance. His ideas have enjoyed a renaissance recently and it isn't hard to see why. He explores how dwelling is intrinsic to being human, but modern economies and technological advances are breaking our links with our sense of home and place, leaving us rootless and disorientated.

The troubling thing about this, though, is that Heidegger was a card-carrying member of the Nazi Party. Hitler understood the emotive power in Heidegger's ideas – how people could be motivated and manipulated by an appeal to a lost sense of home and belonging. The modern far right has made the same intellectual leap. Steve Bannon, the former investment banker turned political strategist, who masterminded the rise of Donald Trump, refers to Heidegger as 'my guy'. Björn Höcke, a major figure in the German far-right party Alternative für Deutschland, has also spoken of his fondness for the philosopher. Heidegger's thinking influences the way the modern far right portrays itself as a defender of 'local traditions, heritage and white national identity'.⁸

This sort of toxic nostalgia is always based more in fantasy than fact – harking back to a world that never was, a halcyon, rose-tinted ideal of how much better things *used to be*. These are often fairytales. The idea of a better world that existed before mass immigration, social media and 'woke politicians' glosses over the very real social challenges and poverty which were endemic in many Western countries in the late twentieth century. But, despite their weaknesses, these fantasies still exert a powerful pull, because they gesture to something real: people are being displaced, ways of life are changing at a frightening pace and the ideas we have of home are being disrupted by a global economic model which places zero value on communities. This is a powerful driver of anger, and progressive political movements will continue to lose ground to the far right if they fail to acknowledge it.

Part of the problem is land. The nineteenth-century economist and campaigner Henry George saw land as 'the great fundamental fact' in determining the wellbeing of a society's citizens. He warned that as more wealth was generated, ordinary people would in fact feel poorer, because those with wealth were increasingly buying the land. His solution was to democratise land ownership, nationalise land as a commodity and use it for the public good. But our economy has leaned the other way.

Margaret Thatcher wanted to create a 'property-owning democracy' – where everyone would have the opportunity to become a landowner and get a share of the wealth the country was generating as a result. This worked for one generation following Thatcher's reforms. But it also triggered a mad scramble for this most crucial, wealth-defining commodity. Now, the conflict between land as a place to build homes and communities versus land as a source of wealth and power has become the defining battle of our age. 'The West faces a decisive challenge: to not become a society divided into two classes, the rich landlords and poor tenants,' said Spain's socialist prime minister Pedro Sánchez, in January 2025. In our biggest cities, we're wrestling with this challenge in real time.

And, as more and more of us live in cities, the challenge is only becoming starker. In 2007, for the first time in human history, more than half the human population lived in urban environments rather than rural ones. By 2050, this is projected to rise to two-thirds. At the same time, cities have swelled into expensive, unwelcoming and isolating places; places where you don't find a permanent home, as much as a never-ending struggle for temporary shelter. In a 2016 UN study of 200 cities across the globe, 90 per cent were deemed unaffordable to live in – based on a ratio of house prices to average incomes.[9]

We need to break out of this trend. If the future is to be urban, our urban environments must be liveable. Places where we can foster community, where we have social interaction, where we can count on our neighbours. Places where we can raise children – not in a tiny cell, isolated from everyone and glued to screens, but in neighbourhoods where they can play and belong.

London's story over my lifetime is a lesson in how quickly things can change. It is a story of the consequences of confusing economic growth with progress. It is a story of a city where the value that can be extracted from its buildings has taken precedence over the humans who live inside them. It is a story of a city which is no longer fit for purpose.

We will go back in time to the 1980s, meet some of the Londoners who occupied the city at the time, and follow their stories through to the present crisis. Then we will look to the future, to the bigger, darker challenges looming as climate change accelerates and a generation of renters ages into retirement. And we will figure out how we might build a different city for the future, reclaiming urban environments as our own.

So while this is a story about London, it is also about what is happening elsewhere – in Manchester, Bristol, Edinburgh, Paris, Lisbon, San Francisco, Sydney, Hong Kong, Nairobi and most of the major cities on Earth. Each has its idiosyncrasies, each has a story to tell about prioritising displacement, disenfranchisement and greed over human wellbeing.

Change in London has been rapid but what this shows us is that change is possible. Cities do not simply grow organically.

They are made by humans, by policies, by the flow of money and the struggle between different interests. Just as London lost its soul within one generation, so it can be reclaimed within the next. Doing so would mean accepting what has gone wrong. As such, we must go back to a city that looks and feels completely alien from the one that surrounds us today.

PAST

1980s

THE BOARD SWEPT CLEAN

London in the 1980s was a city on the cusp of change. The bombardment by the German air force during World War II had left scars which took a long time to fix. An estimated 1.1 million houses had been destroyed or damaged during the war, with some poorer areas of the East End in particular so badly bombed they had to be almost entirely rebuilt. By the time the Blitz ended, roughly one in every six Londoners was homeless. The decades before the 1980s had seen the bomb-damaged city restored – craters filled in, new homes built, burned-out industrial facilities torn down and replaced. But if you looked closely, you could glimpse traces of the devastation. Wooden hoardings still ringed off old bombsites, yet to be remediated and redeveloped. Metal stubs were left where railings had been pulled out during the war's 'scrap for victory' drive. Derelict Anderson shelters remained in many gardens – now repurposed as potting sheds, vines creeping across their corrugated iron roofs. Meanwhile, tens of thousands of Victorian-era houses had been branded slums and demolished, the residents moved out to vast new towns on the edge of the city or new social housing estates within it.

Rapid deindustrialisation was stripping London of its old jobs: the docks were closing and moving downriver to Essex, factories were shuttered and heavy industry jobs, the lifeblood of many working-class communities, were vanishing.

The wreckage remained: the dilapidated red brick and broken windows of now deserted warehouses and factories, overgrown canals, disused goods depots and empty, fenced-off power stations pockmarked the city. The capital was 'suffering more severely than any other British city – even Liverpool' from the transformation away from an industrial economy, as Roy Porter argued in his history of the city.[1]

Unions fought – and lost – battles outside London's factories, just as they did on the picket lines in northern mining towns. Jobs still disappeared – overtaken by new technology, outsourced overseas or to other areas of the country. This translated directly into social deprivation: by the end of the decade, inner London topped national tables for poverty, family breakdown, school truancy and crime. It felt much more dangerous and rougher than it does today. Step into a phone box in Bayswater, Marylebone or Earl's Court and it would be plastered with cards for call girls. Areas of east and south London like Hoxton or Peckham, now hotspots for young graduates, were unsafe, with regular street crime.

It was also much dirtier. Landmarks like Westminster Abbey were coated in the soot and smoke of previous centuries. Rising traffic meant highly polluting cars and thick, dark air. Tube trains which had been in service since before World War II rattled and thundered under the city. Empty homes were left abandoned, no buyers willing to pay the money to fit them up to a liveable standard.

Amid this decline and deprivation, the population was falling, continuing a downward trend since the war. From a peak of 8.6 million just before the start of the war, the number of people living in the city fell to a low of just 6.8 million at the start of the 1980s, as people relocated to the new towns being built in a ring around the city, swapping London's pollution and crime for a quiet life in the suburbs.

It was a tough place to be an ethnic minority. A diverse city for centuries, London became even more multi-ethnic after World War II as the government encouraged immigration from British colonies to provide the workforce needed to rebuild the country. Housing was a major challenge for these new arrivals to the city – with discrimination rife in both private and social housing. As a result, they faced the worst of the private rented sector and were hammered by the unemployment of the late 1970s and early 1980s. There were riots in Brixton in 1981 and Tottenham in 1985 – a reaction to the openly racist policing of Black communities in these areas.

There were also large swathes of the city, like Silvertown in the east and Bermondsey in the south, which were unsafe for many minority ethnic communities, as a rising and powerful National Front capitalised on the dissatisfaction and anger in many of the traditional white working-class strongholds. The fascist group organised around pubs – such as the British Flag in Victoria Dock Road in Canning Town – set up advice centres focusing on white housing issues, which pinned the blame for the housing shortage on immigrants, and pressured councils not to allocate housing to Black and Asian families. Violent racist attacks were a fact of life for the city's minority groups. In 1980, 29-year-old Akhtar Ali Baig was stopped by a skinhead gang on East Ham High Street, who spat at him, racially abused him and then stabbed him in the heart with a sheath knife. 'I've just gutted a Paki,' one of the assailants shouted as he fled the scene.[2]

This was London in the 1980s – a dangerous, dark, polluted, broken, depopulating city plagued by ethnic tension. But also very much alive. There were buzzy backstreet pubs, small live music venues, markets and high streets filled with local businesses – family-owned butchers, street traders, tailors, greengrocers. Communities of Commonwealth immigrants, Irish, Jewish and Cockney residents gave areas of the city unique character.

Developers saw an opportunity to remodel a new city from the debris of the old economy – empty warehouses, docks and markets. 'I believe this is the decade in which London will become Europe's capital,' says the gangster played by Bob Hoskins as he leads a boatload of American investors along the Thames in the film *The Long Good Friday*. 'Having cleared away the outdated, we've got mile after mile and acre after acre of land for our future prosperity. No other city in the world has got, right at its centre, such an opportunity for profitable progress.'

This vision was not just fiction. The regeneration of east London's docks, which closed for good in the early 1980s, was one of the biggest inner-city redevelopment projects in the world. Builders dug foundations for new glass and steel skyscrapers and office blocks for London's burgeoning financial district – where the new trading freedoms which the government instituted in the 1980s would replace colonial trade, which the docks had been the centre of for two centuries, as the primary source of the country's wealth.

The London Docklands Development Corporation (LDDC), which was set up under Margaret Thatcher's government and given control of the land in 1981, led the redevelopment. This was an ideologically driven project: chancellor Geoffrey Howe said the docklands were to be a 'test area' for how 'a return to free market principles could bring prosperity and jobs'.[3] But in reality, it was not the free market in operation. Thatcher was suspicious that local authorities and unions were conspiring against the development potential of the former docklands. Labour-run Tower Hamlets Council, for example, wanted the area to be used to support more blue-collar employment. She saw the LDDC as a way to bypass this and create a base for her new, capitalist vision of Britain. Despite her apparent dislike of state intervention, the project was controlled and funded by central government, with billions in public money used to clear the site of its contamination and previous infrastructure, even filling in some of the former docks entirely. The private businesses that built offices and homes here in the years to come would be the beneficiaries of this spend.[4]

In 1987, a modern, driverless light railway opened in the old docklands – snaking out from the new offices into the east of the city, where those who worked in the financial industries could now live. Development projects cropped up along these lines, catering for this wealthier Londoner. And an airport was opened in the former docklands in the same year – a base for international businesspeople to fly directly between London and other financial centres around Europe.

The new financial district came as Thatcher rebuilt the British economy into one which relied on wealth generated by traders. London's time zone made it a convenient trading base between New York and Tokyo, and the London International Financial Futures Exchange (LIFFE) was opened in 1982 – a huge bear pit of city traders, right in the heart of London, where stockbrokers made and lost their fortunes in a buzz of capitalist energy, and then poured out into the surrounding pubs for boozy lunches and late-night drinks.

There was suddenly a new way to get rich in the UK, a vision of wealth which was (theoretically) open to any kid with a school education, a decent head for numbers and the guts to try. Broadgate, near Liverpool Street station in the east of central London, was then largely derelict railway yards. It was promptly transformed into the base of this trading empire. 'Here in a way we are drawing back the curtain of the future,' Thatcher declared at the launch of the development to build it.[5]

As these markets opened, old ones closed. London's historic markets – Billingsgate for fish, Smithfield for meat, Covent Garden for fruit and flowers – moved, their former premises becoming tourist destinations, shopping centres and office space. The cavernous, empty Royal Agricultural Hall was partially demolished and rebuilt as the Business Design Centre. Smaller markets like the Cutler Street gold and silver exchange also disappeared for redevelopment.

Office blocks for the white-collar jobs popped up throughout the city, on top of old markets or bombsites. There was some local anger. 'London needs a new office block like it needs a new plague' was graffitied on the hoardings of one development site in Swiss Cottage.[6] The Victorian terraced homes in working-class areas were increasingly ceded to more middle-class families attracted by their affordability. People were coming to the city again. The falling population plateaued as people began to move to the city once more for work.

London was hurtling into the future, leaving its history behind. Its empty spaces and vacant buildings were becoming the currency of a modern city, untethered from its past. But who was it going to be for?

ANDY*

As a teenager, Andy Plant lived in a council house in Clapham Park. 'Back then it was mostly working-class, rough pubs,' says Andy. 'It wasn't violent, but it was a working-class area.'

He passed his 11+ exams and got a place at the nearest grammar school, which meant a daily mile-and-a-half walk to school in Battersea. He noticed the signs of gentrification as he walked. 'There were rows of nice Edwardian-type housing,' he says. 'On one side of the road you had the corner shop, the off licence, and on the other side you were starting to get delicatessens.'

After he finished school, he joined the army. But during a drill, his foot went down a rabbit hole, his ankle twisted, his heavy pack fell and his shin bone snapped. 'I'm told you could hear the scream from more than a mile away,' he says. His shin healed but his days in the army were over.

He moved back to his aunt's house in Clapham Park, which had started to turn into a tougher place to live. 'It was rough.

---

* A list of the characters who we will follow through the years can be found in the chapter 'The Londoners' at the end of this book.

It was the sort of estate where everyone had an Alsatian or something so that they didn't get attacked if they just went down the shop,' he says.

At that time, punk music was a huge part of his life. He recalls seeing the Damned at a pub in Croydon. 'For my generation punk set so many people free in terms of expressing ourselves,' he continues. 'This was another thing about all of London back then, most of the working-class areas had loads of record shops. We had Dub Vendor in Clapham Junction, which catered for the younger Black community. Walking past there as a teenager and getting almost bowled over by the bass coming out, that got me into reggae.'

THE WOBBLY PILLAR – THE DREAM OF SOCIAL HOUSING

By 1980, London had achieved something remarkable, something which remains vanishingly rare both historically and globally: it had provided abundant municipal housing, giving its population secure, (largely) safe homes and breaking the grip of exploitative landlords. By 1981, 872,426 London households lived in social housing, 34.8 per cent of the city – more than double the 15.1 per cent who rented privately.[7] To put it in context, New York City had 178,000 social housing households at the same time – and was still the biggest public housing authority in the US.[8] Even more incredibly, this had been done without shipping people to the outskirts: unlike in Paris, where poorer residents live out in the *banlieues*, in London the social housing had been woven throughout the city, even in the centre.

This social miracle had been more than a century in the making. Social housing in London traced its roots back to piecemeal efforts of Victorian philanthropists, churches and almshouses to provide housing to the poor. In the aftermath of World War I, providing decent housing for those who couldn't otherwise afford it became a priority for the state – the British troops were promised 'Homes for Heroes' on their return from France. The plan was simple: central government would borrow money cheaply and provide grants to local government bodies who would use it to build new social housing. Residents would then pay a reduced rent which, over a long period of time, would settle the initial debt.

In this period, London built outwards, stretching into the marshes and farmlands to the east with the vast Becontree estate – a 27,000-home mini-city of smart, large, brick townhouses in long, spacious terraced streets, which accommodated many workers in the Ford car factory and remains the largest single municipal estate in Europe. In more central areas of the city, privately rented slum housing which dated back to the Victorian era was demolished and replaced. Many different visions of estates were built across the city, with the falling population meaning density was never a major concern and green areas and open spaces could be prioritised. Planners in Bermondsey attempted to rebuild the area as a 'garden city' – a development pioneered by Ada Salter, Labour's first female mayor. The development delivered extraordinary cottage-style workers' houses sitting in neat little rows in a vision of housing that seems a world apart from our idea of inner London estates today, although some were lost to the Luftwaffe's bombs during the war and replaced with highrises in the decades that followed.

In the 1950s and 1960s, we built upwards. Futuristic dreams of streets in the sky abounded and brutalist concrete came into vogue as architects experimented with the potential of this modern form of construction. These estates were seen at the time as modern and exciting new ways to live – designed by an army of architects employed by the London County Council (LCC), which was the largest architectural practice in the country at the time. The homes were transformative for the working-class population, used to sharing between whole families and sweating to make rent for the private landlords who had ruled London since the nineteenth century.

Pauline Hutchinson remembers growing up in Stepney, in the East End, in a house which had two rooms, a scullery and a minute back yard and was home to her mum, dad, grandmother and two siblings. The street was full of animal noises: dogs, cats, pigeons, rabbits and the chickens which Pauline's family kept. Her parents were among the east Londoners who moved out of these conditions into council housing – getting a flat on a newly built council estate in 1950. Her parents were 'over the moon' with the home, recalls Pauline. It was a three-bedroom flat with a tiny kitchen and living room together with an indoor bathroom, which felt like an unbelievable luxury in those days. 'We knew everyone and there was a real sense of community. We had Jewish people, Africans, West Indians and Irish and lots of mixed-race families. We lived on the top floor and thought we were living in the clouds.'[9]

These new houses also gave Londoners stable and affordable rents and lifetime tenancies, which meant they had security and, in some circumstances, could pass it on to their children when they died.[10] Oral histories of early social housing in London are scattered with new residents describing the social homes they moved into as 'a palace', 'heaven with the gates off' or similar.[11]

In essence, the provision of housing had become a direct role of the welfare state. It would be wrong to say there was ever complete consensus about this. Throughout the twentieth century, governments also often looked for ways to sell off council homes, increase the rents and reduce the level of capital investment the state put up to build them. Even the 'Homes for Heroes' programme was subject to major cuts. Social housing became seen as the 'wobbly pillar' of the welfare state – never quite as secure in its place as health and education in the social contract between the government and its citizens.

But in London social housing thrived, particularly because of its staunch supporters in the LCC and its successor, the Greater London Council (GLC), controlled by Labour Party politicians who supported council housing for most of the twentieth century. By the 1980s, with London's population having fallen, there was actually too much social housing: in 1981, Lambeth had 3,100 empty council properties, Islington had 2,800, Southwark had 2,700 and Hackney had 2,300.[12] This created financial difficulties because there was stock standing vacant, and no one paying the rent. The GLC would occasionally run 'first come, first served' opportunities to become a tenant at estates where they had too much stock. Young people, some of them students, could simply join a queue at 9 a.m. and become council tenants by the afternoon.[13]

For the most part, these estates were well looked after. Rents were paid to central government, which returned them as subsidy for maintenance, while councils also had business rates and council taxes to invest in housing. 'In those days, Camden had money coming out of its ears,' says Derek Jarman, a long-time council tenant and former councillor, describing a programme of double glazing at one estate. 'There was a resident caretaker. If there were any problems or if the kids were misbehaving he could go and tell them to either piss off or behave,' he adds.[14] This was true of many estates around London. Resident caretakers, good maintenance, high standards of building overseen by the architects at the GLC and abundant supply. Council housing was thriving. But the aftershocks of Thatcher's new economic model were sweeping through London and this would change everything.

HANNAH, ANDREW

Hannah Joshua grew up with her mum on the Samuel Lewis estate in Dalston. 'When I looked out of my window there were lots of trees,' says Hannah. 'I had all my friends on the estate or the estate across the road. Obviously, it wasn't all perfect, but it was a good place to live. The idea that we were poor because we lived on an estate never really occurred to me.'

The estate was formed of three long, red-brick, four-storey finger blocks. One on the east was called 'the electrics' locally, because it was the only one with lifts. Hannah and her mum's flat was small: the kitchen and bathroom were in the same room, separated by a shower curtain. Hannah spent a lot of her time outside. She can still name her friends and their flat numbers. 'There were just loads of kids and we would all play out,' she says: tag, run outs, knock down ginger. 'I feel like I had a lot of freedom,' says Hannah. 'We had a club which was run by women on the estate. It was 20p to go and you'd have pool, table tennis, all sorts.'

The estate had around six residential caretakers who lived there with their families. 'They were quite grumpy, some of them, but they were always around,' she says. 'If there were any problems, like a broken fuse, you would literally walk down to the estate office and someone would come up within half an hour.'

Andrew's dad moved to London from Canvey Island in Essex after the devastating North Sea floods of 1953 submerged the small outcrop of land in the Thames estuary. The floods killed 307 people in the UK, 58 of them from Canvey Island. Andrew's dad lost friends to the waves and watched their bodies floating along the street in the surging water. The family moved to east London not long after, to be further from the sea. It was here, on a small council estate in West Ham, that Andrew was born.

'My dad was the postman for the area, and everyone knew him,' recalls Andrew. 'People think now that the idea that everyone knew each other in the East End is a bit of a myth, but they really did. All the men would finish work and go down the pub: the postmen, the bus drivers, the plumbers. I'm just about old enough to remember the tail end of all that. When you watch old episodes of *EastEnders*, that's what it was like at that point in time.'

Andrew's parents knew most of the other mums and dads in the area, so he had a lot of freedom as a child. He could go in and out of friends' houses and play in the cul-de-sac. It wasn't always an easy community, though. He recalls the story of a young man who lived locally who beat his wife and eventually killed her with a hammer. He was caught trying to dispose of the body with his father on a building site in Bow and both were prosecuted for murder.

'It's always been rough,' he adds. 'But you kind of learned to go with it and knew what you could and couldn't do. And if you weren't involved in any of the trouble, it was actually a really nice area to grow up in.'

EVERY MAN A CAPITALIST – SOCIAL HOUSING UNDER ATTACK

Janice Morphet, a visiting professor at University College London and an expert in local government, explains that social housing was seen as in conflict with the dominant economic theory which gripped the world in the 1980s. 'The feeling was that the private sector had grown as far as it could and in order for it to grow further, it was important now that the public sector needed to be exposed to competition,' she explains.

Trade agreements had seen governments around the world agree to promote this in stages, and housing was one of Thatcher's first targets. In parts of London – like Tower Hamlets – 97 per cent of the rented housing was council-owned.[15] This would not do in her vision of the modern world. Instead homes should be in individual ownership

– with each owner treating their property as an investment, an asset, that might help grow their overall wealth over time. 'I want a capital earning democracy – every man a capitalist. So we start on houses because if you're a man or woman of property you've got something,' said Thatcher, in an interview with the *Observer* in 1983.[16]

First came the now notorious 'Right to Buy'. By 1980, the idea of selling council homes to their residents was nothing new. It could be done on a home-by-home basis with the consent of the local authority (almost 250,000 were sold between 1960 and 1979).[17] But Thatcher was going to supercharge this process. Local authorities would no longer have any discretion in selling the homes, and tenants would be offered huge discounts – 50 per cent if they had lived in the property for twenty years – as well as 100 per cent mortgages, which meant they didn't need to save for a deposit. Within five years, tenants could resell the property at full market value – meaning it offered the opportunity to make a huge, quick profit. And critically, the money raised from the sale would not be retained by the council; it would be hoovered up by the Treasury.

The scheme aimed to reduce the amount of council housing and turn social tenants into homeowners. When he introduced the bill to Parliament in January 1980, housing secretary Michael Heseltine said the objective was 'to reverse the trend of ever-increasing dominance of the state over the life of the individual'.[18] Questions about the impact on the wider availability of social housing were 'dismissed'.[19]

In London, the policy began slowly with just 330 sales in 1980. But ten years later, there were 26,258 homes being sold a year – a third of the nation's total sales.[20] Research shows larger, better quality houses with gardens were more frequently sold under Right to Buy, which means we were cutting the number of homes suitable for families at pace.[21] Year by year, we drastically limited the availability of homes for people who needed them, exactly at the moment that the population of the city and its house prices were starting to grow. Despite having lifetime security, people do not live in social housing forever. Today, the average time spent in a social home fluctuates between eleven and twelve years.[22] If it remains social housing, when one family moves out, a new one moves in. But once the home is sold, this chain of new tenancies is broken: the home will be sold on the market to the highest bidder once it becomes vacant and a family in need of social housing will be left waiting.

And this reduction in social housing stock came just as landmark new homelessness legislation was changing who could get a social home. Driven in part by the Ken Loach TV film *Cathy Come Home*, and major campaigns on homelessness led by the charity Shelter, the UK's first major legislation on homelessness had passed in 1977. Councils suddenly had a duty to rehouse families who found themselves homeless, and provide temporary accommodation to the most needy (families with children, people with disabilities, etc.) while they waited for a new home.

Before this legislation, and before we started to reduce the amount of available social homes through Right to Buy, a wide social mix of people could become social tenants. People in well-paid manual jobs became social tenants. So did new teachers, secretaries and public sector workers. But with a legal duty to house those in most need first, and a dwindling supply of social homes, available properties began to be taken up only by those already in difficult circumstances.

The result was that social housing became reserved for the socially marginalised. In 1980, 41 per cent of social tenants were 'skilled or semi-skilled manual' workers, and 42 per cent were 'economically inactive' (including pensioners). By 1990, just 26 per cent were 'skilled or semi-skilled manual' workers and 61 per cent were economically inactive.[23] In a major report on the impact of Right to Buy, published in 2006, the authors said the policy had rendered the original dream of socially mixed social housing 'a pipe dream'.[24]

Selling off social housing was not the only change Thatcher brought about. She also drastically cut back the amount spent on construction, ending the post-war era of mass building by councils. The central government funding put towards building new council homes fell 43 per cent between 1980 and 1991.[25] And building them became a worthless investment for a council when they could be sold off at a discount shortly after they were finished. In 1980, councils built 74,840 homes across England. In 1991, they built 8,130 – a collapse of almost 90 per cent.[26]

Cuts also targeted the way the existing homes would be looked after. In this era, councils collected the rents from the homes and sent them to the Treasury. The Treasury then used the receipts to pay off debts incurred to build them and returned a subsidy to the councils to pay for maintenance and improvements. But Thatcher slashed the subsidy. In 1980, many councils were allocated less money than the sums they had already committed to spend on management and maintenance, forcing them to start cutting the maintenance spend. The Tory chairman of the Association of District Councils described the situation as 'very grim' and warned 'that a substantial number of the nation's older houses would decline beyond the point of no return'. 'That is part of the legacy that the Conservative Party will pass on to its successors – years in which the housing stock will deteriorate,' warned Labour MP Roy Hattersley in 1980.[27]

In 1984, further cuts representing a real-terms reduction of more than £1 billion a year (£2.25 billion in today's money) were imposed. This was enough to upset even the *Daily Mail*, which described the cuts as a 'bitter freeze' on housing investment that was 'as stupid as it is shortsighted'.[28] A memo, written by then housing minister Ian Gow and uncovered from the national archives by *Inside Housing* in 2014, warned the changes 'would mean an increase in homelessness… increasing disrepair (involving even greater expenditure later on), more overcrowding and more housing conditions which, as I have seen for myself, are unacceptable.'[29]

And the Greater London Council, which had overseen much of London's boom years of council housing development, was also on its way out. The body was scrapped in 1986, with the homes it owned transferred to local boroughs in the years before. Scrapping the GLC was a political decision, described as 'an act of Thatcherite spite' by the historian Roy Porter – the capital's governing body was controlled by Labour's Ken Livingstone and was a vocal and active opponent to Thatcher's government.[30] But it was also a major moment in the history of London's council housing. While the GLC had a huge, experienced housing department, the individual town halls it passed its powers over to were 'ill-prepared and under-resourced' to take on management of what was upwards of 60,000 homes in some cases.[31]

Thatcher's aim was for social housing to be provided by private bodies, funded by private money. At this time housing associations were mostly small housing charities – some established by Victorian philanthropists, like the Peabody and Guinness trusts – or local charities, often set up by minority ethnic communities to meet the needs of people locked out by the racism which plagued allocation of council homes. They were an addition to the mainstream council housing offer – managing around 10 to 15 per cent of London's social housing in the 1980s.

But they attracted Thatcher's attention: because they were voluntary sector organisations rather than government bodies, any money borrowed to build new homes did not appear on the Treasury's balance sheet. This was an opportunity. The Housing Act 1988 allowed these businesses and charities to borrow private finance against the 'assets' they owned.

For Thatcher, this was a masterstroke. The debt could be moved off the government's balance sheet. State-owned and financed council housing would decline, and privately funded housing associations would take over. The act also allowed council-owned housing to be transferred to the management of these new bodies. As Peter Williams, a fellow at the University of Cambridge's Department of Land Economy explains, this was a deliberate choice: 'The government very consciously wanted to shift the burden of finance in the social housing sector, rightly in my view, from a reliance on grant to a reliance on the private market.'[32]

The housing association sector began to borrow and build and grow. In 1988, when the act came in, they had collectively built 10,940 homes around England. By 1992, this had doubled to 20,790.

There were also new ideas about what 'affordable housing' should be. In the 1980 act, Thatcher introduced a new idea: shared ownership. This would allow a buyer who couldn't afford the full price to buy a percentage of the equity from a housing association and pay a discounted rent on the rest, until they could save enough money to buy the balance. The idea of 'affordable home ownership' was born.[33]

These were the changes to social housing Thatcher wanted to see: private money funding private organisations to build smaller amounts of social housing, some of them to encourage home ownership rather than renting and the state-owned properties defunded and sold off.

MANJU

Manju had never really settled anywhere before she came to live in London in the 1980s. When she was seven years old, her family home in the north west of England was destroyed in a fire. One year later her father died, and her mother moved the family from home to home depending on her work. At the age of eighteen, she met a woman from the United States; they became friends and together they decided to work their way around the world with very little money.

They travelled along the Trans-Siberian Railway to Asia, took a cattle ship to Hong Kong and hitched on an oil plane to Jakarta. They did many jobs but never stayed long. Eventually, Manju met a man, Satinder, while she was working in a hotel in the United States, and together they moved to London where Satinder's father was living.

Manju was now working as a shadow puppeteer and an arts practitioner in schools. Satinder initially worked as an accountant for a clothing outlet, which offered them a flat above its premises on Kensington High Street and allowed them to agree a rent based on what they could afford to pay. It was an Edwardian building, and although their flat was small, they loved living in it. They built platform beds, furnished it themselves and made it their own.

'The house was one big space,' says Manju. 'Which is something which only works if you like the people you are sharing it with. But that makes you want to get to know them: if you are going to hear people having a pee and flushing their loos, you want to at least know who it is doing it.'

The community in the flats went through difficult times. While they were multiracial, the London outside was still a hostile place for black and brown people. Manju recalls Satinder turning his car around in the street and a policeman asking him, 'What do you think you're driving, a fucking camel?'

And as the 1980s progressed, a young gay man in the property got sick with a mysterious new illness, and later died as a result. Another of the residents, Barbara, worked at the London Lighthouse, a west London-based residential centre for people living with HIV, many of whom were reaching the end of their lives. 'Ladbroke Grove back then was full of young men who looked very emaciated. Many of them didn't survive, but the Lighthouse was somewhere they could at least live comfortably,' says Manju. 'Barbara used to sit through the night with them and held their hands as they passed away. Some of them wouldn't have their parents with them, because they were ashamed, so they would have had no one if it wasn't for her and the other nurses. We used to joke that everything in her wardrobe was black because she attended so many funerals.'

'But that was when nurses could afford to live locally,' she adds. 'Barbara was working in Ladbroke Grove and she could actually afford to live in W8. What kind of nurse could afford to live in W8 now?'

BACK FROM THE BRINK: THE RESURRECTION OF THE PRIVATE LANDLORD

At the start of the 1980s, private landlords were an endangered species. Just 16.6 per cent of Londoners rented their homes privately – and landlords were declining rapidly, having dropped from housing 45.5 per cent of the city twenty years previously.[34] This was a trend which was in place around the UK, and appeared so firmly entrenched that some commentators were looking towards a new century when private landlords were consigned entirely to history. The Conservative Policy Council wrote in the mid-1970s that the decline of the private landlord was 'quite irreversible' and that 'within a generation' they would be 'as extinct as the dinosaur'.[35]

While many modern commentators attribute this to rent controls, it is hard to make the case stand up. Rent control had been part of the housing system in the UK since World War I and for much of the century, private landlords had thrived in London. What was leading to their demise was that we no longer needed them. Local authority slum clearance programmes had literally bulldozed some of the worst private rented housing and replaced it with municipal properties. Getting a council home was relatively easy, and involved only a short wait for those who needed it. The homes were spacious and well maintained, and the rents were affordable. For those who could afford a little more, the jump up from a council home to a mortgage was much smaller than it is today, and it would take far less time to save for a deposit. So why would anyone want to rent from a private landlord? But a future without private landlords was not the one Thatcher wanted to build.

DAVE, CAROLYN

Dave Hill came to London in 1979. Growing up in a small town, he had dreamed of the London he'd read about in storybooks or seen in films. It became his ambition to move to the city and become a journalist – specifically a music critic. 'I turned up with my portable typewriter. I had no money, no connections, no savings, nothing really,' he recalls. At first he lodged with some friends in Putney, and began looking for a privately rented flat.

'If you were looking for a flat to rent back then, you walked into the centre of town to get the earliest possible edition of the *Evening Standard* and you'd scour the small ads for a flat to rent. Then you'd hope that you could find a phone box that worked and normally, you would stand there for bloody ages, constantly dialling numbers, until someone would answer and say "Sorry, it's already taken",' he says.

After a few days of fruitless searching, he eventually found a small bedsit on the Portobello Road, just north of the Westway motorway, above a shop for £15 a week (about £70 in today's money). 'It was pretty basic, verging on squalid,' he says. 'But for me, it was about the most romantic thing that could possibly have happened to me. I was in London, by the

Westway, near the route of the Notting Hill Carnival. I got a job in a record shop and I could afford the rent pretty easily.'

He started going to gigs, writing reviews and posting them off to any magazine that would take them. Suddenly, he was living the life he'd only read and heard about as a small-town boy. 'My parents were mystified and horrified that I wanted to live in a grubby little bedsit in west London, but if you were prepared to live cheaply, live a bit rough and a bit scruffy, you could do and see things you couldn't find anywhere else,' he recollects.

As a journalist, he tramped around London's small music venues in dirty pubs, reviewing bands playing sweaty rhythm and blues to raucous audiences.

'It was a cheaper city, but in other ways it was failing,' he says. 'The population was still falling and had never recovered from World War II. People were leaving, and they were leaving in some cases because it was a shit place to live. It was still a really dirty city. It still felt like it was in recovery and there was so much really terrible housing. It wasn't quite the golden era people sometimes make it now when they look back.' Still, for someone like him, it was a city where it remained possible to turn up without much money and follow a dream based on luck, graft and talent. Steadily, his music reviews began to get picked up more and more widely and he made a network of friends. Soon, he left his Portobello Road bedsit and moved in with a group of 'amiable social deviants' in a phenomenon called 'short life housing' in Islington, which was even cheaper. This was council-owned housing stock which – for whatever reason – couldn't be let out to council tenants because it didn't meet certain legal requirements. The process was effectively legal squatting, and housed hundreds, if not thousands, of young Londoners during this period. 'I lived in this magnificent five-bedroomed Victorian terraced house just off the Holloway Road and the rent was next to nothing,' says Dave, who remained in short-life housing in Islington and Hackney for most of the 1980s.

Carolyn, meanwhile, had come to London from Walsall. 'I was chairman of my own escape committee,' she recalls. 'I wanted to be somewhere where there was more diversity of life. My parents were great, but the rest of Walsall just wasn't enough for me.'

She rented a bedsit in Crouch End, auditioned for London drama schools and began taking small acting jobs, earning small sums of money, sometimes travelling with theatre companies and performing for children. 'It was terrific fun,' she adds. 'I loved acting for children. Some actors patronised them, but I never did.'

Eventually, the theatre company closed and after securing an Open University degree, she managed to get a job as a civil servant. She continued renting in Crouch End. 'I had some savings, and I did think about buying a place,' she says. 'But banks and building societies at the time didn't like lending to single women.'

She found a room in Finchley, which was 'extremely cheap', in a house shared with six other residents. Meanwhile her civil service career progressed. She worked mainly in the Ministry of Defence and was in the building when Michael Heseltine, then defence secretary, declared his resignation in 1986 and almost toppled Thatcher. She also suffered an injury crossing the road coming out of London Bridge station. 'The heel of my sandal caught the side of a cat's eye and I landed on the base of my spine,' she says. 'I was just lying in the middle of the road, and these men with briefcases were walking by. A homeless man came along and carried me to the centre island.'

The injury would affect her mobility in later years. But she did not worry for the time being. Her rent was affordable, her career was stable and life was good. She hadn't bought a house, but why worry? Prices were affordable, she was on a civil service salary and she was sure she would be able to do so eventually.

THE FREE MARKET UNLEASHED
– THE HOUSING ACT 1988

Thatcher's 'big bang' deregulation of the financial sector in 1986 is widely remembered, but you could argue that her 'big bang' deregulation of private landlords in 1988 played a bigger role in shaping London and the lives of all who lived in it for the coming decades.

A new legal concept – the 'assured shorthold tenancy' – was introduced in the Housing Act 1988. These new tenancies would have a fixed term of six or twelve months, after which the tenant could simply be evicted with the landlord providing no justification at all. So long as they served the legal papers correctly and gave the required notice period, they were allowed to kick the tenant out. At the same time, the rent controls which had been in place in some shape or form for seventy years were abolished.

This was a critical rebalancing of the power dynamic between landlord and tenant. No longer would you rent a home for life, so long as you paid the rent. No longer would you have some certainty over how much it would cost you to live in the same place next year. Instead, your right to the home would always be temporary and the landlord's right to extract as much money as they liked from you would become permanent. As the housing lawyer and writer Nick Bano puts it: 'In economic terms, these assured shorthold tenancies walk softly, but carry a big stick... Easy no-fault evictions are the key ingredient of the profitability of the private rented sector.'[36] They allow the market to very quickly find the tenants who can pay the most, and price out the rest.

The intention was explicit. The government wanted to replace council housing with housing owned by private landlords. They dressed this up in the language of choice. In 1987, as the bill made its way through Parliament housing secretary Nicholas Ridley said council estates were 'monotonous, soulless places in which few would choose to live' and the government wanted 'to encourage the growth of other types of independent landlord in the rented sector'.[37] Another minister, Norman Lamont, meanwhile, insisted the choice offered by the market would benefit tenants as it would 'allow the tenant and landlord to agree any rent they choose'. 'The best way to arrive at a reasonable rent is to allow it to be determined by competition and market forces,' he said.[38]

But behind the scenes, there were concerns. Removing restrictions on rents, at the same time as council housing was being reduced through Right to Buy and grant cuts, would mean more residents claiming housing benefit to help pay the rent to private landlords. And as private rents rose, this would cost the government more money. In 2025, my colleagues at *Inside Housing* uncovered documents in the National Archives which prove Thatcher was aware of this risk. Declassified files show housing benefit spend was expected to rise from £2.4 billion to £8 billion by the end of the parliamentary term in 1991. She was warned that private landlords would raise rents above market rates and 'simply collect the money from the government'. One document specifically warned Thatcher that the impact of higher rents would significantly affect the standard of living of pensioners and families with children. But her government pushed ahead anyway: they argued that the cost in terms of increased benefits would be offset by the reduction in money previously spent on funding councils to build new homes, and income from the homes sold under Right to Buy.[39] Whether or not these sums ever truly added up would be tough to establish. But what it represents was a new path – housing needs would be met by housing benefit payments, instead of the provision of new affordable homes. This was a fundamental change in how the British government thought about housing, and it continues to define the housing crisis today.

After the passage of this act, homes in areas where housing demand was high were suddenly transformed into assets of incredible value. No longer were they simply places to live.

JOHN, PETER

John Hall was born in the Salvation Army Hospital in Clapton. He trained as a teacher and decided to use his profession to travel in the 1960s. Along with his young family, he left London and worked in a series of army schools, in Singapore, Malaysia and finally Germany.

In the mid-1980s he returned to east London, becoming the head of a primary school in Leyton. The local authority put him up in a tower block with his young family as he looked for somewhere they could afford to buy. The place they found was on a small housing estate in Walthamstow, built on a small promontory overlooking the River Lea and the huge north London reservoirs. It had been built by the water board – recently privatised by Thatcher – and the estate was a mix of social and for-sale homes. The house was semi-detached and cost £33,000. John's family got a mortgage from a building society without any difficulty. His wife Jacky was able to find work as a translator and, even as interest rates climbed to nearly 15 per cent by the end of the decade, they could still pay the mortgage. In fact, they elected to keep the higher repayments even as rates fell and ultimately paid off their 25-year mortgage in just twelve and a half years.

Buying a house was an option widely available to people in professions like teaching, local authorities and community work at the time.

John enjoyed teaching at the school in Leyton. The school had children with twenty-two mother tongues, and a mix of nationalities, races and religions. But having taught Gurkha children in Malaya, he was used to teaching children who spoke English as a second language.

He was aware that he was living and teaching in an area with problems. On the nearby Ferry Lane, a road connecting Walthamstow to Tottenham which runs across the reservoirs and river marshes, cars of armed drug runners were often pursued by police. At school, one young girl told her teacher she had been shown a knife by her dad. When John spoke to the father about the incident, he paled. Later that day, police came to the school to tell him the father had stabbed the girl's mother to death on their doorstep. Social services took the girl away to live with other family members. London looked and felt neglected. Su, his daughter, recalls going to the local swimming pool with its cracked tiles, rust and gutters around the edge to drain the water, and feeling like she had arrived in a third-world country compared to the Olympic-style pools she had been used to in Germany.

But the community John lived in was peaceful and tight knit. They lived at the bottom of a cul-de-sac and knew all of their neighbours – both the council tenants and those who owned their homes.

Peter Williams, a geography graduate who came to London to work in Newham Council's housing team, was also initially housed by the council in the early 1980s. With the rent on his one-bedroom flat cheap compared to his salary, he quickly saved up enough to buy a three-bedroom terraced house in Stratford in 1983 for £22,000. 'It was pretty straightforward between my wife and I,' says Peter.

The home was bought from the council, but not via Right to Buy. Instead – amid pressure to stop demolishing the Victorian terraced housing which had been cleared away in huge numbers in the 1960s and 1970s – councils were now refurbishing and selling off homes they had compulsorily purchased for slum clearance to first-time buyers.

'Stratford in the 1980s was a very, very different place to what it is now,' says Peter. 'It was pretty run down, it was cheap and it was beginning to change quite rapidly. The traditional white working-class East End community was leaving the area for the New Towns, unemployment was high, the docks were in terminal decline and, while the private sector was growing, industrial jobs were hard to come by. Plus pollution was a problem, the parks and open spaces were in poor condition, so people were choosing to move out to Essex. The area was thought to be in decline, and the schools were pretty ropey at that time. So people were making the choice to get away. It did lead to an extraordinary change, quite rapidly.'

HOMES FOR PEOPLE – BUYING A HOUSE

The average property price in London in 1980 was £24,037 (a shade over £100,000 in today's money).[40] An adult in a non-manual job would expect an average wage of £7,332 a year, while manual workers could expect £5,772 (£30,000 and £24,200 respectively in today's money). This put house prices and average deposits well within the means of workers on the average income – perhaps with a bit of saving, perhaps together with a partner. But it was possible. House prices in London reflected – as they should in a functioning market – what average working people could afford to pay to live in them.

Buying was also increasingly open to the Londoners who had migrated to the city from the Commonwealth, as the British government tried to encourage workers to move to London after the war. Black and Asian families often reacted to the discrimination they faced in rented housing by jumping onto the property ladder as quickly as they could. They began to buy the old, poorly built Victorian terraced housing in the area – then some of the cheapest in the city – with their own communities forming in particular areas. This was, to an extent, a self-defence mechanism. 'If you took a car ride around south Newham during the early 1980s, you could identify where Black families lived, because they would have no windows, they would have big sheets of wood against them and the letter boxes would be nailed shut to protect them from excrement or accelerant fluid being poured through,' recalls Cilius Victor, one of the founding members of the Newham Monitoring Project, which was set up to record these acts of racism in the face of unwilling local police and local council.[41]

Some of these lower-income families who did buy – both white and minority ethnic – were able to do so because of the thriving building society movement: lending groups owned mutually by members with the purpose of offering affordable mortgages to workers. These were the providers of almost all mortgage finance in the UK at this point, and their model did not lend itself to rapid house price growth. The mortgage loans came from the deposits paid by existing members of the scheme, which kept a limit on what could be borrowed and lent, and therefore a natural cap on what people could pay for a home. Regular banks, meanwhile, were subject to credit controls imposed by the Bank of England, which meant they primarily lent money to industry rather than speculating on growth in the property market.[42] But once more, the system was about to be disrupted.

JOTHI, PATRICIA AND SEAN, RUPHINA

Jothi had moved to London in the late 1970s. She'd come to the UK from Malaysia aged twenty and had been working in Surrey, living in a nursing home and caring for people with learning difficulties. She heard there was work in London and that she could also train as a general nurse, establishing a more secure career. But when she arrived, she realised she had been conned: the woman who encouraged her to move was a landlord who wanted to rent the flat and had lied about the availability of work to get her to move in. She worked initially in a factory in Bow in east London, sewing clothes.

After a while, she did manage to become a student nurse, put her name down for a council property and secured a flat in Bow within a few months of registering. 'Everything was second hand. It was near to walk to the hospital. My mindset at the time was to achieve my qualification and move on,' she recalls. As a student she worked in the A&E department at the now-defunct Queen Mary's Hospital. 'It was exciting because it was very active, a lot of gunshot wounds, knife crime. We used to have policemen with us, and work in the underground bits of the hospital that looked like a dungeon.'

Some of her patients would verbally abuse her. 'They used to say "Get home, you bloody Paki". I used to just think "You silly fool, you are lying in bed being ill and you are speaking like this to the person who is caring for you". I was being spat at, but I just thought "Sorry, mate, I want my certificate",' she smiles.

In 1980, she married Stanley, and the couple moved into a different council flat in Limehouse. They had their first son. An older white couple, Lil and Ted, who lived downstairs bonded with the young family and became regular childminders to their son, and his brother who was born a couple of years later. 'We had just moved into the flat and Lil came and knocked on the door and said hello and said they were our neighbours,' Jothi recollects. 'She was a community leader for that estate.'

But the area still had problems. One day while Jothi was out with her sons, the house was robbed. The flat was cleaned out and they had no contents insurance so were reduced to nothing with two small children. 'I just remember sitting on the floor and sobbing,' Jothi tells me. 'We lost everything, everything, and I wanted to run away from that place.'

She started looking at houses in the newspaper. She wanted a three-bedroom house, with a garden, and a school and church within walking distance. In 1986, between her salary as a junior nurse and her husband's as a junior accountant, this was possible. 'It was winter, we were going round by bus with the two kids looking at all these flats around east London,' she adds.

Finally, the couple found a three-bedroom house in Stratford. 'I remember pushing my youngest in a buggy in the snow, looking for the address in the *A–Z*,' she recalls. 'The kitchen was miserably small, but the garden at the back was long and nice and they had a big swing at the back and two rows of flowerbeds.' The house was £44,500 (£130,000 in today's money). 'I think we probably borrowed money from friends for the deposit. And we rented one extra room out to a Malaysian guy, which helped to pay the mortgage.'

They lived on a small road with ten houses – all of them were families with children. 'It was so different to how it is now,' says Jothi. 'There were not many cars, it was a very happy place for children.'

Patricia was born in west London. Her Irish parents rented privately before the home they were in was listed for demolition and slum clearance. Her family were given three choices for rehousing – a council house in the new towns of Stevenage and Welwyn Garden City or Burnt Oak, a suburb on the fringes of northwest London. 'The first two were just too far out of London for my dad. Even though Burnt Oak was right at the end of the Northern line, he still felt it was London,' she recalls.

When the family moved, they found that they liked it. 'We had a big open space in front of our house, so we weren't cooped up like we were in London,' Patricia tells me. 'Over the years, more and more Irish people came to live there, as homes people were renting privately in London were pulled down.'

They lived in a classic council house – an end-of-terrace property with a shared porch, a sitting room, a big kitchen and two bedrooms, allotments across the road and a small parade of shops at the end of the street. The English couple next door became like grandparents to Patricia and her sister.

As Patricia grew into a teenager and young woman, she relished living in London's Irish community. She knew almost every neighbour in Burnt Oak by name and fondly recalls Sunday afternoons, when groups of Irish expats would take radios out to telephone masts to get a signal for the commentaries of Gaelic football being broadcast across the Irish Sea. 'On Sunday afternoon, across loads of different parts of London, you would find groups of Irish men huddled around one radio listening to the match,' she says. 'There was one across the road from us, so friends used to come up religiously to listen to it.'

The community supported each other: when someone passed away there was a local whip round for a wreath, and 'benefit dances' were held to raise money for those in need. 'For example, a worker might have had an accident, or maybe a parent might die and leave a young family. Tickets were sold on building sites, in pubs and by word of mouth,' Patricia remembers.

She got a job working on the counter at the local post office, began collecting a reasonable wage and was able to enjoy the dance halls and bars where the Irish community would gather at the weekends. In 1983, at a Céilí dance in a Catholic church in Kilburn, she met Sean.

Sean had come to England aged nineteen in the 1960s, having grown up on the Aran Islands off the west coast of Ireland. He had grown up a native Irish speaker and only learned English when he started working at a college, aged seventeen.

At first, he spent time in the north of England, taking jobs on building sites. But many of his co-workers encouraged him to move to London. '"Sean," they used to say to me, "you've got to go to London,"' he says. 'The bright lights, and all the work available.' Eventually, he got a room in Willesden, renting from a landlord who came from the same islands as him. 'When I first came to London there was Irish everywhere,' Sean recalls. 'My goodness, I've never seen so many.'

He would work on building sites around the city during the week and go dancing at Irish bars and dancehalls in the evenings and at the weekends. At one of these, on a Wednesday night, in the hall of a church in Quex Road, Kilburn, Patricia caught his eye. 'There was a good band there. There was a man who played the accordion, and his wife was a singer, you know.' His friend who was calling out the dances encouraged him to ask her to dance, and they did.

They carried on meeting, to go dancing at other Irish events. 'I used to take her out dancing, and my friends would say "Sean, why don't you ask her out?" I was a bit shy, you see, but I took up the courage to ask her eventually.'

After a few months, he decided he wanted to marry her – but he needed to move out of the room he was renting first. 'I told my friend I've met this lovely girl, but I need my own house before I marry her.'

Finding a place proved relatively simple. He found a three-bedroom house in Brent, northwest London, that was standing empty. 'I had a lot of money saved at the time. I had good work, like,' he says, 'and since there was nobody living there, they were keen to sell it.'

The house cost £38,750 (£129,000 in today's money). He got the mortgage easily. 'I was always looking forward to getting married, so I saved my money. A lot of my friends, they loved their drink and they would spend all their money too quickly, but I was putting it away.' With his savings, he could put down a substantial deposit, and the couple married and moved into the home in 1984.

It was not always easy being Irish in London at this time – Patricia's dad was stopped and questioned by the police when he was going to work, their cars were searched. Sean was stopped at customs when he returned from a visit home and interrogated about a wrist injury he'd sustained at work. 'I was there for hours answering questions. They did an awful job on me,' he recollects. 'They must have taken about a hundred photographs of me.'

Ruphina came to the UK from the Caribbean island of Dominica in the 1960s and moved around London living in various rental houses. She kept various jobs. Talented with fabrics, she ran a small personal business making soft furnishings, while also working occasionally as a secretary and child minder.

Good with money and with an entrepreneurial spirit, Ruphina saved enough from these various jobs to buy a two-bedroom home on Brock Road, a quiet crescent street in Plaistow, east London. She was able to get a mortgage to buy the property despite the insecurity of her multiple-sourced single income.[43] Back then, this was an area of working people on low or medium incomes – a part of London which was a little isolated from the Tube network and had a bad reputation. A house like this cost less than double the average wage for an adult in a non-manual job.[44]

This was achievable in London then – with hard work and thrift young couples could work on building sites, behind post office counters, in hospitals or as secretaries, in creative industries, and find their space in the city to settle and raise a family. But times would change.

THE BIG BANG – BUYING A HOUSE

Margaret Thatcher's 'big bang' deregulation of the banking industry in 1986 lifted credit controls on banks, allowing them to provide mortgages without restriction for the first time.

Changes to financial banking rules meant the amount they could lend was also no longer limited by the number of domestic deposits they held. At the same time, the Demutualisation Act in 1986 allowed the building societies to convert into regular banks. Huge money started to be made in a banking system which was not only offering mortgages but developing and trading new financial instruments which tied these profits together.

The result of these complex changes was that it suddenly became much easier for banks to offer larger mortgages to many more people. And so they did: mortgage lending exploded, rising from 20 per cent of GDP in the late 1970s to 55 per cent by the end of the 1980s. As people could borrow more, and banks could lend more, so property prices began to rise. The real price of housing – relatively stable with some ebbs and flows for decades – began to rise sharply. As London's economy changed and white-collar workers increasingly moved into the city, demand for housing grew and the amount people could borrow began to stretch. House prices in London grew 22.3 per cent in 1988, and the ratio between average earnings and average prices rapidly increased, as banks used their new freedom to offer bigger mortgages.[45]

But many of these new buyers were taking big financial risks. In 1989, 42 per cent of first-time buyers put down a deposit of less than £1,000 and just over a third received a 100 per cent mortgage. If house prices fell, neither they nor the banks would have any security.

Neither the bankers nor the buyers worried too much about this. This was the new world, the late twentieth century. It was the time to get on the housing ladder and join in the revolution in the economy.

Building, too, was becoming more profitable. With the banks willing to create new money through mortgages for property, building in a high-demand area was like printing money. Developers no longer wanted to be held back by petty restrictions on what they could build and lobbied for deregulation: the removal of byelaws which stretched right back to the Great Fire of London governing the type of materials, style, form, minimum size and space separation required when building new houses in London. The government obliged – introducing a light-touch regulatory regime where builders would agree to meet various standards but would be left to work out how to do so themselves.

All of these changes, taken together, had set the course towards a new sort of London – one where vast fortunes could be made from the city's housing, but at whose expense? As the decade closed, so did the chapter of London's history which involved industry, established working-class communities and affordable housing. The future was coming.

1990s

A CITY OF CONTRADICTIONS

The population of London grew sharply in the 1990s, as people returned to the city to work in the new professional jobs on offer. In 1991, the city was home to 6.8 million people; by 2001 this had grown to 7.3 million.

And as the population grew, the racial mix of the city increasingly changed too. White residents were leaving the city in greater numbers, while steadily rising immigration was bringing more new arrivals to the UK. As London became the centre of the UK's job market in the post-industrial economy, many immigrants from the global South headed to where the work was – choosing the UK due to its strong currency, its global language and the historic ties made through empire building. The capital was already the most diverse part of the country, which meant it offered those arriving from overseas the chance to join an established community. In 1991, 80 per cent of all residents in London were white, but this began to fall throughout the decade, dropping to 71.5 per cent by 2001.[1]

London, in this era of a falling domestic population particularly among its working-class communities, became increasingly reliant on these immigrants to provide its essential services and keep its economy functional. Immigrant workers were (and are) more likely to take on night shifts and non-permanent jobs. They found employment in transport, hospitality, care and the city's hospitals. London could not have developed in the way it has without them.

Racial tension continued. In 1993, Stephen Lawrence, an eighteen-year-old Black man whose father was a carpenter and mother a special needs teacher, was brutally stabbed to death at a bus stop in southeast London by a gang of white thugs. The failure of the police to catch the killers would ultimately lead to the conclusion that the Metropolitan Police was 'institutionally racist'.

There were many other ways in which the city was changing. Iconic photos of city traders in colourful jackets, chunky phones in hand, celebrating a big win or despairing at a loss are some of the defining images of the decade. One Canada Square, the enormous pyramid-topped skyscraper in the former Docklands, was completed in 1991 and took the mantle of the UK's tallest building.

But the surrounding area struggled – as a community first impoverished by the closure of the docks now faced being driven out of their corner of the city by redevelopment. The new city was becoming increasingly unequal. Despite boasting a direct view of One Canada Square, Newham, in east London, was consistently ranked as the most deprived local authority in the whole of the country.[2] Children from schools in other areas of the country would be driven through the borough on field trips to witness urban poverty – they were not allowed to exit the vehicle for safety reasons. It was very literally a poverty safari.[3]

Poverty was a major problem across inner London in the 1990s, affecting more than half the children in these boroughs, the largest proportion of any region in the UK by more than ten percentage points. Likewise, London also held the largest proportion of children failing to achieve five GCSEs. Statistically, white British pupils in receipt of free school meals struggled the most, often coming from families left redundant by deindustrialisation.[4] Deprivation became hyper-local, as middle-class families congregated on certain streets, often near parks and open spaces or in the areas with the most spacious housing. The city could change dramatically from one street to another. By the end of the decade, Haringey had exactly one quarter of its wards among the richest 10 per cent in the country and one quarter among the poorest 10 per cent.[5] This stark contrast between rich and poor, living almost cheek by jowl with each other, increasingly characterised London.

In 1994, high-speed trains began shuttling passengers direct to Paris from London Waterloo. But the concrete underpasses directly outside it had become known as 'Cardboard City' – home to hundreds of rough sleepers on any given night, living in improvised shelters built on wooden pallets to prevent flooding in the rain.[6] Scenes like this did lead to a Rough Sleeping Initiative in an attempt to turn the tide – although this was as much a PR project as it was born out of altruism. In 1991, Sir George Young, then housing minister, described rough sleepers as 'the sort of people you step on when you came out of the opera', while prime minister John Major said street homeless were 'an eyesore which could drive tourists and shoppers away from cities'.[7]

London was also regularly rocked by terrorism, as the troubles in Ireland cast their dark shadow over the decade. The Provisional IRA stepped up its attacks on mainland Britain in the 1990s, with its sights set on London's new symbols of wealth. There were thirty-five separate bombings or attempted bombings in 1992 alone, including a Semtex device exploding at the Baltic Exchange, the heart of the financial district in central London, killing three, and a major lorry bomb in South Quay, near Canary Wharf, in 1996, which killed two.

Car exhausts belched out black pollutants in much higher quantities than today's vehicles. Rates of asthma diagnoses among children peaked.[8] In December 1991, high levels of air pollution driven combined with an anticyclone event of stagnant air and fog to cause the highest concentrations of nitrogen oxide ever recorded in the city, resulting in an estimated 150 deaths.[9]

But this was the last echo of London's past of smog and thick toxic smoke. Similar weather conditions had killed an estimated 12,000 people in the Great Smog of 1952, an event so severe it had asphyxiated cattle in Smithfield Market. But London – less industrial, less reliant on coal and protected by the Clean Air Act 1956 – was cleaner. It would get cleaner yet as the years passed.[10]

It wasn't just the air that was getting cleaner. In the 1990s, landmarks like Westminster Abbey were scoured of their black coats of dirt and gleamed white for the first time in decades. The city's transport network was also being modernised – new trains replaced the old, rickety, pre-war carriages on several key London Underground lines. And a major extension of the Jubilee line brought swift underground services to previously underserved parts of east and southeast London, massively cutting commuting times to Canary Wharf from several parts of the city. But these changes were also making poorer areas more desirable. One report estimated that the value of homes within a kilometre of the new stations grew by up to £2.1 billion in the six years after the line opened in 1999.[11]

The new, modern, global London was placing its wealth down on top of the city's deeply entrenched poverty. Both Londons vied to find a place for themselves. And once more, these battles were most clearly played out in the field of housing.

DHILLON, MOTIUR

Dhillon lived in a council house with his three brothers, his dad and stepmother in the Isle of Dogs, in east London, in the early 1990s. They were a family of Pakistani Hindus – and the area's local white, working-class community was not happy about their arrival.

'Racism was quite obvious when you played out on the street,' Dhillon recalls. 'The British National Party was out campaigning against Bangladeshi people moving into the area. I got jumped a couple of times just going to the shops, I had chips thrown on me, I was called a Paki. I was actually stabbed in my shoulder blade once.'

At school, PE teachers would separate the boys into Asians and whites for football matches. 'We would hang around with mostly Bangladeshi and Muslim kids. My older brothers had a lot of friends who were Vietnamese. We didn't feel very welcome by the white community,' he tells me.

Amid anger about the allocation of council housing, the BNP won its first council seat on the Isle of Dogs in 1993. 'I remember people campaigning and chanting on the streets, and stickers everywhere saying "rights for whites",' recollects Dhillon. 'There were cars and vans making announcements on tannoys, which was quite scary. You just walked from the shops to your house and tried not to get involved too much, because if you did the backlash would be a lot worse.'

Things improved for the three brothers when they were moved into the Robin Hood Gardens estate about half a mile away. Robin Hood Gardens was a concrete, brutalist block, completed in 1972, which sat in a small enclave in east London just next to the mouth of a busy vehicle tunnel under the Thames. Designed by the architects Alison and Peter Smithson, its noise-reducing concrete fins made it distinctive and instantly recognisable to anyone who knew the area at the time. For Dhillon and his brothers, moving into this community was life changing.

'There were a lot of Bangladeshi families, Kenyans, Vietnamese, Chinese; we all got to know young people on the block quite easily,' he says. 'There was a football pitch, which was a great resource, and a massive green as well. We played a lot of cricket. If it was a weekend and there weren't a lot of people out, you would just go to the intercoms and buzz people asking if they wanted to come down and play football. The estate had a big hill in the middle. When it was sunny, kids of all ages came out and older people came out as well. It had a nice, really nice, community feel.'

The estate had a thriving youth centre, with a pool table and table tennis. Dhillon and his brothers spent quite a lot of time in this club, and Dhillon ultimately became one of the youth workers.

There were problems on the estate – Dhillon recalls drug taking and drug dealing in the stairwells, fights with kids on other estates and territorial gang conflicts. Nor was it in perfect condition; he had nightmares about the lifts, which would sometimes get stuck and often smelled of urine. But despite these issues, the community still made it a good place to live: 'We were all in the same boat, we live in this block, which gets a bad reputation for itself, but if you lived here and you got to know the people, it's actually quite a nice place, But it felt neglected by the council.'

The estate sat on the doorstep of Canary Wharf. 'You could see the sun setting behind Canary Wharf,' says Dhillon. 'I took some amazing photos. But it was a massive contrast. This is like the financial epicentre of Europe, and we're in Robin Hood Gardens and there's loads of people living in these buildings who are quite poor and affected by issues of mental health and poverty.'

One of Dhillon's neighbours was Motiur, whose family got a permanent home in Robin Hood Gardens in 1988 when he was eight years old, after years spent moving between temporary homes. 'It was quite grey and quite grim, but it offered these big rooms, storage space and the balcony. It was just so wide, there was so much space,' he notes. Being able to join a settled community there after so much time moving around made a huge difference to Motiur. 'It was the time of my life,' he adds. 'I've only got fond memories.

'Basically at the weekends or the school holidays, you'd wake up, have your breakfast, head out and the next time you'd come in is for lunch – you'd hear all the parents calling the kids in for lunch. Then you'd have your rice and curry and be out again, and the next time you come home is nine o'clock,' he says.

The estate's design provided a degree of safety. 'At any moment your parents could look out of the window and see you. It was almost like having your own backyard,' he recollects.

In particular, he recalls the fireworks nights. 'I don't think you'll ever see anything like that,' he says. 'The two tower blocks faced each other, you've got the green and the mounds in the middle, and we used to have these firework fights. You split into two teams, I remember my brother making a bazooka with a tube and gaffer tape, you'd put your fireworks in and launch it at the other side.'

Older people would sit outside in the corridors or on balconies. When breaking fast during Ramadan and on Eid, Muslim families would go into each other's houses, sharing food.

'When you're in an estate like that, everybody knows everybody, you watch everyone grow up, all the adults are referred to as uncle and aunty,' Motiur recalls. 'When my brother got married, we had to hire a coach for everyone from the estate. Whether it was good news or bad news, everyone was there to support. You never felt alone.'

Like many other estates at the time, there were live-in caretakers who were able to deal quickly with minor disrepair before it got out of hand. 'I remember Jimmy, a big Rangers fan,' says Motiur. 'He was a real feature of the estate, a real personality. Though over time his role was reduced and the problems started to increase.'

'At one point, it felt like there was a real concerted effort to look after Robin Hood Gardens,' he adds. 'They put double glazing into all the windows, the estate was being looked after. But over time it felt like the council were giving up on it. I remember the council saying things like "We can't get to the root of the problem", or that it's right within the depths of the building.'

CHANGE TAKES EFFECT – SOCIAL HOUSING

After Margaret Thatcher cut the budgets for maintaining housing stock in the 1980s, the decline was rapid. By the early 1990s, capital spending on council homes had dropped to a third of what it had been in the 1970s.[12] With revenue cut back, day-to-day repairs were left undone and planned investment to renovate and maintain buildings was cut back. The live-in caretakers were being replaced with call centres, and John Major's government introduced 'compulsory competitive tendering', under which many repairs contracts were outsourced to private companies.

By 1998, the Chartered Institute of Housing estimated there was a £23 billion backlog of repairs work required to bring council housing up to decent standards.[13] The increasing disrepair was adding to council housing's poor reputation, a growing consequence of the economic deprivation its residents faced. And so a radical solution emerged: even though these homes had been built less than half a century ago, they should be torn down and built again, with different architecture and a different mix of tenancies, hopefully curing them of their sins. Central government money was pushed into 'regeneration' schemes, which really meant demolition.

Some of these early projects worked well: the estates were rebuilt with houses at street level and their residents rehoused in more modern and comfortable homes.[14] But with money limited, not all councils could take this route. Some began to use the powers given to them by Thatcher to transfer their homes to privately run housing associations, which could borrow to invest in their maintenance. For example, in January 1997 Newham Council set up a 'drip feed transfer' of homes which required in excess of £10,000 improvement works to East Thames Housing Association, which would one day join the behemoth L&Q.[15] At the same time, Thatcher's Right to Buy continued to strip London's councils of many of their best homes. London's sales peaked in 1990 at 26,258, but kept up at a sharp pace throughout the 1990s, with inner London boroughs like Lambeth, Lewisham and Tower Hamlets losing thousands of homes through sales every year, the reduced rental income further stretching their budgets.

As costs were cut and maintenance increasingly tendered out to the lowest bidder, problems mounted. On 26 June 1997, the residents of Kerrin Point, a 22-storey block in Lambeth, were woken by an enormous explosion. The communal boiler at the base of the tower had blown up, windows in the block were shattered and hundreds of residents were rendered homeless. The council would later plead guilty to offences under health and safety legislation and pay a £75,000 fine, in a case the judge described as 'an appalling case of neglect'.[16] In a sign of the shape of things to come, the displaced residents struggled to find rehousing in the city – marching a mile and a half from the tower to Downing Street a month later to protest at the fact that they were still homeless.

HANNAH, ANDY

Hannah Joshua continued to enjoy life on the Samuel Lewis estate in Hackney as she grew from a girl into a teenager. 'Once we got older we might have just gone and sat on the wall to chat, and then gone to the shop, gone to the park.' There would be trips of twenty kids to the Rio Cinema for Saturday morning viewings. They'd practise dances to the Spice Girls, E17, the Backstreet Boys. 'There were lots of sleepovers at each other's houses, lots of arguments, lots of "I'm not speaking to you", all of that,' recalls Hannah. It was not always perfect. 'There were definitely characters on the estate I was more wary of: older boys or girls who were a bit more aggressive and intimidating. But it didn't really affect my day-to-day life at all,' she says.

'We knew who lived behind every door. People would bring chairs and sit outside when it was hot. Adults felt like they could parent children who weren't theirs. If I was doing something a bit bad, like climbing up scaffolding, which I quite enjoyed doing, my friend's mum would be the one shouting "Get down from there". When I wanted to go to a sleepover one of the other mums would make it their business to let my mum know that there would be boys there. It was a big sprawling community, and I just remember that we had quite a lot of fun.'

But this was not going to continue forever. In the late 1990s, the estate was demolished. 'We didn't think there was any need for them to do it,' Hannah tells me. 'We didn't think there was anything wrong with the buildings. I was really upset. I was quite a sentimental child. I remember thinking about it: how are they going to do it? Are they just going to rip half of it off, and then will our home just be hanging there, exposed? I still feel sad about it when I walk down that road, because it's all your memories and now they're gone.'

The housing association which ran the estate gave them some money to buy a house when it was demolished. Hackney was too expensive for her mum to consider buying locally, so they had to move out further east. 'I was still very much rooted in Hackney, because I kept coming to school here and coming to see my friends and my dad.' Some of her friends had been moved to a nearby estate on Dalston Lane, others remained in 'the electric', which hadn't been knocked down. 'It did break up the community,' Hannah observes; 'even though they weren't displaced or dispersed that far, they weren't together anymore.'

By 1995, Andy – who had grown up in south London and joined the army before breaking his shin during training – was working as a prison officer at Wandsworth prison and living in a bedsit in Lambeth. He had also got together with his future wife, Ann, who he'd met at an open-air music event in Croydon. 'I got interested in her because she was argumentative,' he laughs. 'We started dating and we both knew fairly quickly that we wanted to be together.' His long-standing knee problems from the broken shin were an issue in a flat that was up three flights of stairs. His GP contacted the council and recommended the couple apply for a social home.

They were offered a ground floor flat on Cressingham Gardens, a small estate on the edge of Brockwell Park, near Brixton. Designed by Lambeth Borough Architects and completed in 1979, it is a simple, well-designed estate – a mix of bungalows, houses and flats, most of which have private outdoor space, set along a series of paved pedestrian walkways and paths that meet at a central 'village green'.[17]

'We just thought, this is great,' he says. 'The place reminded me of the village my paternal grandmother lived in. You have this concentrated community feel.'

TAKING THE STRAIN – PRIVATE RENTING

The growth of London's private landlord sector didn't happen immediately. By 1991, the number of private landlords had actually fallen to its nadir: just 13.9 per cent of the city's households rented privately, three percentage points lower than the figure from a year before.

The increase in renting began as the economy went into recession in the early 1990s. As Londoners fell into financial difficulty, social housing could no longer meet the demands of those who could not afford to buy. It was time for the private sector to step up, in the way Thatcher's ministers had envisioned it would. In 1991, the government was challenged that this would result in increased housing benefit spend in a debate called by the then-backbench Labour MP Jeremy Corbyn. They were explicit that this was their intention. 'Housing benefit will underpin market rents – we have made that absolutely clear,' said housing minister George Young in 1991. 'If people cannot afford to pay that market rent, housing benefit will take the strain.'[18]

But despite the hugely attractive terms to a landlord of an assured shorthold tenancy (which was made the default position by a further change to the law in 1996), investors were not coming in. The trouble was that the only way to build up a property portfolio was to take out a commercial mortgage, and the economic conditions meant these terms were not attractive to those looking to invest.

In 1996, the letting agency industry met with representatives from the banking industry to come up with a solution. They designed a new type of mortgage aimed specifically at small investors seeking to become landlords. The product, branded a 'buy-to-let' mortgage, would allow anyone with a cash deposit to walk into a bank and borrow up to 75 per cent of the value of a property they wanted to buy and rent out, with the mortgage-ability assessed on the potential income in rent the property would offer.

The mortgage repayments were interest-only, which meant big, immediate profits were available from the rental income, at the same time as the landlord would be acquiring a house. Landlords were even able to write off their mortgage payments against tax. It was an extraordinary offer to get rich quick. The new product was launched at the Association of Residential Letting Agents conference in September 1996. 'The rest, as they say, is history,' boasted one of the industry representatives who devised it.[19]

And so it was. Coming as it did at a time when interest rates were low and a generation edging closer to retirement was suddenly realising their investments would not necessarily pay for the lifestyle they had hoped for in old age, this was a golden opportunity to get financial security which they could not and would not turn down. Money began flowing into buy-to-let lending. It happened slowly at first: by the end of the 1990s, buy-to-let lending totalled only 4 per cent of overall mortgage lending. But it would grow, and grow rapidly.

Peter Williams – the Newham council housing officer we met in the previous chapter – was working in enforcement of standards in private rented housing in the east London borough at this time. In the 1980s, private rented housing in Newham had been in sharp decline. It had mainly been provided by big landlords who traced their history back to the days of Dickens, and had made their wealth from the area's industry and invested it in property. The Pears Soap family owned hundreds, and so did the Scruttons, the family who owned many of the properties on the street I grew up on.

But as buy-to-let arrived the profile changed. The former large landlords had rented out to secure tenants on rent-controlled tenancies, and they were now keen to cash in their investments and move on. 'That institutional ownership of property in the borough just disappeared in the 1990s,' says Peter. 'A lot of their tenants were older people who were sort of left behind in the borough – their families had moved out to Essex and they were living in these old, unimproved houses. When they died, rather than do them up, the former landlords were just putting the properties straight up for auction.'

The homes were then bought by the new guard of private landlord – small-time buy-to-let investors seeking a return on a small pot of savings. 'People with quite modest incomes – shopkeepers, small business owners – would buy a couple of houses using a buy-to-let mortgage, become landlords and rent [them] out to people on benefits,' says Peter.

With council housing harder to come by, homeless households seeking a place from the council were also being offered private rented housing. The private sector was indeed 'taking the strain' – and making a tidy profit while doing so, funded by housing benefit. Before Thatcher, the country was spending £21.3 billion a year on new social housing and £1 billion a year on housing benefit. By 2001, this had almost entirely reversed – £4.1 billion a year was spent on new social housing and £15.4 billion went on benefits, much of it to new private landlord investors.[20]

This change – and rush of small private investors into the private housing market – meant that houses in London were not just houses anymore. They were pension plans and investment opportunities for people who would never live in them. As Nick Bano explains, this had a very direct impact on house prices, because the market would start to value homes according to what their expected investment return would be, not what people could reasonably afford to pay to live in them. Driven by a banking sector hungry for credit and property as security, and a generation who wanted a pension and saw an easy opening to financial security, property prices in London began to ratchet up and up and up. In January 1990, the average price was £79,909 (£191,000 in today's money). By 2000, it had risen to £130,411 (£244,000 in today's money). The great 'pricing out' had begun in earnest.

MANJU, DAVE

Manju and Satinder, who had got a tenancy from his job at the clothing company, saw their landlord change in the 1990s. His former employer sold the lease on their shop to another company, who sold it again, with the flats above changing hands too. The relaxed approach to letting the property – where tenants effectively set their own fair rents and made the properties their own – disappeared. A commercial managing agent was appointed. 'Ever since that happened it was a downward spiral for us,' Manju reflects. 'It was a real effort to get anything done. They always sent people who did the shoddiest work.'

Conditions started to deteriorate. A leak in the bathroom of the flat above Manju's began to build up, and eventually the ceiling in the bathroom collapsed. 'There was dust everywhere, it broke the sink, it broke everything. If someone had been sat on the loo at that point, they would have died.'

Around them, the long-term secure tenants started to move out. Their flats were filled with short-term lets or sold to wealthy buyers who did not live there. The group of friends who had sustained them and served London's gay community in its darkest hour was being dismantled.

But the tenants in Manju's building who stayed were still on rent-controlled, secure tenancies. Even though Thatcher had brought in the new regime of short-term tenancies with complete rental freedom for the landlord, those who had started their tenancies before this date were still subject to the old regime. Rents could still rise every two years, but within defined limits linked to inflation. This meant the community could cling on in Kensington, even as the prices rose rapidly around them.

Dave, the music journalist who had moved from a bedsit to short-life housing in Islington, purchased a house with his partner when they had a child. The couple got a small, terraced house in Hoxton – then a dangerous part of east London, famed for its cockney villains and murders. 'A lot of more middle-class Londoners avoided these sorts of areas as a result, which kept the prices down a bit,' he says. 'But it was perfect for family like mine, the houses were great and you could afford to get something quite nice on a fairly regular salary.' He and his partner had two more children and felt like it was time to upsize. In 1992, they moved again, this time into a five-bedroom town house which cost them £127,000 (£274,000 in today's money) – a large sum at the time, but still just about within the means of a couple on middle-class salaries.

'It was a nice spacious house, with a nice bit of garden,' says Dave. 'I never really wanted anything more than that. When I came to London, I thought, "I'd like to live in one of those nice old terraced houses with a big front door and steps going up to it. That will do me."'

BUST AND BOOM – BUYING A HOUSE

At the start of the 1990s, it looked as if home ownership might be the future of London, thanks to Right to Buy and the growth in accessibility of mortgage lending giving many more people a route onto the ladder. The 1991 census showed 57.2 per cent of Londoners were homeowners, up almost ten percentage points from 1981. But this year would in fact represent a peak: home ownership would go into decline and for those who had just found themselves on the ladder the dark side of the boom in credit and the increasing prices which followed was about to manifest.

The end of the 1980s had been a boom time – the economy grew, mortgage lending increased as people turned their new incomes into home ownership, and house prices rose. Banks had piled into the newly available mortgage market, assuming that house prices were stable and would not fall. But towards the end of the decade things had started to go sour. Concerns about rising inflation saw interest rates and mortgage rates rise at the same time as the general economy darkened, restricting people's disposable income. Suddenly buyers who had piled into the housing market and signed up to variable-rate mortgages were feeling the squeeze – their monthly repayments were going up but their personal income was flatlining. Mortgage transactions slowed as first-time buyers found themselves struggling to get onto the ladder, and private house builders slowed their output due to a reduced number of buyers. The mortgage market downturn rippled out and the wider economy turned down in 1991.

House prices in London – which had been growing rapidly in the late 1980s – went into reverse, falling by 5.8 per cent in 1990 and 1991 and then by 9.4 per cent in 1992.[21] The position of those who had just bought was desperate: increasing interest rates meant they were struggling to afford their repayments, but the crashing house prices meant selling the home would not pay off their debts. They were trapped. Between 1990 and 1992, 187,900 homes were repossessed across England and by the end of 1992 more than 350,000 mortgagees were in more than six months of arrears.[22] In London, 41 per cent of those who had borrowed in the late 1980s were in negative equity – meaning they could not move house until prices recovered.[23] The government spent billions in public money on mortgage relief – bailing out homeowners but also the banks, who were able to avoid the losses that might otherwise have resulted from their greed.

This, perhaps, was a warning we should have heeded: lashing our economy and our wellbeing to the fickle mortgage market came with danger. For a functional market, house price growth should be restrained by what people's real-world salaries could maintain and lending by banks controlled by a healthy appreciation of the risk of default. But this was not the path we wanted to take. Instead, banks felt able to lend whatever they liked, and the new mortgages were breaking the link between earnings and house prices. The consequences would hit eventually, but first, prices would inflate out of all control.

JOTHI, RUPHINA

In 1989, Jothi and Stanley had a third child, Rosie. She recalls a happy childhood growing up in the house they had bought in Stratford: 'All I wanted to do was play on the swing in the garden. There was a park at the end of the road and a bigger park round the corner with a basketball court, a skate park and a community centre where we would go to after school. I remember walking to primary school with my brothers, the area was that safe.'

The garden in their house backed onto another one and there was a small hole in the back fence. 'This little white boy used to just peer through the hole.' says Rosie. 'We found out that he used to come in and play with the children who lived here before us.'

Rosie's mum left the hole uncovered, and the boy quickly made friends. He had the same name as Rosie's brother, Aaron, and so the children called him Big Aaron. His mum had passed away, and he lived in the house with his dad. Jothi became a surrogate mother figure to him. 'He was a beautiful little boy with blond hair,' she remembers. 'I would take him with my two boys out to summer events on the bus, and people would stare at me with these two Asian boys and this little white boy. He used to call me Mum. He was part of us, he was part of the family.'

The family stayed in touch with Lil and Ted – the couple they had befriended in Limehouse, who still came to play with the kids in the garden or invited them round to their flat almost every week. Jothi and Stanley did not have many relatives in the UK and so the couple effectively became grandparents to Rosie and her two brothers. 'I think I only saw my biological grandparents four times in my life,' Rosie tells me. 'So Lil and Ted were our grandparents. I developed a lot of English-isms growing up because of them: I loved pie and mash, fish and chips, sticks of rock, the seaside, Southend. That was just normal to us.'

Eli, the son of Ruphina, who had saved up enough money to buy a three-bedroom house in east London from her various incomes as a soft-furnisher, childminder and secretary, was born in 1989. He recalls a happy childhood. 'It was a quiet street without much traffic, so I could ride my bike outside and play with the other kids.' His sister Andrea got a job as a buyer at BHS and, when Eli was six, had made enough money to move out and buy her own three bedroom street property, about a mile away in another part of Plaistow. It had taken her less than a year to save up the deposit.

The area was still majority white – especially a nearby housing estate just south of Newham Way, a large dual carriageway. Occasionally this would pop up as a reality in Eli's otherwise warm memories. 'There was one time when I was riding my tricycle to church, and these two skinheads started chasing me, telling me to swim back to Africa. My mum basically screamed at them and chased them off. There were those odd moments of racism, I'm sure my mum suffered a lot more. But all in all it was OK.'

Towards the end of the 1990s, Ruphina decided she wanted to move back to Dominica for Eli's adolescence. She felt the island would provide a more healthy, outdoor life for a teenage boy, where he would be free from the pressures of racism and crime.

To pay for the trip, and to help build a home and workshop in Dominica, she sold the house. By now properties down the street were getting close to £100,000 in value – more than three times what she had originally paid for hers, so it felt like a good time to cash in. But once sold, and traded in for a home in the Caribbean, the family were off the ladder of rising property wealth in the capital.

'Looking back, if we'd known how the property market was going to go, it feels a bit shortsighted,' says Eli. 'Because once it was gone, it meant there was no equity from the house to help me get back onto the ladder when I came back to the UK.'

But in the late 1990s, people didn't think so much in these terms. London was still a place where you could get a decent job, save for a while and buy. People simply did not realise the goldmine that a three-bedroom terraced house in east London would become.

PRICES START TO ACCELERATE – BUYING A HOUSE

By the middle of the 1990s, the fall in house prices caused by the downturn had brought price-to-income ratios back down to where they had been before Thatcher's deregulation, and even below in some boroughs. For decades this had been the pattern: house prices rose and fell from time to time as bubbles formed and burst, but the house-price-to-earnings ratio usually came back to around three or four to one. 'Generally speaking, in the late twentieth century, that was what you could expect to pay for a house,' says economist Professor Ian Mulheirn. 'But in the late 1990s, that just went out of the window and prices started to accelerate. And we've been stuck in that new world ever since. It's hard to overestimate just how much the twenty-first century has been completely different from the twentieth century in that regard.'[24]

The macroeconomy drove this trend. Economists are divided about exactly why it occurred – perhaps it was savings outweighing investments in East Asia, perhaps it was the deregulation of the major economies and the growth which followed in the 1980s, perhaps it was the end of the Cold War. But what is clear is that since the late 1980s the trend across the developed world has been for interest rates to fall and stay low. This had consequences. For individuals, saving for retirement was now much harder. You couldn't just stick money into bonds and dream of a life of comfort anymore. The money would hardly grow enough to keep pace with inflation, let alone pay for a longer retirement as life expectancy rose.

And for serious, big, global investment funds, their money needed a home which was secure from being reduced by inflation. The result was a wall of money looking for what economists call 'safe assets'. And one of the safest was housing. For individuals, this meant buying up multiple homes as investments through the newly launched buy-to-let programme. For large investment houses, it meant putting their clients' money into property rather than investing in businesses. Housing was now a commodity, sought after by enormous global wealth. Prices would begin to rise accordingly, to reflect the value to investors and their deeper pockets. But this drove a self-reinforcing cycle. The more the price rose, the more attractive it became to invest in housing and the more money was poured in.

With their financial freedom to create new mortgages, banks also piled into mortgage lending and away from business lending at an unprecedented rate. The bubble was being inflated.[25]

JOHN, PATRICIA AND SEAN, CAROLYN

Primary school headteacher John's daughter Su trained as an architect, and was looking to get a place near her parents in east London in 1997. But it was increasingly hard. With her partner, she was renting a small flat in north London, but they couldn't find anywhere they could afford to buy.

'It was a minimum of £75,000 to £80,000 at the time to get a two- or three-bedroom flat, and we just couldn't afford it,' Su says. 'You couldn't really get anything for less than that, unless there was something wrong with it, and we weren't going to have any money to fix anything.'

So reluctantly, the couple looked outside of London, to Frinton-on-Sea, a seaside town in Essex, where Su could commute to work in old slam-door trains. The journey took more than an hour, but it was far enough away from London that the prices dropped right off and the couple could afford a three-bedroom Edwardian terrace. But it meant moving away from her parents, who were now growing older and nearing retirement. They were still happy in their community in east London, and didn't want to leave.

Patricia and Sean, the Irish couple who had bought a house in Brent in the 1980s, decided to help her parents buy. They were reaching retirement age, and she felt Right to Buy offered the best route to a secure retirement. At first, her parents didn't want to. 'Dad was worried about extra bills, and mum liked the fact that if something went wrong the council would fix it,' Patricia says. 'But I had spare money because Sean had already bought our house. So I offered to buy the house for them.'

She put cash in from her savings and her parents got the home where they would live until they died. 'Our wages were better than our mum and dad's wages, so we were able to help them,' adds Patricia.

It is important to remember this sort of story. As well as the harm wreaked by Right to Buy on a national level, for some individuals it has been transformative – Patricia's parents, her dad a labourer and her mum doing casual housework, were able to own property and retire comfortably thanks to this policy.

Patricia and Sean were able to ride out the economic turbulence of the early 1990s, now with two young children of their own. 'We were very lucky, Sean's firm always kept him in work. His boss wanted to make sure all his men had an income.' Sean was building schools, warehouses and residential property – laying the concrete and digging the foundations as London grew and expanded into the modern city it is today.

Carolyn, meanwhile, the civil servant who was renting in Finchley, continued to stay in her shared accommodation. After she'd injured her knee, she struggled with the building. There was a lift, but the steps were tricky if it ever broke down. And it was tough using public transport to commute.

Increasingly her friends were moving to other parts of the city where rents were cheaper, particularly to south London. 'I eventually got to feel like I didn't have a single friend north of the river,' she says.

THINGS CAN ONLY GET BETTER

As the 1990s ended, Britain voted for change. In spring 1997, Tony Blair's Labour Party cruised to victory to the sound of 'Things Can Only Get Better' by D:Ream. The nation was ready for Cool Britannia.

Blair immediately made housing a priority. He delivered one of his first speeches as prime minister at south London's Aylesbury estate. His speech was clear: such a place had no future in his vision of twenty-first-century Britain. 'There are estates where the biggest employer is the drug industry, where all that is left of the high hopes of the post-war planners is derelict concrete,' he told the media. 'There must be no no-hope areas in Labour's Britain.'[26]

But this plan for change in places like the Aylesbury would instead lead to their destruction.

2000s

A TRANSIENT CITY

London's skyline transformed with the arrival of a new millennium. Under Tony Blair's renewed drive for devolution, London saw the Greater London Authority established, a new, seemingly improved, iteration of the GLC abolished by Margaret Thatcher. The erstwhile GLC leader Ken Livingstone returned as mayor of London to a new glass and steel City Hall in the year 2000. Livingstone introduced a planning regime where high-rise building was encouraged. The 1980s and 1990s had seen One Canada Square arrive as the new financial era kicked off. But this was a one-off landmark development. Under Livingstone, things changed rapidly.

His office signed off dozens of buildings more than 300 ft tall, mostly located in the City of London and Canary Wharf. The Cheesegrater, the Gherkin, the Shard, the Walkie-Talkie – these monoliths all began springing from the ground under Livingstone's watch. The Gherkin, or 30 St Mary Axe to give its official name, was built on the site left damaged and derelict by the 1992 IRA bomb. Most of these new buildings were offices, but a small number were also residential. Pan Peninsula, a set of two blocks in Canary Wharf, one of forty-eight storeys and the other of thirty-eight, was built by the Irish developer Ballymore in 2008, and was branded the area's first 'ultra-luxury' residential tower. The penthouse apartment was sold for £7 million in 2006, two years before the tower was completed.

The new towers were irrevocably altering London's appearance. 'The capital's precious skyline is being consciously recrafted into an expression of corporate dominance,' declared historian Tristram Hunt in 2008.¹ But these towers were changing more than just the look of the city and the views of the horizon. Land is priced according to its development potential, and if a fifty-storey residential tower can be built on it, that is how the landowner will price it. This initial cost feeds straight back into the design: to maximise profit, it will need to squeeze as much out of the development as possible. This means packing in as many flats as possible, which in turn means a reduction in space.

In 2005, more change was promised. On 6 July, crowds in Trafalgar Square waved Union Jacks in the sunshine as the city celebrated winning its bid to host the 2012 Olympics. Plans for a giant new Olympic Park and athletes' village were unveiled. Occupying an underdeveloped site of marshland, flood plains, factories, dirty canals and railway yards, the park would sit at the intersection of four deprived London boroughs: Newham, Hackney, Tower Hamlets and Waltham Forest. A legacy of new affordable housing and sporting excellence was promised. A day later, Trafalgar Square was deserted, sirens echoing through the city as the emergency services scrambled to respond to four suicide bombings across the capital, which killed fifty-two people and injured nearly eight hundred others.

Meanwhile London was getting noticeably hotter. In 2003, a heatwave swept through the city bringing record-breaking temperatures. Londoners sweltered in their blocks of flats and brick housing, most without any air conditioning or shuttered window blinds. Tarmac melted on the M25, railway lines buckled and temperatures breached 38 degrees for the first time. It is not clear how many people died as a result, but statistics showed an unexplained spike of more than 2,000 deaths for the weeks during the hot weather, with older people living alone the worst affected. Drenched by extreme rainfall the city also saw floods.² In July 2007, after a month of heavy rainfall which had submerged rural areas and towns around the country, London was subject to its own sudden flash flooding. 'Eyewitnesses reported seeing the sky suddenly turn dark before the torrential downpour of rain and hailstones began,' reported the BBC. 'They were really large pieces of hail the size of 20 pence pieces which tore through the sky, ripping leaves from the trees and flowers from plants. I have never seen anything like it,' said one eyewitness.³ The authorities were concerned. 'Because London's built-up land surface does not allow rain-water to soak away into the ground, there is an increased risk that severe rain leads rapidly to flooding. Because London is so densely populated and developed, a major flood would cause great property damage, with a high chance of loss of life,' said a report commissioned by the London Assembly.⁴

The city grew by almost a million people during the 2000s, rising to close to its pre-war peak population of 8.2 million by the end of the decade. People were coming, as they always have, for work.

It may be worth addressing, head on, the argument that blames immigration for all our problems with housing in London. To some, this story is no more complex than the population increasing due to higher levels of immigration, and the demand for housing rising as a result. But housing is never this simple.

New migrants, especially in London, most frequently live in the private rented sector, and often in rooms rather than whole houses. This means that while they do contribute to an increased demand for private rental housing, they increase the overall demand for new housing more slowly than you might expect, while also filling vital roles in London's economy. It is also clear that house prices are dictated much more by their value as investment assets. House prices in cities have risen globally, regardless of levels of international migration. Increased demand is not irrelevant to house prices, and commentators on the left help no one by completely ignoring it, but equally the tunnel vision among some commentators on the right, seeing immigration as the cause, is misplaced. One major study suggested there is a 1 per cent house price rise for every percentage point increase in the population. If that was all that was going on, houses would have stayed a lot more affordable.

Nonetheless people were coming to London in droves in this period: from new graduates within the UK, seeking higher-paid jobs as university education expanded, to lower-paid workers from overseas seeking a stable income paid in a stable currency. Unlikely to have deposits for a new home, or to be able to access social housing, all of these people were funnelled into the private rental sector, driving up the demand for rental properties.

Rents and evictions rose as landlords quickly replaced poorer tenants with those who could pay more – starting to force the poorest to the city's outskirts. The city's poverty rate stayed at around 27 per cent for most of the decade – always higher than the average in the rest of the country by several percentage points.[5]

And the city's ethnic make-up continued to evolve. By the end of the decade, white British people made up 45 per cent of the city's population – still the largest ethnic group, but the first time in the city's history when they had not represented an absolute majority of the city's residents. This was driven primarily by white British families leaving. During the decade, 620,000 white British people left the city – a figure equivalent to the total population of Glasgow.[6]

For many, this was simply the logic of the property market in action. The homes purchased through Right to Buy or new mortgage lending in the 1980s and 1990s were now worth a small fortune, and could be traded in for a nicer home elsewhere. Selling and moving out to a bigger home, cleaner air and greener surroundings was an obvious choice for many.

The BBC reported on a family in Westcliff, part of Southend-on-Sea, where a family had cashed in their three-bedroom house in Barking for a six-bedroom home by the sea. 'They keep bumping into old school friends, realising that they were joining a sizeable population of migrants from the borough,' the report declared.[7] The communities of the traditional East End were dispersing, cockney London relegated to the history books.

And as the houses they sold were often finding their way into the hands of private landlords, who rented rooms on a short-term basis with rents that rose and rose and rose, it was hard for a new community to form in their wake. With communities moving out, the cultural facilities which had served them started to go. Traditional street markets dwindled and closed down. Long-standing high-street family businesses faded away, replaced by an ever-changing array of chicken shops, bookies and mobile phone repair shops. Pubs also began to disappear, with one in every four across the city closing its doors permanently between 2001 and 2016. The British Flag closed in 2001, and reopened as a west African Pentecostal church.

The loss of security in housing had left London unmoored, and it was becoming a more transient, ever-changing place, somewhere it was hard for anyone to feel truly at home.

ANDREW, MELANIE

Andrew – the son of a postman who grew up in the east London council estate which resembled old episodes of *EastEnders* – became a session musician in the mid-2000s. 'At school I messed up, classic story of having the brains but not the sense to knuckle down and get the GCSE grades I should have done,' he says. 'I wasn't a stereotypical session player, which is basically a middle-class guy with a load of money and a £2,000 guitar. The way I treated it was like a trade – like being a plumber or a carpenter. It's your trade, you learn it. I'd go into the pub on a Friday with my big old bass guitar and prop it up where the builders and plumbers and everyone else left their equipment.'

He was able to make a bit of money from music, but he too kept living under his mum's roof in their council house. 'It was either stay at home with family and share the bills and live in a nice home, or duck and dive and go to a really rubbish, tiny room and share with people you don't know with a landlord that's probably less than brilliant,' he says.

Melanie had grown up in a single-parent home in west London, and left school aged sixteen, looking for a job to help her mum pay the bills. She found herself working as an administrative assistant to the development team at a housing association – one of the private social landlords which had been encouraged to grow under Thatcher.

This housing association had a proud, charitable history – founded in the 1960s to provide decent quality homes in an area of London where poor private rented housing was rife. By the time Melanie joined in the mid-2000s, it was an ambitious developer, taking millions in government grants to either build new social housing projects itself or purchase newly built homes from developers to let out to those on housing waiting lists.

Melanie had lived in social housing for her whole life and had recently moved into her own one-bedroom flat, through a scheme which offered the adult children of social tenants the chance to move to their own property. She loved her job at the housing association – quickly moving up to project management. Melanie was proud of the work she was doing. 'I was really excited by it, because we were doing something which felt quite good,' she says. 'It definitely felt then that we were providing homes for people who wouldn't have been able to afford them otherwise. It felt genuine.'

THE RISE OF PRIVATE SOCIAL HOUSING

With twenty years now elapsed since Thatcher's cuts to council housing, the growing disrepair in social housing stock was becoming a glaring problem. The New Labour government wanted to fix it – but also used the fix to open a door to their own ideological view of social housing.

In 2000, a major 'Decent Homes Programme' was launched by the government, with a view to raising the standards of all social homes by 2010. This offered direct grants to upgrade social homes, with a particular focus on improving them internally. But it came with conditions.

To access the government money, councils had to bring the private sector – and therefore private finance – to the party. There were three options for doing this: a wholesale transfer of their housing stock to a housing association, setting up a private finance initiative (PFI) deal with a private company to do the work (where they were paid a fixed fee every year for decades to complete the repairs) or creating an 'arm's-length management organisation' (ALMO) – a company that would be owned by the council and would run the day-to-day management of council housing for it.[8]

Around the country, dozens of councils transferred their stock wholesale to housing associations, which took on huge borrowing to fund the transfer and the work which would be required as a result. It was a major privatisation of housing management. In some instances, for tenants it worked well – they got improvements to their homes without a change in the rents. Splitting social housing management functions from the state like this is pretty common in many European countries, without major problems emerging as a result.

But privatisation always comes at a cost. The new housing associations paid much larger salaries, and brought a corporate ethos which did not always work. Local management was increasingly replaced by call centres and big contracts with private sector repair companies. In 2002, the government created a new rent formula which saw all social rents increase at rates above inflation to ensure the private debt was paid back. Secure council tenancies were replaced with less secured 'assured' tenancies.

There was significant pushback against these changes in London, led by the Defend Council Housing group. A transfer required a tenant ballot, and with residents in the capital particularly afraid of losing their security and their affordable rents – conscious of how quickly rents were rising around them – some transfers were rejected. Only Richmond and Merton transferred all their stock to a private housing association, following Bromley, which had already done so in 1992. Other boroughs, such as Tower Hamlets, transferred thousands of homes which they could not afford to bring up to decent home standards, but kept others in municipal control.

But this left boroughs with limited options. Some set up ALMOs to take control. Others pushed homes which needed upgrades into PFI deals with private contractors paid a handsome, inflation-linked annual fee to do the work to improve them. Big promises were made to residents about the improvements they would soon see.

And work was done. In Hackney, for example, an ALMO was set up which spent £184 million to deliver new kitchens and bathrooms to 10,800 homes, new roofs to 14,753 homes and new windows to 16,700 homes.[9] But things were being missed. Fundamental problems remained: fire safety, pipe work, watertightness. All of these were starting to fray, and were not covered by the new funding coming in.

And the private deals were not always bringing the rise in standards Blair hoped they would. As we reached the middle of the 2000s, the PFI deals were already going wrong. With guaranteed payments and minimal quality checks, private contractors were able to make a fortune from the work – their profit margin only enhanced by the corners cut. Dr Stuart Hodkinson, an academic from the University of Leeds, who has studied the impact of PFI in social housing in detail, describes it as 'outsourcing on steroids'. His work has exposed the PFI contractors winning big deals to improve social homes and then carrying the work out on the cheap to protect their profit margins, with desperately poor results: hammering nails through water pipes, damage to homes, electrics wired up incorrectly and residents left in shocking conditions.[10]

The ALMOs were also starting to struggle in some cases, with limited oversight of their actions. A review of the body set up in Kensington & Chelsea to manage the 9,000 council homes uncovered serious cases of disrepair, including contractors breaking down a door to the wrong flat, a tenant waiting for twenty years for a leak to be fixed before she was decanted due to the damage it caused, and central heating systems being fitted so badly the resulting noise damaged residents' health. 'Words such as "malevolent", "mistrust", "malaise" and "treated with contempt" were often used [by residents],' the review declaimed. 'This is an unhappy culture and needs to change for the better.'[11] Problems would also develop with ALMOs in Lewisham, Waltham Forest, Hackney and Lambeth – all of which were ultimately shut down.

But there was another big problem. Councils which had not taken any of the routes towards privatisation were left with no money for major repairs. And with no funding, crumbling blocks and unhappy residents, they began to look to another, more drastic option: demolition.

MOTIUR, DHILLON

Motiur was a gifted student at school. He secured a place at the University of Cambridge – the first person in his family to go to university. He left the Robin Hood Gardens Estate during term times, to join a cohort of mostly public school, middle-class and white students. 'It was a real culture shock, but it allowed me to see another side of the world,' he says.

After university he returned to Robin Hood Gardens and got a job teaching in Tower Hamlets. But the estate itself was starting to suffer: 'We knew the talks were happening about improvements and changes. There was always a suspicion that everything has its time. We were so close to Canary Wharf, and you felt the glitz and the glamour might sneak its way over here as well. The estate was starting to feel like such a contrast to the buildings being built around it. So I always had a suspicion that something was going to happen.' In 2008, a condition survey revealed defects which raised 'questions about the cost-effectiveness of future long-term maintenance' and proposed demolition.

Dhillon – who had moved from the racism of the Isle of Dogs to the community of Robin Hood Gardens – was by now a youth worker, working with young people from the deprived communities around London's former docklands. He could feel the area changing: 'You just saw a lot of changes – Canary Wharf popped up and Waitrose and John Lewis arrived and there was a big change in prices.' New housing developments were also changing the landscape: blocks of luxury flats cut off the riverside where previously he had been able to walk freely.

Along with his brother, he had bought his flat under Right to Buy. 'We would have lived there, we were quite happy, but there were loads of carrots being dangled by the council, that you know, you're gonna get bigger property in exchange if this is demolished,' he says.

The building was now suffering from neglect. 'Quite a few people were against the regeneration, but quite a few were for it because the housing conditions were quite poor,' he reflects. 'There were loads of water issues in the building, there was a lot of damp and water leakage. It needed to be modernised. The whole building was neglected for quite a long time.'

Attempts by campaigners to get the estate listed as a historical landmark attracted the support of some leading lights in the world of architecture, but were blocked by government ministers. In 2010, Tower Hamlets Council shortlisted a group of architects and developers who would take part in the demolition programme and build 1,575 homes on the site of the former council block. The blocks were transferred to a housing association, Swan, for the demolition to take place. The tenants would be rehoused once the new homes were built. Remaining leaseholders would receive compensation.

Dhillon and his partner moved off the estate in 2005, but his brother stayed. He continued to endure year after year of exhausting consultation meetings and unmet promises as the building emptied of residents around him. He continued to hold on, believing he would eventually be offered a better property. 'There were lots of leaks, and the drinking water in the building started to taste strange,' Dhillon tells me. 'He had to suffer for quite a long time with that building.'

DEMOLITION OF A DREAM – SOCIAL HOUSING

'Estate regeneration' – as the process of demolishing a council housing estate and rebuilding it at a higher density with more private housing has become known – is probably the element of social housing policy in London that has provoked the most resistance. Seeing families displaced, council blocks knocked down and expensive private apartments built in their place has been one of the most violent visual signs of how the city is failing.

It is worth saying at the outset that not all 'regeneration' is created equal. While some communities have been scattered across outer London boroughs and beyond, others have found themselves rehoused in a newly built block on the same land and relatively happy with the outcome. Similarly, the objective of those involved in 'regenerating' estates was not always the same. I have spoken to many on the local authority side who genuinely felt that what they were doing would eventually deliver better housing and was their only viable option in the absence of proper funding.

Indeed, the real failure with estate regeneration may be here – the failure of the central government machine to invest in keeping places habitable, rather than allowing them to decay. 'Estates built in social problems over many years. But the problems could have been solved,' says Anne Power, emeritus professor of social policy at the London School of Economics and Political Science (LSE). 'They just needed a landlord service on the spot. There needed to be a local estate office and a local budget where the rents were retained and invested. With the rents you could fund one caretaker for every 100 units and a local repairs team, along with other support staff to constantly maintain the estates. You could keep these estates in a spanking good condition with that sort of management.'[12]

But despite the presence of some well-intentioned players stuck in a difficult environment, it would also be desperately naive not to see that there have always been other motives at work with the demolition of social housing estates in the capital. As the price of housing in London rose and rose, the land on which these estates were located became goldmines for developers – especially as many were built at a time when London's population was shrinking and were therefore constructed at relatively low density. To a private developer, the profit to be made from getting control of this land and building it up to the highest density possible was such an attractive proposition that any other social objective would be secondary.

And in the Blair era these projects were never going to be delivered with public funding alone. Instead, if a council wanted to 'regenerate' an estate, it would typically form a partnership with a private developer, who would provide most of the funding for the highly expensive work of demolition and rebuild. But this meant the power rested with the developers, and their incentive was not to rebuild and improve London's ageing social housing stock, but to profit as handsomely as they could from the land on which it stood. 'If the private sector is expected to do the heavy financial lifting, then these things become a vehicle for private sector profit, effectively,' remarks Dr Paul Watt, visiting professor at the LSE's Department of Sociology. 'And that clashes with the needs of the existing working-class communities.'[13]

There was also an unpleasant attitude from some of the councils which managed the social housing in London. They had come to see the estates as problems to be solved. The stigmatising view that estates would function much better with an influx of wealthier residents was in vogue in local authority circles in London. Stephen Greenhalgh, who led Hammersmith & Fulham Council into several regeneration programmes as leader from 2006, wrote in 2009 that social housing 'has become welfare housing where both a dependency culture and a culture of entitlement predominate'. He added that the estates delivered 'a risible return on assets', were 'barracks for the poor' and should be 'broken up'. Sir Robin Wales, the Labour mayor of Newham from 2002 to 2018, described social housing estates as 'social ghettos' and said in an interview that 'I don't want to manage poverty.'[14] Or take the softer words of Pat Hayes, director of regeneration at Lewisham Council, who described the Pepys Estate as 'a monolithic concentration of public housing', which he wanted to 'break up a bit and bring in a different mix of incomes and people with spending power'.[15]

This estate, on the site of a sixteenth-century dockyard on the south bank of the Thames which was sold to the London County Council by the Admiralty in 1955, saw an even more direct form of gentrification than demolition. One of three high-rise towers (the one closest to the river) was sold to the private developer Berkeley Homes in 2002 for the bargain sum of £11.5 million. The tower was emptied of its 144 working-class households. Berkeley then transformed the appearance of the empty building with a shiny facade, converted the top apartments to penthouses and advertised them on the private market, where they were selling for more than half a million pounds each by the end of the decade.[16]

This piecemeal sell-off to private builders also took place in Lambeth. In the previous chapter, I described Kerrin Point, the south London block damaged by a huge gas explosion in 1997. The building could not be repaired and was demolished in 1999. In 2004, the derelict land was sold to private house builder Barratt Homes. This development was completed in 2009, and Kennington Park Square was built: 214 new homes across five medium-rise blocks, replacing the 86 flats of the original tower. Of these, only fifty-seven were for social rent and thirty-five were for shared ownership, purchased by housing association Wandle. Barratt sold the private properties, netting around £250,000 each, and eventually also sold the freehold of the block to a private investor. Years later, it would emerge that the new private building had serious fire defects, costing millions to repair.[17]

But it is where whole estates have been demolished that we have seen the biggest, most controversial changes. The Aylesbury estate, where Blair gave his triumphant speech in 1997, was slated for demolition in 2005, Southwark Council viewing this as a better option than investing an estimated £350 million to repair it. This process continues today – the estate is partially demolished and residents in the remaining blocks have continued to battle the demolition of their homes in the courts. The Heygate estate in Elephant and Castle is perhaps the most notorious example of this. Completed in 1974, its giant slab blocks dominated the skyline around Elephant and Castle station for three and a half decades. It had 1,214 homes, which housed more than 3,000 people at its height. Jerry Flynn was in his late teens when he moved onto the Heygate with his family, after the crowded private homes they lived in were demolished. The family got a four-bed maisonette in the low-rise housing in the centre of the estate. He remembers the Heygate as simply a place where a working-class community could afford to make a decent home.

'I wouldn't get too rose-tinted about it. We knew a lot of our neighbours and they knew us. The teacher from my local primary school lived on the estate,' he says. 'I always say the same when I'm asked about life on the Heygate – it was pretty ordinary. Nothing much different from any other council estate in south London. I used to play football, we knew a lot of our neighbours, but people just got on with our lives. We were secure. Or we thought we were.'

Southwark's former council leader Peter John saw it differently. He described the Heygate as a 'symbol of inner-city neglect, with crime, antisocial behaviour, health inequalities and unemployment the only things that flourished there'.[18] Elephant and Castle at this time was a unique area. Minutes' walk from London Bridge, it has been described as 'one of the few surviving sections of old-school central London'.[19] There was a big Latin American community and a market filled with local traders who served local people. But it was going to change.

As the plans to demolish the estate emerged, residents were promised a 'right to return' and rehousing in new council homes planned around the borough while the work was carried out. But these promises were quickly broken. The council began 'decanting' the residents ahead of the demolition in 2007, before any of the fifteen sites to rehouse them in were complete.[20] They were dispersed across southeast London and the nearby counties, to wait and hope for their promised new homes to be built.

On other estates, the process simply became a gratingly long exercise in waiting for something to happen. Residents were continually called to meetings at community centres, and presented with grand masterplans, which would then be shelved. The anxiety and uncertainty of not knowing what the future of their homes would be grew. On many estates slated for demolition, councils stopped nominating new tenants who would simply have to be 'decanted' again as the process developed. They also cut maintenance spend to almost zero – reasoning that there was no point spending money on a building that would soon be reduced to rubble. But with years elapsing as the planning system, financing arrangements and various other negotiations rolled on, the estates were left to degrade: full of empty homes, leaking pipework, crumbling masonry, peeling paint, broken lifts.

The most glaring example of the time these projects can take can be found on the Woodberry Down estate in Hackney, where the council planned to demolish and rebuild the estate in collaboration with a housing association and private developer after structural surveys in 1999 showed it was 'too costly' to refurbish. But over the next decade, nothing happened apart from planning. Building work for the new homes did not start until 2009.

'It was a stupid decision to demolish Woodberry Down,' Professor Anne Power asserts. 'The flats didn't need to be demolished. Most flats were structurally sound. It was far too big to handle as a single project and doubling the density was a big mistake. There were a lot of leaseholders at Woodberry Down so it was always going to be too expensive, too slow and a big loss of social housing.'

The estate, though, is very attractive to those who want to sell London property. It is close to a Tube station and large north London reservoirs, which mean waterfront properties can be built. 'To a developer, it's a goldmine, it's obvious,' says Power.

SHARDA, ROSIE, ELI, LOTTIE

Sharda – whose mother Manju had found a home in the rent-controlled private rented sector – has fond memories of her time as a child and teenager in west London, living on the fringe of the huge parks. 'Because we lived in a small place, the parks are the most important aspect,' she recollects. 'We'd have picnics and birthday parties in the park, I cycled a lot. In the summer we'd practically live there. It was amazing, especially if you don't have your own garden. Everything was accessible, I could walk right into the heart of central London. I spent so many weekends going to the museums: my brother's favourite was the Science Museum, mine was the Natural History Museum.'

But the invasive attitude of their managing agent on behalf of the landlord was becoming more and more apparent. 'They'd send really rude, threatening letters saying that leaving our shoes outside meant we were breaking the conditions of our lease,' says Sharda.

The community which Rosie had grown up in with her mum Jothi was starting to fray in the 2000s. Families were cashing in on the rising values of their properties and moving out of London to buy bigger homes. An African family they had become friendly with lost their home because they were unable to pay their mortgage. The family had started to build up debts, partly due to the need to care for sick relatives in Malaysia, and they remortgaged the house to help pay off some of the costs. 'That was a very hard struggle,' says Jothi.

As the children started to grow up and leave school, housing was so expensive that they couldn't move out. By the end of the decade, all five adults were living together in the same house.

Eli spent most of the 2000s living an idyllic teenage life in Dominica with his mum Ruphina. But once secondary school was finished, Eli returned to London to go to sixth form and university in the UK. He moved in with his sister in east London and enrolled in a local college, studying music technology. The London he returned to was different: Oyster cards had replaced the 40p bus fares, new blocks of flats had sprung up around the borough he remembered, old pubs and churches had closed their doors and the city was busier and more crowded, with more traffic and less of the community that had defined his childhood.

Nonetheless, he was not that worried about his housing situation. He planned to live with his sister while at college, go to university and then move back to London to find work in the city's thriving music industry and move out into his own place – just as his mum and sister had before him. 'No one foresaw how bad the housing market was going to get. We still looked at Newham as an affordable place to live,' he says.

Charlotte – Lottie to her friends – grew up in the Medway Towns in Kent. Her dad worked in London – an engineer working on air-conditioning units – and her parents owned their home. She had what she describes as a happy, normal, working-class childhood. After leaving school, she got a job in London as a receptionist at a recruitment agency and began commuting into the city while living with her mum and dad. Eventually she found a job which paid enough for her to rent a place in south London – closer to work but still not too far by train from her parents.

She was never entirely happy renting. 'I always felt unstable,' she says. 'A year goes by so fast, and you never know if the landlord's going to hike the rent or say they want the property back.'

Lottie met Joe, now her husband, and the couple wanted some security as they started their new life together. They began to save as much as they could, trying to keep up with the ever-rising price of flats around the city.

THE RISE AND RISE OF THE 'SMALL-TIME SIDE-HUSTLER' – RENTING PRIVATELY

The seeds that had been sown with the deregulation of the private rented sector by Margaret Thatcher in 1988, and the launch of buy-to-let mortgages in the mid-1990s, finally sprouted into the hideous knotweed they always threatened to become in the 2000s. Continuing low interest rates, the collapse of the dot-com bubble and the failure of many pension funds encouraged many small-time investors that the best place for their money was property. And they were right.

The number of landlords was growing and growing. From the start, this was what Nick Bano calls 'small-time side-hustlers' rather than big real-estate capital. A survey from 2001 showed 65 per cent of private rented sector dwellings were owned by individuals, less than one in ten were owned by property companies and only 9 per cent of landlords saw it as a full-time occupation.[21] 'Despite the government's wish to draw large-scale company landlords and institutional investment into the private rented sector… the sector is increasingly dominated by small-scale private individual landlords renting property as a sideline activity,' concluded the survey. This remains the case today, with more than 2.5 million individual landlords – more than the number of teachers or NHS workers in the country.[22]

This really began in the 2000s: the number of homes rented privately increased by almost 125 per cent over a fifteen-year period from the year 2000 onwards. And this was not happening because new homes were being built. Instead, existing homes were being bought up by those chasing a bigger property portfolio. As one study from 2016 observed: 'This growth came through the change of tenure of existing housing, as owner-occupied and social rented units were purchased by landlords – mostly private individuals.'[23] We were handing our housing stock over to side-hustlers to replace their flatlining pensions.

It is worth saying here that it would be wrong to demonise the people who made this choice – tempting as it may be for those in my generation who have seen their annual salaries eaten up by rent. All they were doing was making a logical economic choice: a low-wage, low-interest economy offered little other chance of a secure life and a stable retirement. There are many landlord investors who come from immigrant and working-class backgrounds and turned to the property market after the economy removed the stable, skilled, unionised labour and guaranteed pensions enjoyed by the previous generation. We set up a system where this felt like the only choice available. But it came at a huge cost.

The plan for this type of housing to 'take the strain' of providing for those on the lowest incomes was starting to show its frailty in the 2000s. Housing benefit was getting dangerously high, as rising rents forced more people to claim it, and pushed up the cost to the state. In 2008, in a bid to get it under control, ministers introduced a new rule called 'local housing allowance'. This meant those seeking benefits to help pay their rent would be able to claim no more than 50 per cent of the local market rate, the aim being 'to control public spending on housing support [and] prevent rises in unregulated rents from being fully covered by Housing Benefit'.[24] But we had started down a dangerous path: rather than control rents, the government was allowing them to rise freely, instead clamping down on the amount offered to benefit claimants. This meant councils in wealthier areas could not find enough housing for their homeless families, and would place them in poorer boroughs in the city instead. The poorer boroughs began to look for locations outside of London altogether. These policies laid the groundwork for an enormous crisis in London and beyond.

And something else was happening. Rather than simply buy a house and rent it out to a single family, landlords were discovering the potential to increase their earnings by turning a family home into several flats. Fit a lock on each bedroom door, and suddenly you have four rent payers rather than one, increasing yields by around 50 per cent. What one analysis termed a 'smash-and-bash crowd' were actively seeking larger properties to 'completely reconfigure to house up to six or seven tenants'.²⁵ This hunt for larger properties further drove up values. This mass conversion of homes into flats has happened before in London: in the aftermath of both world wars in particular, housing shortages led to the conversion of huge Edwardian and Victorian houses into flats by both individual private landlords and local authorities — with limited oversight and regulation, resulting in some seriously poor quality housing.²⁶ But these conversions were focused on large town houses in particular areas of the city (Kensington, Camden and Islington for example), and in response to the specific post-war pressures. What was happening now was different: regular family homes right out into the suburbs were becoming bedsits, and the driver was the messy combination of permanently high housing demand and the economic incentives for investors, neither of which was going away any time soon. Behind closed doors, the city was being transformed from one of family-sized homes into one of single rooms, locked doors and communal kitchens. 'You started to see this really take off in the 2000s. Landlords saw an opportunity to maximise their income, so instead of letting to a single family, they would let out individual rooms to several households,' says Peter Williams, the former Newham Council officer.

However, the picture wasn't completely bleak. As the Olympics approached, the city decided it needed a renewed focus on helping people off the streets. This was partly inspired by the national vanity that accompanies an Olympic Games — a desire to show off London as a modern, sophisticated city, not one where poverty was pushing people into the gutter. But the effort to achieve this entailed real improvements.

'This was a pretty wholesome attempt to do it properly,' Michelle Binfield tells me. She is now director of programmes at the Centre for Homelessness Impact following a thirty-year career working at all levels of the system to reduce homelessness — including with the government. 'We started to get initiatives like "No Second Night Out" off the ground for the first time. It was genuinely an attempt to try and use the Olympics as a jumping-off point to achieve something good, and it worked. The numbers did start coming down.'

In 2007/8, rough-sleeping numbers fell to an estimated 249 in London.[27] Eliminating rough sleeping was – from there – an achievable aim. We would take a different path.

JOHN, PATRICIA AND SEAN, CAROLYN

For John, the schoolteacher who had bought a house in Walthamstow in the early 1980s, the distance from his daughter Su, who had moved out to the coast, was starting to nag. He wanted to be closer to his grandchildren.

John and his wife Jacky sold their house for £207,000. They had bought it for £33,000 twenty years previously. 'The young family we sold it to had great difficulty raising the mortgage, despite working in finance,' John recalls. 'But they were just about able to do it.'

Su's mother-in-law, another east Londoner, refused to move. She was too settled, too at home and too old to feel like she could move to a new place. But without her younger family members around, she began to feel isolated, especially after her husband died. 'Although it's an hour and a half away, it's too far to look after an old person,' Su reflects.

Patricia and Sean noticed the Irish bars and dancehalls they'd once loved closing down rapidly throughout the 2000s. 'By the time our daughter was eighteen, a lot of those places were gone, and our son never got to go any of them,' she says. The legendary Galtymore in Cricklewood closed in 2008, after over fifty years as a dancehall, with planning permission put in to transform the site into a mixed-use development of apartments, retail units and a hotel complex, which the *Irish Times* heralded as 'the end of an era'.[28] 'When the Galtymore closed down, that was a real shock to all of us,' Sean tells me.

As the end of the 2000s approached, Sean realised it was time to retire. He was still working in construction, for the same firm he'd worked for in the 1980s. 'It's hard work, working on the building site, I tell you, shovelling concrete and digging trenches. I was fit, I could have stayed with them for another ten years, but I thought, "We're only passing through in this world, why kill myself? I will get the pension now, that will keep us going."' With a secure home, and a mortgage paid off years before, this was a decision he could comfortably take.

For Carolyn, the Ministry of Defence civil servant who had been renting in Finchley, little changed until the end of the decade. In 2008, now in her fifties, she had become exhausted with life in Whitehall. An early retirement scheme was made available, and she took it – happy to start a new life supported by the civil service pension that would comfortably pay rent on the shared housing she'd been living in for twenty-five years.

In May 2009, she went to visit her mother, who was now living by herself in Norfolk and increasingly struggling to cope independently. 'She was eighty-six and her vision was deteriorating and she didn't drive, but she was living in the middle of nowhere,' says Carolyn. 'I started thinking about getting a place for the two of us.'

But when she returned home, something strange was going on: 'There were a lot of messages from people asking where I was and wanting to speak to me.' When she spoke to the landlord, he told her he wanted to sell the property. But since she was a secure, rent-controlled tenant, having a tenancy which had started before 1988, he wanted her to leave to allow the sale to go ahead. 'Well, I knew once someone wants to sell, you might as well just go,' she says. 'Otherwise they will make it uncomfortable for you, by turning the heating off in the middle of winter and so on. So I took the compensation they offered and left.'

The next morning, she got another phone call. This time it was from Norfolk to tell her that her mother had died in the night.

BOOM AND BUST – BUYING A HOME

With the rental market turning family homes into honey pots for investors, low interest rates keeping credit available and the demand for living in London higher than ever before, the price of homes at first bubbled up – sitting at around £170,000 for the first four years of the decade – but then took off. Prices doubled in three years, reaching an average of £340,000 by 2007, now drastically outstripping wages – the house-price-to-income ratio across London soared from 7.17:1 in 2002 to 9.22:1 in 2007. The whole city was becoming less affordable: even in Barking & Dagenham – the cheapest borough in London relative to average salary – the ratio had skyrocketed from 4.68:1 in 2002 to 7.05:1 by 2007.[29]

This was made possible because of access to credit. New home buyers were indebting themselves, and banks were dishing out ever larger mortgages, creating new money with each loan, basking in the wealth and allowing prices to shoot upwards without a thought for the consequences. The mortgage market was breaking the link between incomes and house prices.

A mortgage basically bridges the gap between the money a buyer has and what the home costs. If banks make it very easy to access mortgages, prices can grow *almost* indefinitely. Unrestrained by regulation and able to create new mortgages at the click of a button, banks around the world became hooked on this type of lending.

Up until 1995, most bank lending across advanced economies was invested into businesses – the money was provided to firms who used it to grow and then repaid the bank. But from

1995 onwards, this shifted. Gradually, more and more bank lending pooled into mortgage credit, and less into genuine investment. 'Lending to a firm is a risky business, with no guarantees that the loan will be repaid,' explains the economist Josh Ryan-Collins in his book *Why Can't You Afford a Home?* 'But when a bank makes a mortgage loan, it almost always demands the property as collateral in case the borrower defaults.'[30] As Ryan-Collins writes, across advanced economies, the amount of mortgage debt shot up from around 40 per cent of GDP to almost 70 per cent by the end of the decade. House prices rose at almost exactly the same pace.

Banks were losing their grip on the risk they were taking as this process accelerated, increasingly believing that the investments were inherently safe. If the buyer defaulted, they had the house as security – and house prices were only going up. The collapse in the early 1990s was long forgotten, and there were big bonuses to be made from cramming the lending books full. In the US particularly, the subprime market – lending to those on low incomes with a poor history of paying debts – took off. New financial instruments bundled together stacks of mortgage debt, which were then traded en masse. The whole system of finance became reliant on mortgage lending and house price growth.

With huge demand to live in London, and supply around it constrained by planning laws, the only place for this money to go was into the existing housing. As Alistair Darling, chancellor from 2007 onwards, would later reflect: 'When you have got a lot of money available to lend and a supply of housing that's not as high as it should have been, that's a lethal combination.'[31]

While the conversation about the cause of London's housing crisis often focuses on the lack of new homes being built, it often misses this point about the role of mortgage finance in inflating prices. This is a critical mistake. Countries such as Spain and Ireland, which saw massive construction booms in this period, also saw huge rises in house prices as banks poured money into the new builds. To quote Ryan-Collins again: 'However fast you can build, banks can create new credit faster.'

And this was a trend the government was aware of and actively encouraged. The expansion of mortgage debt meant more homeowners, who were willing to spend money in the economy furnishing their home, which drove growth. Rising house prices were simply too politically attractive to curtail: those on the ladder liked getting wealthier every year, and the rising value of their assets also solved another pressing political problem – policy makers hoped it would pay for their care into old age.

Rather than take any action which would curtail rising prices, Labour looked for ways to offer new home buyers a leg up, while letting the prices soar. The party fought the 2005 election on a promise of a new 'Homebuy' scheme, where buyers would get half a home with a traditional mortgage and be given a government equity loan for the rest, which would be paid back only when the home was sold.[32] A scathing article in *The Economist* warned these new buyers would be acquiring homes 'just in time for the crash'.[33]

But Tony Blair and Gordon Brown did not share these fears. House price growth was too important. During the 2005 election campaign, Brown said homes were 'not just places to live' but were 'becoming ever more important as assets'.[34] Unlike other forms of inflation, rising house prices were seen by fiscal policy makers as a mark of success.

And there were powerful commercial figures making huge money out of this economy, which began to wield an increasingly large influence over government policy. Landowners, banks and volume house builders all have similar interests when it comes to government housing policy, and together represent an enormously powerful lobbying operation. They all want taxes on land to be kept low, more land released to the private sector for development without any restrictions on profit, and government policy which promotes home ownership where they make their profits. This trifecta of economic interests began to employ a vast network of consultants, thinktanks and industry bodies to speak to politicians on their behalf. The academic Bob Colenutt has described them as the 'finance housebuilding complex' and describes their operation as 'one of the best organised, well-funded and well-connected political lobbies in the UK'.[35]

Labour promised these groups precisely what they wanted with its 'growth areas' initiative. Land was packaged up, public money was spent to make it suitable for house building and the sites were sold to volume house builders, who were given control to build them out on their terms. Derelict areas of London left abandoned by deindustrialisation – Nine Elms and the space around Battersea Power Station in southwest London; the 'Thames Gateway' area of old dockyards, warehouses and the broken-down railyards and heavy industry between Stratford and Hackney in the east – came under the auspices of this programme, or others like it. As the decade came to an end, these old industrial areas were being ringed off by hoardings bearing the names of large property developers and CGI-generated images of huge, new blocks of flats, green spaces and blurry images of smart-looking commuters heading to their office jobs in the city. Press statements about the new schemes made promises about large numbers of affordable homes, green space and environmentally conscious development.

But there would be nothing to enforce this. The house builders had agreed to meet specific targets in terms of affordable housing and environmental development in these new schemes, but in reality they represented what Colenutt calls a 'blank cheque'.[36] Family-sized homes were also less prevalent in the new developments, as builders looked to maximise the number of units in every development. At the start of the

2000s, around a third of the homes being built in London had three bedrooms or more, but by 2010 this had plummeted to a shade over 10 per cent as the share of smaller flats increased.[37]

This was the final clearing out of old London. Rathbone Market in Newham had been a thriving part of the community when I was growing up, with a history that could be traced all the way back to the thirteenth century. But in 2009, the market was mostly closed off and the land was handed over to a private builder – part of New Labour's 'growth area' in the Thames Gateway. A blue and yellow tower block on its eastern side was demolished along with around 1,700 other council homes in the area, in a plan to invest £3.7 billion to build 10,000 mostly private homes. A budding student journalist when this happened, I dropped by the market and spoke to the traders, moved over to one side by the building site, with little footfall and their previous customers gone. 'At the end of the day, this is prime real estate in one of the best cities in the world,' one told me. 'They weren't going to let us stay here forever.'

And as the builders cashed in, quality was also starting to take a hit. At one new, luxury riverside development near Canary Wharf called New Atlas Wharf, residents moved in to discover that they could hear everything going on in the neighbouring flats, and the flats were smaller than advertised. It emerged that no soundproofing had been installed, and residents moved out for twenty-six months while it was fixed.[38] Many years later, it was revealed to also have life-threatening fire safety defects which required £10 million of repair work.

Buying a flat also meant these new purchasers would be entering a new kind of legal agreement, which dated right back to the feudal era of England's property laws: leasehold. Instead of owning the flat, they would buy a long lease on it of at least ninety-nine years. This meant that, despite not owning the building around them, they were responsible for paying any service charge the freeholder (usually an investment firm) demanded for its maintenance.

This constellation of market dysfunction and bad behaviour was sowing the seeds of a huge crisis which would be reaped in the next decade. But first, the fragile financial model on which the whole system was built would come close to complete collapse. Defaults on subprime mortgages in the United States kicked through into losses which rumbled through the banking system in England. We should have seen this coming: the process of lending infinite money, and making higher and higher profits would not go on forever. By the end of 2008, nearly 47,000 homes were repossessed in the UK as homeowners struggled to keep with their mortgage repayments.[39] The banks' appetite for mortgage lending nosedived and private builders scaled their development back to almost nothing, as their potential profits collapsed.

Again we stood at a crossroads. It was the end of the 2000s. The modern world was just arriving. Students began sharing their photographs on a new social networking site called Facebook, and watching videos on YouTube. A new mobile device produced by Apple – the iPhone – meant people increasingly had the internet in their pockets at all times. In east London, new Overground railway routes were opening up previously neglected parts of the city like Shoreditch and Hoxton, and young graduates and artists flooded into the Victorian terraced houses and council flats which had been sold years before under Right to Buy the remaining old boozers converting into bars and coffee shops.

The housing model we had followed to this point had led us to financial disaster, the greed which had seen the banking sector gamble everything on the mortgage market had backfired and led to an enormous bailout which, effectively, temporarily nationalised them. It was an inflection point – an opportunity to enter the forthcoming digital age with a different economic model, one that did not simply entrench the growing inequality which was most acutely apparent in London and driven by the growing housing crisis in the city.

For a brief moment, it looked like this might happen. With the economy flatlining and house building grinding to a near halt, Labour suddenly rediscovered its historic appetite for building new socially rented housing. In the 2009 Budget, Gordon Brown tripled the amount being spent on social housing, with a target of 110,000 affordable homes to be built across England within two years.[40] This was the chance to set out on a different road. But instead, in the 2010 election voters rejected Gordon Brown, and the New Labour project he embodied, and the Conservatives came back into power for the first time since 1997, as part of a coalition with the Liberal Democrats. The forces they would unleash turned the budding housing crisis into something much, much worse.

2010s

COFFEE, UBERS, SKYSCRAPERS, HOMELESSNESS AND VIOLENCE

In response to the huge sums of money borrowed to bail out the banking system, the new Conservative-led coalition government immediately introduced a bruising regime of economic austerity, sharply reducing public spending in a manner which would have immediate and permanent consequences for London.

Inner London boroughs, where poverty was already the most severe, were the hardest hit. Westminster, Newham, Tower Hamlets, Hackney, Camden and Wandsworth all saw their budgets cut by more than 25 per cent in absolute terms.[1] It amounted to a dismantling of many of the services millions of Londoners relied upon. Across the city, £400 million was cut from library services, £71 million was cut from sports facilities, £126 million was cut from funding for young people as councils closed eighty-one youth centres and made 800 full time posts redundant.[2] Cuts to budgets for public parks led some to be sold off to developers.[3] Schools in London saw cuts equivalent to more than £1,000 per pupil[4] and social care services were left with a £1 billion black hole.[5]

Public services across the board were left to decay. There were major cuts to the teams needed to plan and control the quality of new-build housing. The London Fire Brigade suffered some of the steepest cuts of any fire authority in the country, its backroom staff numbers slashed and fire stations closed. The Metropolitan Police was forced to find £850 million in savings, with police stations shuttered and sold, sometimes to residential developers, and police numbers reduced.[6] Cuts to mental health services resulted in a vicious spiral of increasing costs as conditions worsened and expensive agency staff were brought in to cover gaps on the rota.[7] Anger over austerity, combined with bubbling rage over police violence, contributed to the city's biggest riots since the 1980s in 2011.

Meanwhile, the city's skyline continued to change. The trend for new tall buildings which had sprung up in central London in the 2000s spread out across the city, as the 'growth areas' were filled with towering residential buildings.

Transport around the city became nimbler. A cycle hire scheme arrived in 2010, using what were immediately christened 'Boris bikes', after the city's new floppy-haired and flamboyant mayor, Boris Johnson, despite the scheme having been designed by the preceding regime. In 2012 the private car hire app Uber was granted a five-year licence to begin operating in London. The number of Uber drivers grew rapidly to 45,000 – the trademark Toyota Prius ubiquitous on the city's streets, a totem of the kind of irregular, gig-economy employment that new immigrants to London the city were being offered, and a world away from the demanding 'Knowledge' tests the city's iconic black-cab drivers were required to pass. The difference in skill was also reflected in pay, security and housing. I grew up with the children of black-cab drivers who converted the profession into a mortgage and a decent-sized London family home. As delivery apps took off, a whole new workforce emerged, shooting around London's streets to collect passengers or deliver huge bags of takeaway food and groceries. Many of these workers would find temporary housing in shared rooms across the city's under-regulated private rental sector – the most modern manifestation of the capital's ever-changing working class.

Coffee shops began to boom in the city, the centre of a nationwide trend which saw more than 10,000 branches in operation by the end of the decade – on course to outnumber pubs nationally by 2030.[8] In London, where pub numbers continued to decline rapidly through the 2010s, that threshold has almost certainly already been reached.[9]

In the east of the city, the Olympic Park rose from the site of one of London's last post-industrial wastelands – becoming the home for beautiful, wild green space, children's play facilities and wildly expensive, densely packed private housing. The area was given a whole new London postcode, and a new Westfield shopping centre opened on its southern edge in 2011 – the fourth largest shopping centre in the UK. It brought new bars, restaurants, a cinema and more than a million square feet of retail space to the east of the city, and the centre hummed with visitors from London and beyond, their number quickly reaching more than fifty million a year. Families, young people, tourists and football fans on their way to see games at the West Ham football stadium, which had moved from its traditional East End home to the new Olympic Park, thronged through the centre, which also became the site of gang violence, with several stabbings, some of them fatal, and regular clashes between its security staff and the gang members who would hang out in its food court.[10]

Outside the shiny new Westfield Centre, Stratford's former shopping mall – a jumbled mix of small local hair and beauty shops, takeaways, butchers, second-hand tech stores and cheap clothing sat beneath an ageing multi-storey car park. Its status as a public footpath meant its doors stayed open at night, and it became the site of London's new cardboard city – hundreds of rough sleepers bedding down there every night. On the roof of this old shopping centre, a new pop-up bar and cinema opened, with young people stepping past the rough sleepers to access the lifts to the car park and drink expensive cocktails as they looked out at a sea of red lights twinkling from the cranes building the new city. And just over the railway tracks, one of the area's largest council housing estates, the Carpenter's, lay half-empy – most of the residents having been decanted to make way for a demolition and rebuild which had not yet happened.

In many ways this small corner of east London held everything the capital had to offer at this juncture in its history: the vast excess of consumerism in a globalised economy, the disruption and displacement of a working-class community in its wake, the creative and mobile young generation toasting their success and ambitions while fretting about their rising rental payments, other young people cut adrift and left to fend for themselves in the violent underbelly of an unforgiving city, the forgotten social housing dream of decades past left to decay and those who could simply no longer afford a roof over their heads congregating in the last small space of shelter which was still open to them.

A GOLD RUSH: THE AFTERMATH OF THE FINANCIAL CRISIS

The global financial crisis would prove a game changer to London's housing market – but not in the way you might expect. In the immediate aftermath of the crisis, property prices in the city briefly fell. But they would soon rise again.

To spark the economy back into life as the recession hit, the Bank of England pulled two levers. The first was to cut interest rates towards a historic low. The second was to essentially create new money, £875 billion in total, and use it to purchase UK government bonds, a process known as 'quantitative easing'. The hope was that both of these efforts would encourage investors to seek yields by pushing their finance into creating growth – new business ventures, infrastructure projects, start-ups.

But in reducing interest rates and the yields on government-backed bonds, the government was creating an enormous demand for other safe investments. If the returns from UK government bonds and interest savings were low, those with capital didn't want to take risks by investing in new projects with uncertain returns. Instead, they wanted another safe haven for their money.

And this meant property. In particular, it meant property in big cities where there was a large demand for housing. With central banks around the world taking a similar approach, a wall of international and domestic money suddenly wanted a piece of London. There was only one possible outcome – prices were going to soar. 'Capital was searching for yield and it was going to find it in London housing,' Professor Ian Mulheirn explains.[11]

This would take the form of billions being poured into a model of house building known as 'speculative development', where the developer takes on debt to build a housing development and effectively gambles on the profit that will be made on its completion. 'London is probably the most speculative of all the markets in the country,' observes property analyst Neal Hudson. 'In London, especially in the 2010s and under Boris Johnson, you had all sorts of people and different kinds of financial interests speculating in the market and trying to make a profit.'[12]

This creates a certain model of house building: the land is bought at a very high rate, in anticipation of high sales at high prices. As many flats as possible are then sold 'off plan' (before they are built), to recoup cash as quickly as possible and provide finance for the development of the building. This means marketing them around the world, in East Asia, the US, the Middle East, Russia and anywhere else where big money is looking for a secure asset in a major capital city. 'The model would require that you need to sell 60 per cent to overseas buyers before you can even build it,' Hudson continues. 'So we became incredibly reliant on that model.'

This model pushed directly against what London desperately needed at this time: affordable housing. Since the 1970s, the law has allowed local councils to require a certain percentage of homes in a new development to be 'affordable' as a condition of their construction. Known as 'Section 106 requirements' after the legislation which requires them, these homes are generally sold by the developer at a discount to a social housing provider, which then lets them out to people on a waiting list for housing.

This was a pivotal moment for London. Billions of pounds of investment capital was about to flow into new housing in the city. The UK government could have tapped the profits to ensure an adequate supply of affordable housing as these new developments sprang out of the earth.

But the opposite happened. Speculative development hates affordable housing requirements – and is actually geared towards reducing them. If the original developer could buy the land based on an expectation that 35 per cent would be affordable housing, they would have paid the landowner a sum which reflected this. But if they then drive the number of affordable units down to 20 per cent, their profit margin widens.[13] This is precisely what they started to do in London.

The government – under the influence of the property sector's sophisticated lobbying arm – was hoodwinked into thinking that development was only possible if as many 'burdens' as possible on developers were removed. As a result, David Cameron's government oversaw changes to planning regulations in 2012 which created, in the words of one major review, 'a national planning policy environment that was favourable to land promoters and housebuilders'.[14] The rules included a presumption in favour of development, meaning local authorities faced crushing and expensive defeats at planning tribunals if they said no to proposed schemes. The second key reform was the introduction of 'viability assessments' – which allowed developers to insist on a reduction in affordable housing to protect their profit margin. With huge resources to plug into this process, developers were able to present misleading data to reduce or entirely remove the obligations placed on them to include affordable housing in their schemes. Experts quoted in the *Guardian*, which received one such assessment under Freedom of Information, said the process 'threatens the very foundations of the UK planning system' and was a legalised practice of fiddling figures that represents 'a wholesale fraud on the public purse'.[15]

Land that had previously been public was sold off to private builders in this climate, with pitiful amounts of affordable housing built as a result. In the 700-home development at the old Mount Pleasant Post Office sorting depot in central London, for example, personally signed off by mayor Boris Johnson, the developers refused to include anything higher than 10 per cent affordable housing, despite local planning targets seeking 50 per cent.

Councils, battered by austerity and desperately under-resourced, were blinded by the same philosophy, thinking they had to cave in to developers' every demand for anything to get built in their area. Planning committees started to see their role as encouraging investment – not as a democratic filter to ensure it was appropriate and affordable. Council planning departments were stuffed with politicians with links to the development industry; members of planning committees were wined and dined by development companies and flown out to MIPIM, a luxury annual property conference in Cannes. 'London is open', read a banner on the London tent at one such event in the 2010s, with Croydon Council's stand proudly telling investors Croydon was where 'it's happening'. A huge, partially three-dimensional map of the city spread through the room, as investors sipped complimentary alcohol and considered which sites they would purchase and rebuild to the maximum profit margin.

A revolving door began to spin between council planning departments, developers and the consultancies which worked to broker relations between the two – staff would move on from their council roles to lucrative jobs in development consultancies, using their connections to win favourable results from their successors. One London council source showed me a text message they received, shortly after being appointed to a planning committee, from someone who had previously been a big figure in their party. 'I now have my own consultancy business and have a client who is interested in a site in your town centre that could potentially provide much needed homes,' the message read.

Development in London gained a ferocious pace. Blocks of new residential housing were popping up all over the city, particularly in the 'growth areas' identified and pushed by the previous Labour government. In the east, the major Olympic Park development was coming together and, in the west, Nine Elms, the area around Battersea Power Station, was being transformed.

In Nine Elms, the original promise was that 50 per cent of the housing would be affordable. But this collapsed to 18 per cent. Much of the money earmarked for affordable housing was eventually dispersed on an otherwise needless extension to the Northern line, which mainly served to increase the value of the planned homes, and therefore the developer's profits. In the Olympic Park too, social housing numbers were cut and tenures shifted to homes for higher rents or homes to buy. Both sites were snapped up by international funds: Nine Elms was built out as a joint venture between Irish developer Ballymore and EcoWorld, a huge property company based in Malaysia. Much of the housing in the Olympic Park was sold to developer Delancey and a fund owned by the ruling family of Qatar. These developments had been assembled by the state, helped through the planning process with generous public sector support and ultimately converted into investment pots for international finance.

As residential skyscrapers rose, prime properties were snapped up by buyers who would never live there – they simply wanted a home for their money. London flats became the equivalent of a fine wine, kept in a billionaire's cellar and never drunk; just another way of storing wealth. This money was coming from all over the world – sometimes from extremely suspect sources. Transparency International identified London property worth £4.2 billion bought with suspicious wealth, such as that stolen from state budgets and extorted in bribes.[16] Its research showed that in some areas of the city which were particular targets for 'super prime' investment, around 5 per cent of the properties exhibited abnormally low energy use – suggesting these 'buy-to-leave' investments far exceed official figures and account for tens of thousands of newly built homes in the city's most expensive areas.[17] The report found businesses closing in the areas where this practice was thought to be at its height due to lack of footfall – the city being bled dry and converted into a sterile investment asset.[18]

This international wealth – huge pension funds and shady high-net-worth individuals – was only able to keep the very top end of the market afloat. The sums they were willing to pay rippled out, raising the value of land, and therefore housing, all over the city.

But this raised a problem. For these developments to be profitable, they needed buyers. And if people couldn't afford to pay the rates which speculative developers wanted, the party would be over. The answer was to turn to the government, and to use the national balance sheet to bridge the gap.

ELI

After returning from university in Leicester, Eli, the son of Ruphina, who had moved to the Caribbean for his teenage years, began to rent privately. His work was in a primary school – practising music therapy for children, but being paid a teaching assistant's wage – and making rent at the end of the month was possible but challenging. Just before Christmas 2014, his landlord's agent arrived at the property with bad news: the landlord had decided they needed the house again, so Eli and his housemates would be evicted.

He moved back in with his sister, and began to look for other options. This was a difficult time in his life: losing the home along with other external pressures prompted a psychological crisis, ultimately resulting in a short stay in a mental health unit.

When he came back to work, he found employment as a mental health advocate – supporting people struggling with their mental health and speaking on their behalf in hospitals and prisons. The work was draining – vitally important but dreadfully paid. In order to find somewhere he could afford to live, he and his then-girlfriend entered the messy world of guardianship housing.

This was not unlike the 'short-life housing' music journalist Dave Hill used in the 1980s. But since then guardianship housing had changed. Back in the '80s, it was a collective of former squatters making formal and informal agreements with the council. Now, like everything else in the housing market, it had become big business.

If a property is going to be abandoned for a period of time and the building's owner wants to limit the risk of it being squatted, they can enlist a guardianship company to fill it with occupants, ostensibly to guard against that threat. But in reality, these companies are letting the space out to those who cannot afford to rent in the private market, with the bespoke arrangement allowing them to dodge many of the protections and requirements that come with a formalised tenancy.

For Eli – and thousands of other priced-out young people trying to make their way in London at the time – guardianship meant a steady tour through the abandoned buildings that were waiting to be swept away as property developers raided the city for its assets. He moved from empty offices over shops to disused council homes awaiting demolition. 'The communal aspect of it in your early to mid-twenties was quite fun,' Eli concedes. 'It was mostly trendy young people living in the first one I lived in, people into arts and music.'

But living in vacant council estates awaiting demolition was not always pleasant. 'The places would be emptying out. Every now and then a removal van would turn up, one of the old council tenants and leaseholders would pack up, you'd never see them again and the house would be left empty. It's like you're watching the stages of gentrification play out. You can't help but feel bad about it – like you were part of the problem, but I just couldn't get out of it. By the end of the 2010s, it was nearly £1,000 for a room, and I just couldn't afford that.'

In the mid-2010s, after yet another eviction, he found himself in an abandoned care home, this time in Stratford. 'For me, that was the lowest of low,' he says. 'The state of it was absolutely dire. The bathroom and shower area was floor-to-ceiling black mould. The whole place stunk so badly that it was hard to breathe. You had to open your windows or burn incense just to make it liveable. There was dust everywhere, electrical appliances that had just been left behind when the home was abandoned. It was so run down, it was a really horrible place to live.'

In this home, the residents were no longer the young, bohemian artists he'd stayed with at the start of his guardianship journey, but families – couples and recently arrived immigrants, including one who had a baby in their room. 'They always try and present it as this young, trendy thing, but I met all kinds when I was doing it – families, older people, people with mental health issues. People who don't want to uproot all the time and have no security, but basically feel like they don't have any other option.'

Eventually, with a new partner and a new, secure job, Eli was able to scrape together a deposit and finally try and find a flat in the regular private rented market which they could turn into more of a home. 'I did think about moving out of London entirely,' he says. 'But all my friends and family are here, and I needed that network to cope with the mental health struggles I went through. I don't know what would have happened to me if I'd moved out. It's hard, but if it's where your home is, you fight to stay.'

Eli had similar economic circumstances to his mum. But where she had been able to buy a house and put down roots, London's housing market left him in the wind, surviving at the edges of a property market from which enormous profits were being extracted.

KICKING AWAY THE LADDER: HELP TO BUY

Aside from austerity, Help to Buy was arguably the most significant economic policy of the early 2010s. Introduced in 2013, the scheme was designed to assist buyers who could not otherwise get onto the property ladder and afford the now exorbitant house prices. It was, essentially, an expansion of the Homebuy initiative brought in by the previous government but on a much bigger scale. It was a means to keep a steady supply of buyers coming to private house builders, without them having to lower their prices.

In London, the policy involved offering buyers a 40 per cent equity loan so that they could buy a new-build flat. This loan was provided by the government, which meant buyers could borrow lower amounts from the banks, pay lower rates of interest in the early years and get a flat with a lower deposit. Over the next ten years, the government poured an astonishing £24.7 billion into these equity loans.

The trouble was that this just sustained high prices. New homes could be built and sold at much higher rates, and the market did not need to correct towards what people could actually afford. 'In London and those hotspots of demand, [the government investment] has gone straight into price. That's been the problem,' said the chair of a parliamentary review of the scheme in 2022.[19] Other reviews concluded that the scheme had 'increased house prices by more than the expected present value of the implied interest rate subsidy' and was 'an ineffective policy in already unaffordable areas'.[20]

The policy helped a very narrow category of buyers: those with a big enough income to pay the huge combined monthly cost of the mortgage and the equity loan, but who wouldn't have been able to put together enough money for a deposit unless it was reduced. In many cases, it was simply state help offered to affluent households who would have been able to purchase anyway. By 2018, only 37 per cent of people who used the scheme said they wouldn't have been able to buy without it. As prices rose and rose, the dream of buying a home in London slipped out of reach for anyone in a profession that didn't offer the highest salaries.

'[Help to Buy]'s main impact was in pushing up the price of housing, kicking away the ladder that middle income households were climbing and enriching the directors and executives of the big property developers,' Vince Cable, the Liberal Democrat business secretary in the government that introduced it, told a BBC documentary in 2023.[21] The state itself was taking a risk. By 2019, the total size of the Help to Buy loan book was equivalent to a medium-sized building society. If another financial crisis struck, it wouldn't be Northern Rock going bust, but the UK government. 'At points when the market turns down (whether over the near, medium or longer term), the taxpayer could lose out significantly, as the government's investment in housing capital would reduce in value,' said the National Audit Office in 2018.

The winner, instead, was the private house-building market. It could build homes and sell them, almost risk free, to buyers whose purchasing power was artificially inflated by the state. The biggest three volume house builders had a boom decade in the 2010s, experiencing 'supernormal levels of profitability, with gross profit margins reaching 32 per cent and never falling below 17 per cent'.[22] Berkeley Group, which operates primarily in London, made a grand total of £4.57 billion in profit across the decade, its annual profits rising an extraordinary 900 per cent from a mere £110.3 million in 2010 to a peak of £934.9 million in 2018.[23] In the 10 years from 2015, Persimmon, one of the biggest builders, made pre-tax profits in excess of £7.5 billion – including two years where its profits exceeded a billion in a single year.

London was transformed by the homes built in the 2010s. The capital saw 340,560 new homes built – enough for almost two new boroughs and 80,000 more than the previous decade. The skyline of the city was changed, with twenty- and thirty-storey blocks appearing in almost every neighbourhood. But social housing was sidelined, homes got more expensive and those who could not afford them were left with fewer options.

And amid these profits, corners were being cut. The developers' focus was on the bottom line, and completing developments in time to get good numbers out for the next quarterly update to the London Stock Exchange. The long-term quality of the homes was a secondary consideration – particularly in an environment with little protection for buyers.

While the new developments looked nice from the outside, life inside them was often quite different. Buyers quickly found that the system of warranties and guarantees meant little – if the home was badly built, they were often stuck with it. Improperly fitted plastic pipes leaked. Soundproofing was poor. Insulation was either too intense – meaning overheating in the summer – or insufficiently installed, meaning draughty and cold winters. District heating systems were badly built and poorly maintained, which made the homes crushingly expensive and often without heat. The cheapest materials were picked for the external walls, to keep costs as low as possible and margins high. And fire safety rules were overlooked. This would have a cost.

LOTTIE

Lottie, the renter we met in the previous chapter, then saving money to buy her first flat, was finally able to get onto the ladder in 2016. Her husband Joe's family were able to provide a bit of help for the deposit. Joe came from a big Irish family. His dad worked in the aviation industry and had been careful with money, making sure they had something to put away for their kids. 'Joe's parents planned their money that way because they grew up with so little, they wanted to leave something to their kids,' explains Lottie.

In 2016, some of this money went to Joe and his new wife, allowing them to start a family. They found a one-bedroom apartment in Bow, with a small balcony. Having been independent from such a young age, Lottie felt pride that she had managed to find somewhere of her own. 'I felt like I've worked in London for so long, I can actually put my roots down here now,' she says. 'Obviously, there's the caveat that we'd had financial help, but we had worked hard to get to this point. You get a sense that "I'm really an adult now".'

But this dream was about to take a turn for the nightmarish. Lottie was surprised to be offered a 'lease' on the flat, rather than full ownership, but assured herself she had little to worry about. This was the normal way to buy a flat, she was told, and the lease was so long it would never expire. She put it out of her mind. 'I think so many young people in London go into these contracts not knowing what they're signing up to. That was definitely the case for us. We were totally naive to the whole thing.'

In June 2017, she watched Grenfell Tower burn on the news. 'It's like 9/11, you remember where you were when you first saw it,' she says. 'But I felt disconnected from it somehow, like, even though it's in the same city, and I'm living in a block of flats as well, you never think it's something that could happen to you.'

Two years later in 2019, Lottie spoke to a neighbour on the ground floor who was trying to sell their flat. 'They were being asked for all sorts of documentation that they hadn't heard of before,' she says. 'And neither the developer or the freeholder could provide it, so they went round and round in circles and eventually the sale fell through.' They were seeing stories on the news about other buildings being discovered to have similar cladding issues to Grenfell and not being sellable as a result. 'I remember my neighbour saying to me that they have a horrible feeling that something here is wrong,' she says. So it would prove.

THE RENT IS TOO DAMN HIGH

For those who could not afford London's soaring property prices, the only option was private renting. But here too, the changing economy would supercharge the existing problems. The low interest rates which pushed global finance towards real estate had the same impact on individual savers, who were left scrabbling for a decent return in a climate where traditional savings accounts and bonds would pay out a fraction of the returns they would once have offered.

For many, the answer was the property market. Buy two or three properties, and suddenly the retirement plan was taken care of. Buy-to-let lending for new purchases shot up, from around £20 billion in 2010 to more than £50 billion by 2018.[24]

London's population passed its pre-war peak of 8.5 million in 2015.[25] In 2010/11, the percentage of Londoners renting privately exceeded those in social housing for the first time since the 1970s, and would continue to rise for the rest of the decade. More and more family-sized homes were being bought up and converted into HMOs (houses in multiple occupation). In 2013, a shade over 5,000 HMOs were registered with councils, and by the end of the decade there were more than 15,000 – but this was a tiny fraction of the number of HMOs in the city as only the largest need to be licensed.

With no rent controls in place and a huge pool of potential tenants who wanted a home, landlords were free to keep putting rental prices up and up and up. By September 2013, the median rent in the capital had reached £1,300 per month, more than twice as high as the median in England as a whole.[26] Londoners in the private rented sector were spending more than 40 per cent of their income on rent.

And the quality of what they were paying for was often dreadful. Tenants struggled to get landlords to carry out repairs and faced the threat of eviction if they complained. There was almost no oversight, while cash-strapped environmental health teams at local authorities could do little to police the fragmented market of small-time side hustlers. Some launched mandatory registration schemes to try and get a handle on the market, the first launched by Newham Council in 2013.

'We had estimated there were around 4,000 private landlords in Newham, but when we got the scheme up and running we realised there were more like 24,000,' the former housing officer Peter Williams tells me. 'Sitting in the housing department, we hadn't been able to see what market forces had been doing right under our noses.

'The conditions we found, especially in the HMOs, were so poor. There were all sorts of informal buildings which had been added to homes, often without planning permission. A lot of the tenants were single men, mostly from abroad, a lot of them working in the black economy or doing minimum wage jobs. They weren't going to complain. But the conditions they were living in were extraordinary,' he adds.

'One that sticks in my mind was a butcher's shop which had been closed down. One of our environmental health officers went along and found six people sleeping in the old commercial freezers, with no natural light, no ventilation. It was miserable and if there had been a fire, it would have been a death trap.' London's gig economy workers, a growing sector upon whom the city was increasingly reliant, were being relegated to housing reminiscent of the Victorian era, the type the city had tried so hard to eliminate in the decades after World War II.

At the other end of the market, though, private renting was becoming a more luxury pursuit. Developers began to specifically capitalise on this demand, with the rise of 'build-to-rent' developments backed by investors like pension funds and insurance giants, which were seeking the long-term cash flow from the rents. Investment in this sort of housing passed £2 billion in 2016 and doubled to £4 billion by the end of the decade, having been virtually non-existent before the financial crisis. Around 20,000 build-to-rent homes were built in the decade.

But with land prices in London hugely inflated due to the speculative development bonanza in the city, these new developments were only targeted at the wealthiest. They sold a lifestyle as much as a home, with pools, gyms, Instagrammable roof gardens, block parties in the communal areas, and boutique bakeries and flower shops installed on the ground floor. Research by the London Renters Union found that Grainger – the largest player in the build-to-rent market – set rents 20 per cent higher than the average local rent.

Student housing too was starting to attract the attention of big investors for similar reasons: vast student housing developments began popping up around London, backed by major finance, which wanted the hefty returns, secured by student loans and wealthy international students. 'Students, especially international students, are a massive driver of the demand for rental housing,' says property analyst Neal Hudson.[27]

There was money to be made – and glamorous rented housing was being built for those who could pay for it. But many could not. And that meant they had to claim benefits to pay the difference. Three decades before, Margaret Thatcher's government had foreseen this – with the intention that housing benefit would 'take the strain' of rising rents. Her successors in the 2010s would break this promise with devastating consequences.

ROSIE, CAROLYN

Rosie, the daughter of Malaysian nurse Jothi, was now working as an actress and starting to make her way in London's competitive world of theatre, TV and commercial acting gigs. She had regular bookings for stage shows, TV ads and medical role play, as well as holding down jobs in theatres, ushering or behind the bar, and various teaching gigs. But she could never earn enough money to move out from under her parents' roof.

'As I got older the friction of needing your own space became a really big thing. I remember just butting heads with my dad so much. You're finding your independence, you're finding your voice, but you are still living in your parents' house with their rules and expectations,' she says. 'I started to feel like I couldn't breathe in this place.'

In 2012, the London Olympics landed right on their doorstep. Jothi joined the local council's Olympic Committee to be consulted on the plans. She had been a school governor and volunteered on homelessness outreach projects and anti-gang and knife crime projects, so was invited to take part. 'We would be invited to go for breakfast at these posh hotels, and they would have glasses of champagne,' she recalls. 'I used to think, "Whose money are you playing with?" My fight with them was to give residents of Newham affordable housing. We had this image in our head, that maybe for our children we would have affordable housing. They were promising us so much.'

But this was not what was delivered. The homes in the Olympic Park, once built, remained wildly out of reach of Rosie and her brothers. Eventually in 2017, her parents decided to move out themselves and effectively gift the home to the children. They accessed their pension pots and looked for somewhere they could rent for £600 a month. They searched around Essex, looking at tiny flats in dreadful condition. Estate agents were openly racist, sometimes changing the terms of the offer when they heard Jothi's accent on the phone or making sly comments about the smell of the curry she would cook. Eventually, the couple were able to get into a part-rent, part-buy shared ownership scheme targeted at pensioners in Basildon, a town about twenty miles outside of London. From the security they had worked so hard for as young professionals in the 1980s, they had come almost full circle as pensioners: renting a small, expensive flat in a white community, surrounded by people who did not welcome them.

Carolyn, the former civil servant who was evicted from her home of twenty-six years in the late 2000s, was able to find a new home in Catford, south London, on the top floor of a terraced house. She filled the shelves with her books, her collection of soul and rhythm and blues records and easels to pursue her hobby of painting. She had her civil service pension, and her state pension. 'The rent was £650 a month,' she says. 'And I could afford that comfortably, I even had a bit of extra money to help my friends out.'

The rent was creeping up steadily – rising to £875 a month by the end of the decade – but she could still survive.

A BROKEN LINK – THE LHA CAP

By the time the Conservative-led coalition took power in 2010, housing benefit expenditure was £24 billion a year – a very substantial chunk of overall welfare expenditure.

In reality this hefty bill was out of the claimants' control; it was the logical result of the policy decisions made by previous governments. A lack of social housing and unregulated private rents meant housing benefit would ratchet ever upwards as rents rose. The new administration did not want this to continue.

Housing benefit claimants were demonised in aggressive media reports in the early 2010s, which focused on individual cases where large families claimed big sums for a family-sized home. Ministers promised to clamp down on what was portrayed as individual greed at the public expense, instead of a badly designed housing system which left people with no other option and offered landlords a blank cheque. Instead of trying to increase the availability of social housing or rein in out-of-control rents, the government simply cut benefits.

In 2011, the government capped the amount that could be claimed by councils to provide 'temporary accommodation' to homeless families the councils had a duty to house. And its next set of policy changes would send the number of families needing precisely this sort of support spiralling.

The local housing allowance (LHA) rate, which Labour had introduced to limit how much housing benefit tenants in private rented housing could claim, was cut. Where it previously covered the cheapest 50 per cent of properties in a given area, the coalition cut it to merely the cheapest 30 per cent. From as early as 2014, experts were warning that this was pricing poorer people out of the most expensive parts of London.

But it got worse. From 2016 onwards, LHA rates were frozen, so that even as rents rose, the benefits did not. Suddenly, there were no areas where benefits would cover the cost of a private tenancy. This, combined with an overall cap on benefits, meant that anyone with more than two children would not be able to claim enough benefits to rent a home. Those on benefits – many of them in work, but simply in lower-paid professions – had no choice. They had to leave the city. Even mayor Boris Johnson seemed uncomfortable – warning his political peers in central government of 'Kosovo-style social cleansing' if they persisted with benefit limits.[28] The warnings fell on deaf ears. Landlords, meanwhile, became less willing to rent to those in receipt of benefits, fearing (correctly) that they wouldn't be able to make the rent.

This created a very serious problem for London's local authorities. They had a legal duty to find housing for those who were made homeless and came to them for support. But because there were no private rental units available at rates which people could afford on benefits, and not enough social housing, they had nothing to offer.

Those in 'priority need' – a parent, a domestic violence survivor or someone with a serious health condition – had to be offered temporary accommodation while a permanent home was found. But with no permanent homes available, these people were stuck. And councils, with the rates they could claim for this accommodation capped, were forced towards the cheapest, most inadequate emergency housing they could find.

The number of households in this position rose and rose throughout the decade. In 2010, there were 51,310 households in temporary accommodation. By the end of the decade there were 88,310, with 58,730 of them in London.[29] A city within a city, one filled with homeless families stuck in cramped, desperate conditions, had started to form. And for those who were not considered in 'priority need', the only options were to leave the city or sleep on the streets.

Michelle Binfield, the homelessness policy expert whom we met earlier, says that this period fundamentally changed the characteristics of homelessness and rough sleeping in London. 'In the past, broadly, it was people with unaddressed support needs,' she explains. 'In 2009, when I was working for government, I could have found flats for every person sleeping rough in London. A lack of housing wasn't why people were sleeping rough then. But in the 2010s, when we broke the link between housing costs and benefits, it became economic. It's not just people with loads of support needs, it's people who can't afford housing – an absolute rush of people coming out of the private rented sector and into homelessness.'

At the same time, austerity cuts were destroying the tools local authorities previously had to prevent and address homelessness. 'Austerity has absolutely killed our ability to tackle homelessness,' says Binfield. 'There is no debt support, no housing advice. It's all been closed. I used to work in a local authority, where we had a law centre, a Citizens Advice Bureau and loads of advice and tenancy support. If you got into trouble, there was someone you could talk to. But all of that just went into the black hole of council savings when budgets were cut in half. We stripped back everything that was a safety net for vulnerable families, and just watched the dominoes fall in the years that followed.'

MANJU, CONALL

Steadily throughout the 2010s, the row of blocks neighbouring the one which Manju and Sharda lived in were sold to private investors. Because the tenants were secure, investors had to pay large sums of compensation to end their tenancies and gain full possession of the building, but the new owners saw this as a price worth paying for the prize: prime real estate.

Some residents accepted the first offer, others clung on, went to court and eventually accepted six-figure payouts. But the new landlords did not always want to play nice. 'They used pretty horrific means: threatening to cut people's water off, sending these scary, threatening letters. A lot of people I know ended up getting displaced,' Manju recollects. Step by step, the buildings were cleared out, refurbished into luxury apartments and gated off. The community disappeared. In 2017, the secure tenants who remained in Manju's building got sent a thick paper document telling them the building they had called home since the early 1980s had been sold for £56 million to an investment fund which managed pensions for a large UK utilities company.

In the late 2010s, Satinder, Manju's partner and Sharda's father, died after a short illness. The investors immediately saw it as a potential opportunity to get hold of the flat without compensation. 'Within a week of my dad dying, the eviction letter landed,' says Sharda. 'While we were looking at funeral arrangements and grieving, my mum was having to scan in her marriage certificate to prove she had a right to inherit the flat.' Manju remembers representatives of the court coming to visit in the aftermath of the death, as they considered her claim. The representatives saw the flowers, the cards and heard neighbours wishing her well and consoling her for her loss.

'But they said nothing, nothing,' she says. 'It's dehumanising. Nobody cares who you actually are as a person, with real lives and real personalities. They just see you as something they need to get rid of to get to the value in the property.'

Sharda herself began to work in museums after university and was thinking about becoming a curator. But witnessing the changes to her community, she decided to do her research on community heritage in Kensington: the local shops that were being replaced, the local businesses that were being cleared out by the rise of shops like Whole Foods, which were completely out of reach of the local community. She is now an academic researching the impact of gentrification on London, and the impact on the remaining secure tenants specifically.

'We were feeling physically as well as symbolically displaced,' she observes. 'Public spaces were being cordoned off, the area was becoming heavily securitised, the shops were changing. It was that growing feeling like "It's not for us anymore".'

It was not just those who had been in London for years who were struggling, those who were coming to the city faced difficulties too. Conall, a young hospitality worker, moved to London from Dublin in 2019 – already effectively priced out of his home city. 'We had a lot of huge institutional companies come into Dublin and buy up whole apartments. In Dublin, you would see a whole queue around the block very regularly when homes come up for rent. It was just too expensive for me to rent on the income I was on.'

In London, he rented a space in a warehouse in Haringey which had been converted to residential living. 'It was affordable, but it wasn't in the best condition,' he notes. 'We didn't have any heating, and the bedrooms were so small that I couldn't even stand up straight in my room. We used to pick up wooden pallets off the road, chop them up and burn them in a wood burner to keep the place warm.'

After a year, he was evicted but managed to get what by now amounted to a good deal in London's property market: a two-bedroom apartment for £1,400 a month. With two couples sharing, the rent was manageable between them and they settled in. But the conditions in the flat, again, were harsh. 'There was jet black mould about a metre and a half up on our bedroom wall.'

Mould is a regular hazard in homes that are not properly ventilated – especially in colder countries. When they are overcrowded, when poor building work is carried out or pipes spring leaks, it can become out of control. In London, a densely packed, cold city with poorly maintained rented homes as standard, it was becoming a chronic problem.

Sure enough, in Conall's home a survey of the property revealed it was due to structural issues causing internal leaks, but the landlord told them it was due to them drying clothes in their bedroom. 'It was pretty demoralising,' he tells me. 'My partner has asthma and she had bad breathing issues the whole time we were in that flat. It was also a really hot summer, and the building was just not ventilated – if you touched the walls, they felt like radiators.'

Just thirty years had passed since Sean – who we met in the 1980s – had come to London from Ireland seeking work. But where he could labour on building sites, save enough money to buy a home with his new wife and start a family, a new generation of Irish and other immigrants were left stuck in the expensive misery of a deregulated rental sector.

A FULL FRONTAL ATTACK – SOCIAL HOUSING

Like Thatcher thirty years before, the new Conservative leadership of David Cameron and his chancellor George Osborne brought overt hostility to the idea of social housing. According to Nick Clegg, then deputy prime minister and leader of the Liberal Democrat Party, when his party suggested building more social housing 'the prime minister and chancellor rebuffed them with the stark message: "All it does is produce more Labour voters."'[30]

Initially Osborne intended to remove the public grant for social and affordable housing completely. But warned of the consequences for housing benefit spend if more poorer people had to rent privately, he confined himself to a huge cut. A 60 per cent reduction in the money paid to housing associations for building new houses marked the nadir of state expenditure on building social housing since 1919.

To compensate for the cut in state funding, the rents on any newly built social homes would have to be higher from this point forward. Unlike the old 'social rents', which were set according to a formula based on average local incomes and property values, the new rents were set according to the local housing market, and could be anything up to 80 per cent of what it cost to rent privately. In London particularly the hike could be huge, meaning the monthly rent could be close to £1,000. A new Orwellian term entered the UK housing market to describe this new regime: 'affordable rents'. And this wasn't just newly built housing – existing social homes were converted to the new rent regime as tenants left. Over the course of the decade, more than 16,000 social rented homes in London were converted to the new higher rates when they were re-let.[31] Home by home, social renting was becoming more expensive, the options for people on lower incomes shrinking away.

The government no longer felt a responsibility to help the poorest with housing. 'The government and the particular ministers of the time believed state-funded housing should be for a different client group – it was seen as an intermediate product for people to take a step up into home ownership,' Steve Douglas, a former chief executive of the government's Housing Corporation, told me in 2018.[32] As for those who could not afford the new rents, well, they should simply move somewhere cheaper and stop asking the state to keep them housed in an expensive city.

This was particularly true given that an overall cap on benefits was introduced – meaning that larger homes would be unavailable to those out of work or on the lowest incomes. In 2014, nine London boroughs went to court to try and get the rules changed, presenting evidence which showed affordable rent properties 'will not be affordable for a large proportion of the eligible households, who have low incomes or are on benefits and subject to the benefits cap'.[33] They lost.

As it pulled away from social rented housing, the government began to invest much more in shared ownership – where buyers purchased a share of the equity and rented the rest. This was already an established part of affordable housing programmes – having been introduced by Thatcher and grown steadily under Blair. But as house prices had risen – especially in inner London – calling it 'affordable housing' was increasingly ridiculous. During the decade, shared ownership homes with a value of more than £1 million went onto the market, while many others had monthly costs of more than £2,500 – due in part to inflated service charges to pay for luxury facilities in blocks designed for high-end buyers.

At the same time, welfare changes were restricting the ability of social tenants to make rent. The welfare cut which became known as the 'bedroom tax' penalised those who had a spare bedroom – including the recently bereaved, disabled people who used the extra room to store medical equipment and parents who shared custody of their children – and the introduction of Universal Credit introduced further cuts and a painful six-week wait for the first payment. Arrears began to soar and – even in social housing – evictions became more and more common. Housing associations stopped letting homes to tenants on the lowest incomes, saying they couldn't afford the rent. For London's poorest there was nowhere to turn.

But as the options were taken away at one end, councils were faced with ever increasing numbers in need of help. With huge competition for every available social home – especially those which remained on the old 'social rents' scheme – only those in the greatest need were housed. Increasingly, social housing estates became the destination for people who had suffered trauma, experienced severe disability or had significant mental illnesses.

As state funding shrank away, landlords which managed social housing became increasingly commercial. These housing associations were mostly charities – not-for-profit bodies set up to provide housing to those on the lowest incomes. But they now needed to derive a 'surplus' from their balance sheets to cover the gap previously funded by government grant, and pay the interest on the loans they had taken out. For those based in London in particular, this meant building housing for outright sale, cutting back day-to-day spending on the social housing estates they managed and merging into bigger structures.

And all this came at a cost: it meant shedding staff, piling more pressure on remaining housing officers and neighbourhood managers, and cutting the cost of repairs and maintenance services by procuring the lowest-priced private contractor. The standard of services began to slip. The neighbourhood caretakers of the 1980s were a long-forgotten dream.

Some also began to 'sweat their assets' – selling off the most valuable homes they owned when they became vacant at auction to private investors, instead of placing new tenants in them. One source explained to me how this process operated at the organisation she worked at. When a home became vacant, a review was carried out by the commercial property team and if it was worth more to sell than the organisation would get in rent from putting a new tenant in, it would be sold. Properties she had worked to refurbish and bring back into use just six or seven years before were put under the hammer and went off into the hands of private landlords. Because these sales were targeted at areas where values were highest, it meant the social housing in London's richest areas was being sold. 'One of the guys in my team was seconded to go around and look at all the homes we owned and find what were informally called "the crown jewels" to be sold off,' she says. 'I understand we weren't getting as much funding as we used to, so decisions needed to be taken, but a lot of good social housing was sold to fund the building of new properties which just weren't as affordable.'

The system was starting to slide. And no one was there to keep an eye on the provision of basic services, because that too had been cut. In 2010, the government scrapped the

Tenant Services Authority, a regulatory body set up to keep an eye on the performance of social landlords. Regulation of social housing providers was now limited to ensuring they were 'financially viable' and well governed, to keep the confidence of the private lenders. Professor Martin Cave, who had written a report into social housing regulation for Gordon Brown's government, said this was 'my worst fears realised'. 'I feel it will leave tenants without the protection they need against incompetent landlords,' he said.[34]

Stories about serious disrepair in London's social housing were starting to become more and more commonplace – the large housing association Circle was engulfed in a major scandal over the condition of some homes it managed in 2016. In early 2017, I visited some of its residents on an estate in Bow who had been left without heating for months throughout the winter. 'We had to have extra clothes on all the time,' one resident told me. 'We've all been ill – coughs and colds and chest infections.' The association responded by merging with another large London housing association to become Clarion – the country's largest social landlord and the custodian of 125,000 homes. It promised its residents the repairs issues they had experienced would be fixed.

These changes were changing the ethos of social housing. While many people who worked for housing associations did so out of a desire to make a difference, the sector increasingly became a home for commercially-minded professionals who cared much more about new development than providing decent services to those who needed a home. This was cheered on by a government whose ethos matched this agenda entirely. 'We kind of had this mental drift process where we lost sight of what the sector was supposed to be about. It became a really weird kind of ego-driven industry, which was all about who can build more than anybody else,' reflects one source who worked at a senior level at many organisations in this period. 'There was an inherent discrimination and stigma against actual people that need support at the bottom of the housing rung. People thought "Those people don't deserve it and therefore we don't need to worry".'

Funding was also being stripped out. In 2016, the government announced a four-year cut to the rents paid by social tenants. While this might sound like a benevolent policy, it was actually a very direct funding cut to the social housing providers, who used the rents to fund new-build homes and maintenance projects. Repairs and property investments were delayed, grassroots staff were laid off and associations pushed even harder into the private market to generate new income.[35] London Councils estimated that the policy cost boroughs £459 million in lost income, and most of this came straight out of investment in housing.[36]

In 2016, when I interviewed Neil Hadden, then chief executive of north London-based housing association Genesis, which traced its roots back to charities set up to provide homes to poor residents around Paddington in the 1960s, he talked up his organisation's record of selling off the social housing it owned in Camden, doing what it could to 'get our hands on that value, changing its tenure, by churning it, by selling it and using those proceeds to build more homes'. He said the organisation would no longer build 'affordable' rented homes and would focus instead on those who wanted to buy. Asked where this would leave those who could not afford to buy in London's property market, he replied, 'I could be really harsh and say that's not my problem.'

MELANIE, HANNAH, ANDREW

Melanie, who had started work in a housing association development team, noticed the changes coming through. 'The housing association I worked for started obtaining new types of funding, and the focus began to change as well,' she says. 'Suddenly we were putting in really swanky designer kitchens and bringing in sales and marketing executives on high salaries from big estate agents to sell them. It really started to feel like the management were much more excited about that than the social homes. When I started, I felt like I was working for a third-sector, governmental-type organisation. But by the time I left, it felt like I was working for a developer.'

She was also concerned that this focus on development meant the organisation she worked for was taking its eye off the ball regarding the management of its existing homes. A social tenant herself, she empathised with the struggles the residents were experiencing. 'Having raised complaints with my own housing provider, I could really relate to the frustration of tenants, and it was something I felt a lot of guilt about actually. I think there was a massive attention diversion. Everyone on the board and in the senior teams were so focused on the new and shiny developments that they just didn't want to know about the estate in Peckham which was run ragged and was in dire need of funding.'

Hannah, who grew up on the Samuel Lewis estate in Hackney before it was demolished, got a place at university to study English Literature, but when she came back to London she struggled to find good work. 'I just went back to what I knew, which was temp work in the NHS,' she says. She lived with her mum for a few years, and then got a social home of her own aged twenty-four in around 2010.

The experience was far removed from her time growing up on the Samuel Lewis estate. 'It felt more isolated,' she says. The estate is in a central area of London dominated by offices and nightlife. 'It's a place where people come to go out,' she says. People would spill onto the estate from the bars nearby to 'drink or fight or have sex basically'. The housing association which managed the estate would not respond to calls for a gate, and did not initially allow the residents to form an official tenants' association.

'I felt they put a lot of barriers in place,' Hannah notes. 'Every now and then they would attend our meetings and we'd go through a list of actions, but nothing ever got done.

There just doesn't seem to be any accountability. We just don't see them on the estate, and they have such a high turnover of staff it's hard to keep up with who we should be speaking to. One person will tell you something, then you come back and you'll speak to somebody new. When a contractor is booked, they don't turn up, and when you call the housing association office they don't even know there was a booking.'

One night in 2014, Andrew, the session musician who had grown up on a traditional East End council estate, met a young woman called Katy at a pub in east London. After they struck up a conversation at the bar, he gave her a business card which he'd recently had printed. 'It was a pack of 200 and I think I only ever gave out five,' he says. It was a good one to hand out, though – she texted him, and they started a relationship which quickly became serious.

The timing was fortunate, because Andrew's life was getting difficult. His mum had major mental health issues, and she ended up clashing with the warden who looked after their estate. As a result, he made some checks and realised Andrew shouldn't be living there. 'Technically we were bang to rights,' says Andrew. 'It was only my mum and my brother on the rent book, so I was technically subletting from them and that's not allowed. So even though it was a three-bedroom flat, they made me move out and I became homeless.'

Six months into his relationship with Katy, he phoned her and asked if he could move into her bedroom at her mum and dad's house in nearby East Ham. 'I don't know what I would have done, if I [hadn't given] her that business card. I wouldn't have had anywhere to go.'

SOLD OFF AND DEMOLISHED – SOCIAL HOUSING

As well as cutting funds for new build and changing the business model of social housing providers, the government also accelerated the process of sell-off and demolition for the housing that remained.

Right to Buy sales had been dwindling under Labour – rising house prices had put the option out of reach for many of those who had held off. But in 2011, David Cameron announced plans to supercharge the policy. Right to Buy discounts would be raised to a maximum of £75,000 nationally and £100,000 in London – and would rise with inflation every year thereafter. While he promised 'one-for-one' replacement of any 'additional' homes sold, this hasn't happened. London has seen more than 25,000 council homes in the capital sold since, but just 13,000 replacements started, many of which will be smaller with higher rents.[37]

The journey of Right to Buy homes sold in the 1980s was now becoming clear. While originally they were purchased by the tenant who lived in them, now many of those tenants had sold and moved on and the homes were increasingly shifting into the hands of private landlords. By the middle of the decade, data I collected revealed that more than 40 per cent of former council homes in London were being rented privately. In Westminster, Harrow, Enfield and Tower Hamlets it was more than half.[38]

This has made council estates a quick source of profits for those who want to make money out of London's housing shortage. 'Over the years, I have seen many of our estates become virtual honey pots for estate agents and landlords,' Pat Callaghan, former cabinet member for housing in Camden, told me in 2015. The ability to make such startling profits has attracted the attention of criminals. Callaghan told me she had seen companies flyer whole estates, particularly seeking older tenants, promising to support them to buy their home. The companies then fund the purchase and kick the tenants out, and the property goes straight into the private rented sector. 'It is usually people who are in desperate need of money or who are quite vulnerable who are particularly encouraged into these deals,' housing solicitor Giles Peaker – who had advised some clients caught up in these scams – told me in 2016. Meric Apak, now cabinet member for housing in Camden and a lifelong social housing resident, has seen this first hand on his estate. 'In short, they say "Do you want to pay rent for the rest of your life or do you want to own your home? We can help you",' he says. 'But they are basically mafia. They send heavies round and intimidate the tenants and eventually people give in.' The dream of Right to Buy was being hijacked by profit-hungry criminals.

And many homes that were not being sold off were being demolished, with the estate regeneration programmes which began in the 2000s finally reaching the stage of bulldozers and wrecking balls in the 2010s. And the promises made on affordable housing were being broken. At the Heygate – the south London estate we encountered in the previous chapter – just 100 of the 2,924 homes ultimately built to replace the estate by developer Lendlease were for social rent.

Instead, the development comprised two-bed flats, with access to a private yoga and gym room, and 24-hour concierge, which cost more than a million pounds each. Meanwhile, Heygate's social housing tenants were scattered and dispersed across Southwark. Leaseholders, mostly those who purchased under the Right to Buy, were offered a paltry £122,140 on average for a two-bed home, with some getting as little as £32,000 for a one-bed flat. Like many former leaseholders from demolished estates, they have been scattered as far away as Sidcup, St Albans, Chelmsford, Croydon, Bexleyheath, Ilford, Romford, Dartford, Cheshunt, Mitcham and West Thurrock. It would emerge that Southwark Council had sold the Heygate to Lendlease for a catastrophically low sum of £50 million, barely recouping the £44 million it spent 'decanting' residents. Peter John, the council leader who had steered the project to completion from Southwark's side, would become chair of Terrapin – the private lobbying firm which had represented Lendlease during the regeneration – when he stepped down from his council role in 2020.³⁹

At Woodberry Down, in Hackney, the project which had started in 1999 was still grinding on. Some of the estate had been demolished, other blocks were left to decline in a seemingly endless wait. Those who did move into the new-build blocks that had been completed were not entirely happy. Their prison-like corridors and sterile, hotel-style layout are nothing like the communal buildings that existed before the demolition. 'You come up in the lift and you go along the corridor and its door, door, door, door, carpet, but you don't see anyone,' a resident of one of Woodberry Down's new blocks told Dr Paul Watt in his research for his book on estate regeneration. 'I think they've killed the community,' added another.⁴⁰ Meanwhile, the blocks built by Berkeley where the estate once was are marketed as 'luxury' homes sitting in the 'spectacular natural surroundings of two existing reservoirs'. They are priced between £550,000 and £1.8 million.⁴¹

A review by the Green Party in 2015 assessed fifty estate regeneration projects across London, planned or completed. These started with 30,000 socially rented homes. By the time they are completed, for all the money spent, lives upended and carbon released, we will have 22,135 socially rented homes – a loss of almost 8,000. In their place, the density of the estates will have doubled – with 36,000 new market sale homes built on the land which was once council housing.⁴²

There is an alternative reality where this situation simply got worse and worse. When Cameron won a majority at the general election in 2015, he embarked on even more aggressive reforms to social housing which would have further decimated London's social housing sector – a mass sell-off of the remaining council homes to investors, social rents jacked up to market rates if tenants' incomes rose, deeper benefit cuts and much more private-finance-led estate demolition. But while this vision passed Parliament, it was never enacted.

The vote for Brexit in 2016 led Cameron to quit and Theresa May replaced him as prime minister. She shelved his plans and even made some modest moves towards building more council housing. With Boris Johnson also losing City Hall to Labour's Sadiq Khan, the decade ended with some signs that we were turning a corner: more social housing was being built and residents of existing estates were promised ballots before their homes could be demolished. But these changes were paltry compared to the size of the challenge – and much of the damage had already been done.

ANDY, DHILLON

In south London, Andy Plant and his neighbours caught the first hint that their estate might be listed for demolition when, in 2012, two Labour councillors were overheard talking outside a resident's window. 'He was saying, "We're going to demolish here, so we don't need to continue doing any major works,"' Andy remembers. 'So when they actually announced it in 2013, we were prepared for them.'

Basic work, like clearing the gutters, stopped. 'Unless you maintain the roof, you get problems everywhere,' says Andy. 'Water starts to get in. Our gutters were designed for 1970s levels of rainfall, not what we get nowadays. So it's essential that they are maintained.'

Many of the residents decided they did not want the homes they loved to be knocked down. 'The community on this estate bonded people together so they thought "To hell with Lambeth Council, we'll fight".' His wife Ann got involved very early and went to a lot of the community meetings. A judicial review had the first consultation overturned, but Lambeth re-ran the consultation and tried to push ahead with the redevelopment. More legal challenges followed. Ann was heavily involved in this process. For both of them, the stress was taking its toll. 'It was affecting our health,' says Andy. 'I always thought I was in worse health than her, but we didn't know the impact it would have.'

By the mid-2010s, Ann's illness had become severe. Andy expands:

> My wife was dying by then. We didn't know, but she had a slow-growing bowel tumour. A couple of weeks before she died, the oncologist said he had never seen this particular cancer grow so fast, and he asked if she had been under a lot of stress. We explained about what was happening with the estate, and he said, "Unfortunately tumours tend to like cortisol. So the stress hormones your wife is producing have fed that tumour." A tumour which should have taken three or four years to grow to the size it had had done so in about a year.
>
> She loved this place. So we brought her home for the last couple of weeks. Our flat looks out towards Crystal Palace and you can watch the sunrise. She wanted to see it and be where she loved being and say goodbye to her friends. The community were fantastic, people were coming to see her, they kept her spirits up.

Ann died at home in November 2016. Before she died, she made Andy promise never to let the council knock down the estate.

'I never expected to be here without her,' he says. 'The people round here pretty much saved my life after my wife died. They didn't let me sink into myself.'

In the east of the city, Dhillon's brother was still living in Robin Hood Gardens, his block half empty and leaking. When the demolition of the estate started in the mid-2010s, he was finally moved into another run-down property as temporary accommodation – once more a council block that was facing demolition. His mental and physical health began to suffer. Finally, he was moved into the new property he had waited so long for. But a year later, in 2018, he was dead. 'He died really suddenly of a massive heart attack,' Dhillon tells me. 'I really feel sorry for him. He stuck with it waiting for this new property that he was dreaming of and he only lived there for eight or nine months before he died.'

Dhillon links his brother's death to the housing conditions and the stress of waiting for a new home for so long. 'He had an addiction. He had poor mental health. He didn't have very good discipline in terms of his health,' he says. 'So it's not just one thing, it's lots of things that contributed to it. But quite a lot of that came from the conditions he lived [in].'

ONE ESTATE IN WEST LONDON

To grasp the cumulative impact of the forces which assailed social housing in the forty years after Margaret Thatcher's reforms began, let's consider the case of one estate in west London. It was built in 1974, to replace local private rented housing which was so notorious for its overcrowding, poor conditions and exploitative landlords that it had been described as the worst slum housing in the whole of England.[43]

The 1,000-home new estate started well, offering a melting pot of working-class people the chance to build a thriving community, with better housing than they had ever previously experienced. But this community started to come under pressure. In the 1980s, as homes started to be sold under Right to Buy, maintenance budgets were cut to almost nil. The condition of the buildings on the estate began to degrade: leaks, damp and draughts multiplied. Management was handed to an ALMO to pick up the funding offered by Tony Blair's government in the 2000s.

But the money given under his Decent Homes programme was insufficient. In 2008, a board report for the management organisation said there was a shortfall of funding and that it faced 'an impossible situation in that funding falls far short of the level of investment needed to maintain the stock'. The ALMO tried outsourcing the repairs to a private provider, but the provider went bust. The estate's live-in caretakers and front desk were removed. To report repairs, residents were required to phone a central call centre where they would be left on hold for hours and spoken to rudely when they finally got through. 'It was like [the call handler] was angry with me that I was making a complaint,' one resident later recalled. 'I felt like they thought I was a "troublemaker" because I had been making complaints about these leaks but I was incredibly stressed, had to take time off work, and [the ALMO] did not seem to be doing anything else about it.'

In 2009 a draft masterplan recommended 'demolishing most of the existing housing' on the estate to make way for new-build homes, noting that there would be 'significant' interest from private developers, and describing the appearance of the estate as 'a blight' on the surrounding area. This was ultimately never taken forward but with the possibility on the table, investment dried up entirely. As the 2010s developed, residents endured miserable conditions: unfixed leaks caused mould so serious mushrooms grew in kitchens. Pensioners lived on microwave soup for days when their gas supply was interrupted. A resident with bowel cancer had to walk to a local leisure centre to use the toilet. Disabled residents placed on upper floors of the estate's main high-rise tower block were trapped in the building when the lifts broke.

This tower was in particularly dire need of investment. Eventually, after years of complaint, money was cobbled together through the sale of some surplus property the council owned elsewhere in the borough, and a refurbishment project was announced. But this was done on the cheap and focused on the external appearance of the building – using the cheapest external cladding panels available to give it a cosmetic facelift with little benefit to the people inside. Meanwhile, repairs essential to maintain the safety of the block internally were left incomplete.

Maybe you have realised by now that this estate is Lancaster West and the building is Grenfell Tower. On 14 June 2017, a fire ripped through the block and the decades of poor maintenance were exposed with lethal consequences for the seventy-two people who would be trapped inside as a result.

I wrote in my previous book about how deregulation and corporate greed gave us the fire, and the seventy-two deaths which resulted from it. The neglect and deliberate marginalisation of social housing and its residents in London, the process which had started almost forty years previously and accelerated with every decade that passed since then, was central to this story too.

PRESENT

Social housing

You may feel like *no one* needs reminding of how bad the housing crisis has become in present-day London. Those who live in the city engage with it every day. Those who don't can hardly miss the regular news reports about the plight of homeless families, the poor condition of social housing or the crushing, Sisyphean struggle facing those who are fruitlessly saving up to buy.

Nonetheless, some reminders are necessary. The dominant political narrative paints London as elite, aloof and wealthy in contrast to the struggles of the rest of the country – somehow missing the fact that the city's uniquely dysfunctional and dominant rental market makes it home to much of our most extreme poverty.

We lose a frustrating amount of energy debating the consumer-focused lifestyle of young people (Netflix subscriptions, takeaway coffees, avocado toast), and too little on the fact that today's market means a 21-year-old graduate moving to London for work will have spent in excess of £100,000 renting a room by the time she reaches her thirtieth birthday. Meanwhile, political debate gets sucked into a culture war between so-called NIMBYs (who oppose new developments) and YIMBYs (who think that all of our problems can be fixed with mass building), neither of whom have real solutions to today's crisis. If things are going to get better in London, we need clarity about the state we have found ourselves in. So let's take a short – and admittedly bleak – journey through the city of today, as well as catching up on where the individuals we have followed through the years find themselves.

DHILLON, MOTIUR, HANNAH

Dhillon, whose brother died after the demolition of Robin Hood Gardens, has moved to Scotland with his family. He misses the multiculturalism of his hometown, but is glad to be able to afford a decent home to raise his children. Motiur, his former neighbour, has decamped to Ipswich where he is the headteacher of a primary school. He worries about the impact of precarious housing on the children in his care, many of whom come to school hungry or move regularly as their housing situation changes.

After speaking to them both for the last time, I visited Robin Hood Gardens – the estate which they described so fondly. One of the blocks was still standing, though abandoned. A few posters on windows suggest it might be in use – perhaps illegally. The mound where Dhillon, Motiur and their friends used to play remained. But now it was derelict, overgrown and strewn with beer cans and cigarette butts. The noise reduction built into the estate still worked. Despite being between two major roads, it was almost eerily silent and tranquil. Twenty years ago, the noise would have been children and young people – Motiur, Dhillon, his brothers and their friends – celebrating goals, playing cricket with taped-up tennis balls, joking and play-fighting. But now it was silent.

Around the corner, I knocked on doors at the smart-looking new-builds where some of the residents of the estate have been rehoused. I found some residents from the former estate. They told me the new flats are nice, but suffer from snagging defects – cupboard doors falling off hinges, unusable and unsafe balconies. From the outside, their building looks slick and modern, but inside it looks neglected. Flyers pour from postal boxes, a plasma screen displays what it says is 'fire safety advice', but the words are placeholder Latin. The communal, outdoor life has been replaced with sterile, enclosed corridors.

Hannah, meanwhile, still lives on the housing association estate in the centre of the city. Now a mum herself, she struggles to find shops selling reasonably priced groceries: 'The supermarkets aren't proper supermarkets, they're the mini ones that sell expensive sandwiches to office workers.

'It can feel quite depressing with all these huge buildings surrounding us. In terms of talking to neighbours and that kind of community that I remember, it doesn't really exist.' She adds, 'I don't see kids playing out ever now, and that is quite sad. There's maybe one or two families who will bring out a deck chair. People are more insular now, there's less of a community vibe in society in general. People are working more to afford their bills and they spend a lot less time having a chat.'

CRISIS

It is early January, not long after Christmas. There are still lights on the high streets, trees in living rooms and tinny music playing in the shops. The city is wet, tightly swaddled in grey clouds, and it is freezing cold. After a warm autumn, winter has arrived suddenly, and temperatures have dipped down towards freezing.

A council home in Southwark is home to a family of five. The second youngest daughter is Meghan, a seven-year-old girl with round glasses and a bright smile. Meghan is sick. She has kidney failure, needs twelve hours of dialysis a day and is awaiting an operation for a transplant. Her house is freezing, she is shivering alongside her family and every shower she has taken for the last fortnight has been stone cold. The family's boiler broke down four days before Christmas, and the council has so far been unable to replace it.[1]

We move to another council flat, in Croydon. Here we find a leak spreading across the ceiling, water cascading out of light fittings, soaking floors and destroying the carpets. In the kitchen, there is black mould so thick that there are furry spores on the walls and ceilings, growing in the plug sockets and on the family's food.[2]

Next, we travel to the Eastfields estate in Merton, south-west London. This estate like so many others has been listed for demolition for years, without any work taking place. In the interim, it has been neglected by Clarion, the housing association which owns it. Here, ceilings are collapsing after persistent leaks, the debris falling down around children doing their homework, kitchens are caked in mould, there are holes in the walls where plaster has simply fallen out. Mice, rats and cockroaches run riot. Residents are so frustrated at the lack of action from their housing association they have purchased bags of concrete and are attempting the repairs themselves.[3]

In Barnet, north London, we find a block where the door entry system is broken, so rough sleepers line the corridors and needles are scattered all over the floors. Doors, marked 'danger', hang, rotting off their hinges, and the walls are split by jagged floor-to-ceiling cracks. The building was listed for demolition in 2003. It is seething with pests and vermin and in 2021, it made the news when a mother took her newborn baby to the BBC and showed the presenter a cockroach bite on her child's eye.[4]

This short tour is a snippet of the worst of London's social housing in the 2020s. As we have seen over the previous chapters, these problems have been building for years, as homes were neglected and investment cut and then cut again.

This problem, of disrepair and inaction from the landlords responsible, is not unique to the capital city. Indeed, the story that really threw these conditions into the national spotlight was the death of Awaab Ishak – an otherwise healthy two-year-old boy who died from breathing difficulties because the mould in his family's social housing flat in the northern town of Rochdale had become so severe.

Yet London is the epicentre of this crisis. The most recent English Housing Survey says there are 72,000 social homes in the city with damp and mould problems, a shade under one in every ten, and more than double the next highest region.[5] Hackney Council alone had 1,400 open complaints of damp and mould at the time of writing.[6] The city has almost 90,000 social homes considered 'non-decent' and 37,000 with a hazard so serious it poses a risk to the tenants' life.[7] According to the London Councils group – which represents the thirty-three local authorities in the capital – London has the lowest social housing standards of any region nationally, with satisfaction nineteen percentage points lower than the national average.[8] Residents are left stuck, facing non-responsive corporate bureaucracy when things go wrong with their homes. Lambeth Council was sanctioned recently for taking, for example, 197 weeks to fix a broken pipe and 187 weeks to fix a seriously cracked window, despite the residents chasing fruitlessly, spending upwards of ninety minutes per call on hold to the customer services desk.[9]

In short, the cuts, mergers and outsourcing drives described in prior chapters have left social landlords – both councils and housing associations – struggling to keep up with the hundreds of thousands of homes their understaffed operations are responsible for. A stark example of this came in 2022, when 61-year-old Sheila Seleoane was found dead and decomposing in a social housing flat in south London. She had been there for over two years. Despite repeated warnings from her neighbours that she might have passed away, her landlord had simply sent multiple rent demands and capped off her gas when she stopped paying the bills.[10] The landlord was Peabody – a famous and historic housing association, established in the nineteenth century with the intention to provide quality social housing to London's poorest residents. At her inquest, the failure to discover her body earlier was blamed partly on cuts which destroyed the landlord's model neighbourhood management of homes – leaving staff in charge of 1,200 homes each.[11]

At the same time, as local authority enforcement teams have been cut back by austerity, they have stopped policing social landlords, and focused instead on private landlords where money can sometimes be clawed back through licensing schemes. 'All the legislation is there, it just needs to be enforced,' says one retired housing enforcement officer, who spent his whole career working for London boroughs. 'About twenty-five years ago, we used to serve notice on social landlords for disrepair all the time. I would do two or three a week for damp and mould. But all that fell away and we never do that now because of resource pressure.'

Meanwhile, the cost of renting a social home has gone through the roof. The most expensive family-sized homes let under the new regime of 'affordable rents' introduced by David Cameron sit at £1,420 a month,[12] only a shade below the UK's average cost of a mortgage repayment.[13] Even for those who have not moved into one of these new homes, rents have risen sharply – shooting up by 15.2% between 2023 and 2024. Service charges – which can be charged to some social tenants – have also climbed sharply. This, coming at a time of rising costs and stagnant wages, means residents are in poverty: 40 per cent of social housing tenants are struggling to make ends meet, going without basic needs or relying on debt to pay for them in 2023, while 51 per cent said they worry that they will not be able to meet their housing costs.[14]

And this is just those who can get social housing. In 1995/96, London's councils and housing associations offered more than 50,000 new social tenancies. By the start of the

2010s, this had collapsed to 11,620. With so few getting in and demand so high after years of rising rents and a rising population, the time spent in the queue is now literally a lifetime. Waiting times for a social home are fifty-five years on average in Greenwich, thirty-eight years in Newham, thirty-five years in Brent and thirty-one years in Merton.[15] 'Nineteen years and nothing. I'm a 40-year-old man now, I'm tired of living like a dog, sleeping on floors,' one of the thousands on the waiting lists told *Inside Housing* in 2023.[16]

The lack of availability also stops people moving up into decent-sized housing as their families grow. As a result, overcrowding has spiralled – 14.8 per cent of social homes in the capital are considered overcrowded, a figure which has risen steadily from 12 per cent in 2011, and compares to 6.6 per cent of the overall housing stock.[17] 'Our whole family spends our life in one room. More suitable accommodation would change our lives,' Mohammed, from Ilford, told *Inside Housing* in 2023. 'My children could play freely.'[18]

Recent years have seen some pushback against this state of affairs. The disrepair in social housing briefly became an issue of national concern following the death of Awaab Ishak and the campaigning of Kwajo Tweneboa, who lived on the Eastfield estate until his father's death drove him to fight back. In response, the government implemented a beefed-up housing ombudsman, a new regulator with power to sanction landlords for widespread failures and a new law (yet to come into force at the time of writing) which sets maximum timescales for fixing the most serious disrepair. There has been some impact. Social landlords have doubled what they spent ten years ago on their existing homes. After forty years of neglect, it is limited, slow progress, which will not cure everything overnight, but it is a start.

But this has come at a price. With more money being poured into fixing historic disrepair, as well repairing a shocking list of fire safety defects which emerged through checks carried out after the Grenfell Tower fire, there is little money left for anything else. With inflation and interest repayments soaring after Covid-19 and the war in Ukraine, the social housing sector is edging towards going bust.

London's councils are budgeting for £170 million of cuts to housing management which will leave them 'focusing only on the most urgent repairs and delaying much-needed improvements'.[19] Housing associations have pulled right back from building new affordable housing as their funds have been eaten up elsewhere. The number of new affordable homes built in the city dropped an astonishing 91 per cent from 25,658 to 2,358 between 2023 and 2024 – a catastrophe for those waiting for a new home.[20] The consequence may be further sell-offs. Around 300,000 homes owned by social housing providers around the country – many of them in the capital – are no longer considered 'viable', as the rental payments do not meet the cost of managing them, particularly given the forthcoming costs of complying with decarbonisation targets.[21]

Amid this financial strife, we have seen the rise of new 'for-profit' housing associations – where large investors stump up money to directly buy up or develop new social housing in London, replacing the financially stretched not-for-profit or public bodies we have today. Once purchased by an investor, these homes can be traded like any financial portfolio, sold and resold to the highest bidder as investors try to drive a profit out of the rental yield. This hardly feels likely to result in a good outcome for the people who live in the homes. But the for-profit sector is growing relentlessly – from virtually nothing in the mid-2010s, it owned 28,164 homes by 2023. By 2028, the estate agency Savills predicts it will own 113,000. Some of its leading investors are lobbying government to authorise full-scale transfers of social housing stock into their ownership, seeing the potential for lucrative returns from the rents social tenants will pay in future years. 'Housing associations have assets which are worth something of the order of £200 billion, on the basis of existing social rents in perpetuity,' one wrote recently.[22] One of the largest of these new entrants is Sage, a housing provider backed financially by Blackstone, which has $881 billion of assets under management globally – more than twice the GDP of Denmark. It has previously been linked to scandals in Spain, where it bought up rental housing at low cost after the financial crisis and then hiked up the rents and forced tenants to leave. This has not yet happened in the UK. But the for-profits are coming. Legal and General Affordable Homes is openly seeking the transfer of existing social homes into its ownership.[23] Octopus Real Estate, a fund with £3.7 billion under management, has done some small deals.[24] With the financial circumstances they face, traditional housing associations have little choice but to get on board. 'Working with the for-profits and other sources of patient capital has to be an integral part of what we are doing, moving forward,' the chief executive of Peabody told *Inside Housing* in 2025.[25] We will only see the impact of these new for-profit investors on peoples' lives as the next decades pass.

MELANIE, ANDY

Melanie – the social housing tenant who also worked for a social landlord – has had a difficult journey through the 2020s. She left the housing association she worked for when she started being asked to develop shared-ownership homes valued at more than £700,000 each. 'We were taking cash deposits off people of more than £100,000 and calling ourselves charitable,' she says. 'I just couldn't do it anymore.'

Frustrated, she decided she might as well work for an organisation that simply admitted it was acting for profit and paid her a salary which reflected that. She found herself at one of the larger for-profit providers entering the sector. 'That was even worse. It was almost like working for a pension fund.

It's just numbers. They buy up as much as they can. I was supposed to be making sure the properties we were buying from private developers were up to scratch, but it was a fruitless task. All that mattered was the value and the return. We were buying absolute crap. They have no interest in becoming long-term housing managers.'

Adding to the irony, she herself has faced serious housing disrepair at home – a collapsing ceiling, damp, woodlice, rotting floorboards. 'Each time [my landlord] has sent out a different operative from a different department. They've never sent a building surveyor. I'm in construction myself, I can see what they need to do, but they just can't work it out. I'll come home and the whole carpet is soaked, I've had to throw out a mattress, there are timber props in my room so half the bedroom is unusable.' It has been a year since she first reported the leak that caused the damage to her housing provider. 'I sit in all these industry conferences or hear people boasting about what they're doing on LinkedIn and I just get so angry,' she says. 'It just doesn't reflect that reality that people are living through.'

Andy, meanwhile, still lives in Cressingham Gardens. After a formal review of Lambeth's housing services in 2022, which led to damning conclusions about its housing management company Homes for Lambeth, the council put the plans on hold. In 2024, it awarded a £1 million contract to property consultancy Montagu Evans to write an options appraisal. More than a decade after the intention to demolish it was first announced, its future remains completely unclear. 'We'll keep fighting, every inch of the way,' Andy told me the last time I saw him. 'We don't have a choice. It's our home.'

Private renting

CAROLYN, MANJU

For Carolyn, the former civil servant who was renting privately in Catford, things started to go wrong in 2024. Her rent was still just about affordable on her civil service pension. But in February of that year, the landlord told her he was planning to sell, and that she was going to be evicted. By now, rents in the area had doubled while her rent had not kept up. Getting a new tenancy in a similar home would cost her around £2,000 a month – far in excess of what she could afford.

She told Lewisham Council she was facing eviction and kept them up to date with the process. She stayed in the home for as long as she could and was eventually evicted by bailiffs on 1 April, following a court process. With a friend, she walked down to the town hall with the note from the bailiffs saying she had been evicted and asked for help. 'It was a very stressful situation,' she says. She got the telephone number of a housing officer, but when she called him it went straight to voicemail, and if she called the switchboard, she was told she was on the system and 'someone would get back to her'. 'But they never did,' she says. 'Everywhere I turned I was met by silence.'

She stayed on her friend's couch for a while, and was intermittently paying for hotels or short-term holiday lets out of her savings. She moved her belongings from place to place with her in bags – the moves made difficult by the legacy of her injuries, which now meant she needed a stick to walk. Now in her mid-seventies, she felt the council should consider her case 'priority need' and offer her accommodation, but they said her needs were not severe enough. She was left homeless – a sofa-surfing disabled pensioner who had spent her whole career working for the British state.

In late 2024, the council finally made her an offer of permanent housing. But it was in County Durham, over 250 miles and a five-hour drive from London. Carolyn has no friends, family or connections in the north east.

Lewisham's letter to her was remarkably brisk. 'We notified you that we owed you a duty to take reasonable steps to help you secure suitable accommodation,' it said. 'I am pleased to inform you that to end that duty we have been able to arrange for you to be offered a final accommodation offer for a private rented tenancy in Bishop Auckland, County Durham. I am satisfied that the offer is suitable and reasonable for you to accept and this will bring the duty owed to you to an end whether you accept or reject the offer.'

In December 2024, I volunteered to drive her across south London, from a short-term let she was staying in to a Premier Inn which she had booked in Lewisham. With her physical ailments, carrying all her belongings on public transport was impossible. On a brisk, cold Saturday morning not long before Christmas, I met her at the door of her rental accommodation. The flat she was renting a room in had once been social housing. Carolyn had found a few nights' shelter in this room at the cost of several hundred pounds. But now time had run out and she had leave by 11 a.m.

I helped her carry her bags to the car – a lifetime's possessions reduced to a rucksack, a bulky laundry bag and a suitcase. They barely took up half the boot. We drove into Lewisham town centre, which became the southerly terminus of the Docklands Light Railway in 1999. Since then, it has been 26 minutes away from Bank and 17 minutes from Canary Wharf. As such, it has transformed from a down-on-its-luck working-class area to an enclave of residential skyscrapers around the station which provide homes to city workers and the high-end student housing beloved of property investment funds. Carolyn looked up at the tall buildings as we drove towards her hotel. 'Every time I come through here, it seems like another one of these towers goes up,' she reflected.

In the hotel lobby we passed a family on their way out – a mixed-race London clan with three kids, two of them in Arsenal shirts. A few seconds eavesdropping on their conversation told me they too were stuck in the temporary accommodation cycle: they were leaving the hotel, but were waiting for the council to tell them where they would be sleeping that night. The mum and dad were arguing about what they should do in the meantime. The children looked despondent.

I sat with Carolyn in the lobby and chatted about what her next steps would be. Would she take the property in Bishop Auckland? 'London is the place that I've been for fifty-four years. I've got friends here. I need them, but they also need me. One of my friends has really serious depression and anxiety and I look after her. My life is here, but I know nothing about Bishop Auckland and I know no one there. So I'm going to stay and fight. I want the council to put me in temporary accommodation. At the moment I'm running out of money from staying in hotels, so I will have to do something eventually.'

Carolyn can appeal. She can argue that the offer of the place in County Durham was not appropriate. She can argue that the council should have regarded her as in priority need. There is every chance that she will lose both of these arguments. Maybe the council will make a closer offer – Peterborough, say, or Luton. But it won't be London.

In Manju's building, she and her neighbours are still clinging on. Manju, who celebrates Thanksgiving from her time in the States, recently held a Thanksgiving party for the block where they put tables in the corridors, made soup and bread and asked neighbours to bring items and had a building-wide feast. The leftovers were donated to a local foodbank. They also leave food parcels and other gifts outside each other's doorways. But the landlord has pressured them to stop doing so. 'The property manager has said to us, "The hallway is our domain, you don't rent the hallway,"' says Manju. 'So I said to him, "What do you want me to do to get out of my flat, jump out of the fucking window?"'

Their building is the last one standing in the row of what used to be secure tenancies for people on low incomes. In one of the buildings that was cleared out, Manju and her neighbours now glimpse a Saudi princess in the morning, as she is led into a limousine by her Filipino maid. Some of the families who had been evicted had lived in the building generation after generation for more than 100 years. In a place where young nurses once lived, houses now sell for an average of £2.5 million.

'All the other buildings are gentrified and gutted. We had to watch as all the beautiful things our neighbours made were cleared out and thrown into skips. It's right up to our door. When they can get our building, they will gut it for sure. It's just a case of them getting it.'

At Manju's building, the owner is making a careful financial balancing act. If they clear out the tenants now, they will be required to pay them compensation. But if they hold out and wait for them to die or move, they will get the building for free. Strange visitors come to the building, phoning properties at random to ask for specifics about who is living there, enquiring about people's ages and health conditions, presumably to calculate how long they might have left to live. In one instance a man arrived, buzzed all the intercoms and got into the building. Sharda asked him who he was and he said he'd been sent by the landlord. She asked to check his ID but noticed when he pulled out his wallet that his business card said he was a private investigator.

'They're just waiting for us to die,' Manju sighs. 'It's just property to them. Nothing to do with human beings. But we're holding on. We won't be told that we don't belong here.'

For Sharda herself, she has moved out of her mum's flat to a rented home in Clapham with her partner. The rent was about £500 each per month. But at the end of their most recent contract, the landlord emailed to say the rent was being hiked to £2,100 a month before bills. Neither Sharda or her partner could afford it. 'It has been awful, the mental stress of it,' says Sharda. 'Just the idea of having to go through the whole process of having to find somewhere else and knowing that the next landlord might just say the same thing. And when we started looking, we realised there were just no alternatives. So we just said to her, "Fine, we'll pay it." My partner got pretty depressed. We were looking for new jobs just to help pay the rent. At one point, I was working five jobs to pay the rent. So I was just exhausted.

'I long for the security that my mum had,' Sharda continues. 'It was never perfect, but to not have that feeling that at any moment now my landlady could send an email and force us out and everything we have built up here would be completely gone. And we just don't have the same communities my mum had: it's such a transient community, people are only here for six months at a time, so you can't build up any connections.'

Sharda is aware that she will not be able to stay forever. 'I'm a Londoner, through and through. I'll really miss it when I have to go. It really pisses me off when people say "Why don't you just buy a home in Sheffield?" I just feel like this is my home, this is where I grew up, why on earth can't I stay here? I just want to stay here. I just try not to think about the day when the landlady increases the rent or kicks us out. I know it will happen. But it just makes me freeze: I can't get on with my day if I'm thinking about it.'

CHAOS

Covid-19 was undoubtedly harder for private renters – especially those in shared homes, where lockdowns confined them to their bedrooms and social distancing was nigh-on impossible. In the early stages of the pandemic, poor housing conditions correlated directly to deaths. But for the city's 2.7 million private renters, the pandemic was just the start of their pain.

During the pandemic the cost of renting actually fell a little, but in 2022, prices started to go up very fast. By June 2024, they were growing at 9.85 per cent a year and showing no sign of slowing down. Advertised rents in inner London rose from £2,288 to £3,010 a month between 2020 and 2023.[1] Londoners were forking out an average of £1,000 a month for a single room. This was the fastest rental rise in recent history, and a far more significant contribution to the cost-of-living crisis for renters than the increase in energy bills.

A lot of factors were combining: a rise in the number of international students coming to the city, a drop in the number of vacant properties as fewer people moved, and a reluctance to put new properties on the market amid higher taxes and forthcoming regulatory changes for landlords. Between April 2021 and December 2023, 45,000 rental properties were removed from the market without replacement in the capital, with those which were previously the cheapest to rent being removed most quickly. This has had 'a particular impact on the ability of low-income households to access the [private rented sector]', according to a report by Trust for London.[2]

But this left multiple tenants competing for every house. The increased competition meant landlords were able to drive prices relentlessly up. 'We've offered £200 over [the listed price] and not got it because someone else offered six months upfront. I've heard of people offering £500 or £600 over, or offering to pay a year upfront in cash,' a 23-year-old civil servant told the *Guardian* in 2022.³

The lack of rental restrictions creates a trap where improving London comes at an immediate cost in terms of housing affordability. As soon as an area gets better, it also gets more expensive and people are forced out. Abbey Wood, in southeast London, was previously a tough and neglected part of the city – cut off from its major transport network. Then the Elizabeth line opened in 2022, and suddenly it was only ten minutes away from Canary Wharf and less than half an hour away from central London. Rents rose 55 per cent between 2019 and 2024.

Short-term tenancies and no-fault evictions have long been the gun which private landlords wield to carry out these heists on our incomes. But – in a small kernel of hope in an otherwise bleak picture – this era is now coming to an end. Since 2019, the government has been promising an end to the no-fault evictions introduced in 1988. Amid lobbying from landlord groups, this has been delayed and delayed again. So when the huge rise in rental costs hit after Covid-19, those who could not pay had no protection. They were simply kicked out – and continue to be. No-fault evictions are now 98 per cent higher than they were before the pandemic in London, running at a shade under 3,000 a quarter.

But this may be the last hurrah for this definitive housing policy. The new Labour administration, elected in 2024, has started to push this legislation through the House of Commons, and it is due to be on the statute books by the time this book is released. This will mark the first genuine reform to private renting since Thatcher, but it comes with substantial weaknesses that might limit its impact in the real world. There will be wide freedom for landlords to end tenancies even after the law is introduced. With landlords having complete freedom to hike rents, tenants will still likely find themselves forced to leave if a landlord wants them out. And new renters' rights come with a missing ingredient: enforcement. Research I carried out in 2025 shows there were just 108 environmental health officers focused on housing working across twelve London boroughs. This equated to one officer for every 7,900 private rented homes.[4] A retired enforcement officer explains that as local authority cuts stripped funding away in the 2010s, the money that remained was prioritised for children and adult services. Enforcement across the board – whether housing standards or trading standards – was 'wiped out'. 'It's just been stripped to the bone,' he adds. This has come amid a broader culture of a reluctance to regulate private businesses. 'There's not an enforcement culture like there used to be. I was in court every week when I worked for a London borough twenty years ago. But the same borough probably doesn't even go to court once a year now. Over time, the regulation of business went out of fashion. You were told not to prosecute, to go easy. So we got polluted rivers, we got badly built homes and we got private landlords doing what they want,' he explains. Another enforcement officer, who currently works at a London borough, explains that some resource has been built back up due to licensing schemes bringing in finance. But he explains that this is often not enough. 'If you think about the officer time required to investigate – the writing up after a visit, the preparation of documents for court, the work with lawyers, and then potentially an appeal – people just don't have the time,' he says. 'So they just don't do it – they will try and deal with the issue by sending an email and asking the landlord to comply, which works sometimes but is often just ignored.' Research by the Chartered Institute of Environmental Health found that 87 per cent of councils are relying on agency staff for enforcement and 56 per cent have had vacancies unfilled for more than six months. Most now rely on non-specialist staff with limited training or practical knowledge. 'Traditional environmental health departments have been largely dismantled,' said one academic analysis in 2023.[5] This poses a major threat to the success of the new legislation.

But even in this world of limited enforcement, new regulations, new taxes and requirements for licensing are pushing some landlords who only wanted to hold the property as a stress-free pension investment to sell. This may lead to increasing consolidation of private rental homes in the hands of a smaller number of landlords who want to develop big portfolios. Institutional landlords are starting to move in and buy up some of these properties, with a record £1.5 billion spent by investment funds on single family homes in 2024.[6] The biggest private landlord on Brent's licensing scheme, for example, is IV One (GP) LLP, which owns 180 homes in the borough.[7] Its directors are companies owned by the Realstar Group – a Canadian real estate investment giant with $9 billion of assets under management globally. The increasing attention of big capital on family-sized homes means families will increasingly be competing with the global real estate market when they try to get a home.

An increasing number of landlords may also choose to flip their property into 'short-term' or holiday let accommodation, like Airbnb instead. There are no official figures, but estimates of the number of short-term let properties like these in London range from 82,000 to 117,000. The growth has been rapid – and is rising most quickly in inner London.[8] The profits available here are larger, with nightly rates far outstripping monthly rental fees. In the borough of Westminster, a hotspot of this new market, 40 per cent of the private rental properties were short-term lets in 2025, while the figure reached 35 per cent in Kensington & Chelsea and 25 per cent in Camden.[9] The Greater London Authority has warned 'there are signs that short-term letting platforms are becoming increasingly commercialised and used by property investment companies and landlords to rent properties that would otherwise be available to long-term residents'.[10]

These trends mean the capital's poorest renters are being priced out of the rental market altogether. Research in October 2024 revealed that just 5 per cent of rental homes were within reach of someone claiming local housing allowance.[11]

While renting a room is now a common experience for Londoners in all income brackets – and has been for many years – those on the lowest incomes face the worst of the conditions, with some exposed to the kind of slum housing of Dickensian London, the sort of homes we worked so hard to eliminate from the city after World War II. In 2023, I visited a privately rented block in Harrow in northwest London, where a single landlord owned the entire converted office building. He had attempted to add an additional floor to the roof of the property to boost his income further, but in doing so he had apparently damaged the building, allowing water to penetrate deep into its structure. The resultant mould spread throughout the building so thoroughly that it would grow on toothbrushes overnight. I met the father of a six-year-old boy who was soaked in filthy, freezing water when it burst through his ceiling in the middle of the night. Council officers had told a pregnant woman she would not be allowed to bring her baby home to those conditions. Shortly after hearing the news, she miscarried.

A letter written to the council by volunteer medics at the charity Medact, who inspected the building, said: 'A number of infants have also been provided with inhalers due to the new onset of respiratory conditions and wheeze. None of them required inhalers before moving into the property. This is deeply concerning and appears to be a direct result of the conditions the landlord is housing the tenants in.'

The local authority inspector quoted above explains that boroughs struggle to carry out the investigative work that would uncover this kind of behaviour. Landlords actively hide them, only putting two residents down for council tax purposes, not licensing as an HMO and not giving the residents formal tenancy agreements, which means they can be evicted at the drop of a hat. 'We know that tenants in these properties are unlikely to complain, because of the vulnerable situation they are in,' he says.

This can cost lives. In Shadwell, in the East End, a two-bedroom flat in Maddocks House was rented out to twenty men at any one time, most of them recent arrivals from Bangladesh who had been recommended the place by fixers when they arrived. They paid in cash: some paid £25 per night, others paid £500 per month, meaning the landlords were taking somewhere in the region of £150,000 cash per year from the property. In an interview, one of the former tenants told me the conditions in the house were 'worse than a prison'. He slept in a bunk bed in one of the bedrooms, which he shared with another man. The tenants were not allowed to use the kitchen to cook. 'Every day the landlord used to bring food,' the former resident told me. 'There were seventeen people there, but they would only bring food for ten or eleven. If you weren't in, that was too bad.'

On 5 March 2023, one of the many cheap e-bikes stored in the flat by the men who worked as delivery drivers ignited. The rapidly spreading blaze caused pandemonium and in the chaos Mizanur Rahman, a 41-year-old father of two, was trapped and killed. The landlords of the flat pleaded guilty to breaches of housing law in November 2023.

This home used to be a council flat before being sold at a discount under Right to Buy. We built council housing to eliminate London's slum landlords, and then handed the keys back to them.

CONALL, ELI, ANDREW

In the 2010s chapter we met Conall, who had come to the UK from his home in Dublin to work and found himself stuck in a mouldy and frequently overheating two-bedroom flat he shared with three other people. In 2020, he moved on to a home by Seven Sisters station in north London for £1,250 a month.

This was an area of the city Conall grew to love. It is a centre for London's Latin American community, with 'the same significance for Latin communities as Chinatown [has] for [East Asian] communities'.[12] 'I love going to that part of Seven Sisters, picking something up from the butchers, having a little beer out the front,' says Conall. 'You can practise your Spanish in these places, there's a whole football league at the weekends in the park down the road and there are restaurants where you can get a full three-course meal for £10. At this point I was doing lots of volunteering with local food banks, and I was working for a mental health charity in Haringey. We'd embedded ourselves in the community.'

But Conall would not be able to stay. As his tenancy was coming up for renewal, a new 'build-to-rent' development planned by Grainger opened just opposite – complete with gym facilities and a pool. Rents on the new flats were close to £2,000 a month. When Conall and his flatmate's tenancy came towards its end, their landlord told them he was going to put the rent up to £1,895. 'So it was about a 50 per cent rise, which was just completely unaffordable for us,' Conall explains.

When they asked the landlord why the rent was increasing, he showed them a screenshot of the new Grainger block, and said that the rents being charged in the new apartments represented the 'market rate'. 'We couldn't pay the rent he was asking for, it was basically an eviction notice,' Conall tells me. 'It just shows the impact these developers can have on communities. They build places with all these facilities, that no one from the local area can afford, and it creates a licence for all the landlords nearby to put their rents up as well. But cities aren't places that belong to corporations. Cities are places that people live in and build communities and want to exist and thrive in.'

Eli – the son of Ruphina who had a traumatic journey through guardianship housing – was finally able to find a rented flat in the regular private market just at the start of the pandemic. Now, he and his partner pay more than half their salaries to stay in a small flat on the very outskirts of London, above a Greggs. Neither expects to live there for long – the rent is already at the maximum they can afford. When it goes up again, Eli is resigned to leaving the city.

'I think the London we all grew up with and loved has changed completely and is gone,' he says. 'There's this huge almost sterilisation of London. Buildings left empty, estates that should be knocked down being left for years. It's one big money pit. It feels like you're up against this really terrible mindset that just doesn't have a place for you anymore.'

Katy and Andrew, the couple who had met in an east London pub just before he was made homeless, lived with Katy's parents' throughout Covid-19. After the pandemic, the couple's financial situation was improving: Andrew had given up playing bass to get a more stable income as a teaching assistant in a primary school and Katy, who had been a teaching assistant herself for ten years, qualified as a teacher. Finally, they could scrape together enough money to rent their own place.

But shortly after moving into the first place they found they were evicted – not long after they had complained about the landlord's failure to fix a leak in the roof. They moved into a block of flats instead, but this too suffers from leaks – which pour through the ceiling into the bedroom. 'We have to put bin liners and a bucket on the bed or move our mattress into the living room to get to sleep,' says Andrew.

The couple want to buy, so that they can stop seeing their money being eaten up by rent, and to escape the conditions in the block of flats they live in now. But they are resigned to leaving London to do so.

'In my school, half the staff come from outside the area, and they've come into this really deprived area,' Andrew says. 'It's a bit of a cliché, but if you're not from around here, you don't know what it's like. But we know exactly what it's like for the kids and the families and what they have to put up with. When I speak to parents at the school gates, they get it. They think "He is one of us." But I don't think we're going to have any choice but to move out of Newham. It just isn't right: we serve our community, but we just can't afford to live in it anymore.'

Buying a home

LOTTIE

We left Lottie, who had managed to cobble together the money for a small place on the lowest rung of London's housing ladder, in 2019, worried that fire safety issues with her block may prove serious. In 2020 these fears were realised.

A 'waking watch' of 24-hour fire wardens was imposed on the building, at a cost of £20,000 a month – paid for by the leaseholders. Suddenly, the already difficult financial balance many of them had arranged to get a flat in the first place was thrown out of whack. And things would get worse. Their building had been assessed by a surveyor who turned out to be a fraudster. The signature on the bottom of the form was not his – it had been lifted from a wholly different surveyor in another part of the country who had never seen the building and would not have been qualified to assess it anyway. The assessor had simply been a grifter, someone willing to mop up the big money which was suddenly available to assess the fire safety of high-rise buildings.

But when the building was finally, properly, assessed even more serious issues were found. It had 'HPL' cladding – not the same as that used on Grenfell, but still an extremely combustible material, essentially made of wood and glue laminated together at high temperatures. There was also combustible insulation and missing fire breaks. Fixing it would cost millions, possibly tens of millions. And the cost of this work would be chopped up into forty-two slices and passed on to the leaseholders.

For Lottie and Joe, this would have been the end. They had no major savings, no family wealth left after the deposit for their house. They would have been wiped out, left with nothing and thrown back into the private rented sector to start again.

Eventually, after a long and arduous public campaign – in which Lottie became a key figure – the government did impose protections to prevent leaseholders from paying and order the original developer, in this case Bellway, to put their hands in their pockets to assess the building and repair any 'life safety' defects.

Lottie has been wrapped up in this battle for five years, and was continuing to have to fight to get the work started when I spoke to her in 2024: 'I find it hard to put into words how much of an impact it's had on my life. These were supposed to be the happy first few years of married life. I've never been dead certain on whether or not I wanted kids, but this has taken the choice out of my hands. We couldn't bring a child into a dangerous one-bedroom flat, and we couldn't afford to with the bill hanging over our heads. But I'm thirty-six now, and I have to face that it might not ever happen.'

She pauses. 'It's like a weight you carry around all the time, sometimes it's all I can speak about.'

BROKEN

Before the pandemic, buying a home in London was extremely difficult, but still just about possible – at least for those with a bit of help from parents, a decent job and access to a scheme like Help to Buy or shared ownership. But even that aspiration is now out of reach for most. After some sharp rises following the pandemic, London's average house price reached £523,000 in June 2024. This, combined with the rise in interest rates, means mortgage repayments are way beyond the means of first-time buyers, even those on reasonable salaries. There were 37,280 loans to first-time buyers in London in 2023, the lowest figure since 2012, when the financial crisis was still putting a brake on deals.

Those who did buy were only able to because extraordinary family wealth brought the cost of the mortgage down. In 1997, the average deposit put down by a first-time buyer was £5,200. In 2023, it was £140,000.[1] You would need to give up Netflix for 1,944 years to save this sum.

And even for those who did buy in the previous decade, the relative security they have found may not last long. As they shift from fixed-term mortgages signed in the low-interest-rate era to higher rates, which will persist for some time to come, their bills will increase, by upwards of £6,500 a year in many cases. At the end of June 2023 there were around 718,000 outstanding fixed-rate mortgages in London that were due to come to the end of their fixed-rate period by the end of 2027.[2] Many will tighten their belts and pay – others may find themselves kicked off the ladder they only just scrambled onto.

As for those who got one of the new-build flats, built with enthusiastic state support since 2010, the experience has often been miserable. London, with its disproportionate share of the country's high-rise residential buildings, has also been the centre of the safety crisis which has emerged since Grenfell. Thousands, probably tens of thousands, of young buyers have been chucked into the same boat as Lottie: the discovery of fire safety issues followed by a nightmare of desperate emails, refusal to take responsibility, incompetent management, downright fraud and crippling bills. Lives have wasted away with no resolution in sight.

And even without fire safety issues, the capital's 584,000 leaseholders often face struggle. Catastrophically high service charge demands with little to no transparency are a feature – not a bug – of the system. In 2021, one leaseholder in west London, where the service charge had increased 67 per cent to about £5,000 since 2012, told the *FT* he had been diagnosed with throat ulcers due to the stress of the never-ending requests for more money. 'It has been non-stop stress and you are totally disempowered,' he told the paper.[3] The new government's promise to abolish the leasehold system, made in March 2025, may rid us of some of the worst abuses, but those who live in badly built blocks of flats will still be stuck with the problem of how to fix them. As 'commonholders' they will have more control over this process, but that doesn't always help when all the choices are bad.

Among these leaseholders are an increasing number of 'shared owners' – those who bought into the 'part buy, part rent' housing model launched by Margaret Thatcher in 1980. While the lower deposits required to access this housing make it an attractive option to buyers without huge cash backing from a wealthy parent, all of them are sold on a leasehold basis and the monthly costs are linked to inflation, which mean they have risen rapidly in recent years. The result can be a financially crushing nightmare for those first-time buyers with the least ability to cope with it.

As the new Labour government seeks to build our way out of the problem of unaffordability by removing planning restrictions and granting a presumption in favour of development, it may find its efforts thwarted by a London market that remains in thrall to investment demand. Predictions suggest new-build housing will be targeted by investment funds, with huge funds such as Blackstone, Carlyle and Citra all striking big deals to buy in bulk from UK housebuilders in 2023 – helping keep prices high, even though demand from individual buyers has been suppressed by higher interest rates. The future demand for newly built homes such as these from investors was estimated at £25 billion. 'The arrival of institutional investors could mean home ownership is a never-fulfilled dream for young UK savers,' said the *FT*.[4]

These investors are also pursuing money from international students, whose numbers have risen exponentially in recent years, from 126,000 in 2020 to 417,000 in 2023.[5] By summer 2024, starts on purpose-built student accommodation projects had increased 78 per cent year on year.[6] Walk around London in early 2025, and you will likely see the logos of student accommodation providers attached to hoardings around the concrete core of a future skyscraper. The companies driving this include the FTSE-100-listed Unite Group and IQ, owned by global giant Blackstone. The homes they build are not cheap. The average rent for a student room in the capital now exceeds the maximum maintenance loan, while one in seven costs more than £20,000 a year – up from one in twenty just two years ago.[7] Those who are not supported by large parental wealth will need to fight it out with low-paid workers for a room in one of the converted terraced houses, not live in the plush new accommodation rooms being developed thirty storeys above the city.

As the housing crisis has intensified, the aftermath of the pandemic has also seen London hollow out. As costs rose and demand fell, 3,011 pubs, bars and nightclubs closed across London between 2020 and 2024, along with an estimated 76,300 small businesses also departing – the highest number anywhere in the country.[8]

The city is increasingly resembling a playground for the tiny minority of extremely wealthy residents. Estimates put the city's number of 'ultra-high net worth' individuals (someone with at least $30 million worth of net investable assets to their name) at between 4,500 and 5,000 residents.[9] This means they account for just 0.05 per cent of its population, but their influence is disproportionate. Sales of homes above £10 million rose to an eight-year high in 2023.[10] The 2020s have been branded a 'golden decade' for the development of 'super-prime' property by the luxury lifestyle magazine *Spear's*. 'I've never known in my career more new hotels, more new clubs, more new restaurants – we are the centre of the world,' one high-end property developer told the magazine.[11] There were 16,740 private helicopter flights in London's airspace in 2022,[12] and 50,000 flights on private jets from its airports.[13] The city has more five-star hotels than anywhere other than the casino city of Macau,[14] and eighty Michelin-starred restaurants.[15]

PATRICIA AND SEAN, JOHN, DAVE, ROSIE

Patricia and Sean, the Irish couple who got a house in Brent in the 1980s, have continued to hold onto an Irish community through their Catholic church. They are members of the Brent Irish Advisory Association, who meet twice a week. 'A lot of older people who are living on their own come in and talk about old times,' says Patricia. 'They have an office where people can get advice about housing or other issues if they're having problems.'

The couple still live in their house in Brent, the mortgage paid off decades ago. But they may not stay for long. Their son has married and moved to Lisbon with his Portuguese wife. Their daughter and her husband and three children have also moved out of London, to Norfolk – the only choice they had to afford space for their family.

Patricia and Sean still see their grandchildren regularly – they were in town the weekend before I spoke to them to see *The Lion King* in the West End – but the family would like to be closer together, as the grandparents age and the grandchildren grow up. 'We will probably move to Norfolk eventually,' Patricia adds. 'The grandchildren are asking for us. We used to see them twice a week, now it's once a month.'

For John, the retired headteacher who moved out to Frinton in Essex, he likes his new life and his proximity to his daughter and grandchildren. But he notes that the town he lives in now is full of ex-Londoners – not all of whom are as happy to have left. 'Frinton, Walton, Clacton are all full of people who used to live in the East End,' he says. 'And they're almost all white, it's just been this big cultural shift of people out of London. I don't think it's a coincidence that [Reform Party leader] Nigel Farage got elected out here. There is a lot of resentment among people who feel they had to leave.'

Meanwhile, Dave, the music journalist who rented a flat in the Portobello Road before buying a place in the early 1990s, still lives in the five-bedroom home he bought with his family in Hackney. He now has six kids, all of whom live in London. In different ways, almost all of them have had help from him and his wife – whether financial or through living rent-free at the family home – and all of them have found a home in London as a result, apart from the youngest who is still at university. 'It's almost impossible for young people to buy somewhere in London these days without help from mum and dad,' he notes. Listening to Dave, I cannot help be struck by the contrast with Carolyn's story. Both came to London at around the same time. Both worked hard and got decent jobs. But while Dave got onto the property ladder, Carolyn didn't. Now, while Dave has security he can pass down to the next generation, Carolyn is left homeless; chewed up by the system, and spat out alone in a northern village she has never been to before.

And for some families, having accessed the property ladder is still not enough. Rosie, whose mum, Jothi, moved out to Essex and gifted her home to her children, left the former family home when her brother started a family and bought her out. But even with the cash from this, she is struggling to find a bank which will accept her for a mortgage given the instability inherent in acting. 'There is no chance in hell I could have done this if my parents didn't work so hard to get the house and then help us in this way,' she says. 'But I'm just so frustrated. They've saved so much and still it's barely enough for a one-bedroom flat in the area I was born and raised in.

'You are brought up in this school system, you follow all the rules, you never do anything wrong, you try to do everything right,' she adds. 'Since I was eighteen, I've never had less than three jobs at any one time. I don't go to flashy restaurants or buy designer clothes. I don't smoke or do drugs or drink excessively. All I want to do is have enough money to survive and live in London, and it's just suffocating how much of a struggle it is.'

Homelessness

You could argue that the fundamental question of government housing policy is 'What support do we offer to those who cannot afford a home? In London, in 2025, there are thousands asking that question and no longer any real answer to it.

Instead, people are finding themselves homeless in droves. In 2022/23, 11,933 people were found sleeping rough in London – the highest figure on record.[1] This figure included 7,974 people seen sleeping rough for the first time, another record. Many more of these are sleeping rough for multiple nights than in the past. 'We're seeing a lot more stable people rough sleeping' rather than 'typical, entrenched' rough sleepers, one outreach worker in Lambeth told *Inside Housing* in 2023.[2] Research by the charity Shelter in December 2018 found that the overriding reason for rough sleeping was the loss of a settled home, often through eviction but also through relationship breakdown or the loss of a family member. And many of those bedding down on the streets had approached their local authority for help and been told they were ineligible or intentionally homeless.[3]

The city is increasingly full of canvas villages: under flyovers, on the verges of cycle paths and among small clumps of trees on the edge of the city's parks there is another city altogether, one of grubby tents, damp sleeping bags, sodden cardboard and faces desperate for warmth, shelter, toothpaste and dry bedding. 'There are people making an active choice which is linked to the cost of accommodation,' homelessness expert Michelle Binfield tells me. 'Housing eats up so much of people's income, especially for those working casually, that they end up sleeping in a tent as their only real option. In the past, some of these people might have been in shared houses, or rotating beds with co-workers in a flat. But once even that becomes unaffordable, you just push the bottom rung even further down.'

Binfield says London had twenty-two deaths among the priority list of people sleeping rough it was targeting for support last year. 'For so many, it is the destitution that is killing them,' she says.

For those who are considered in 'priority need' – parents, people with disabilities, people fleeing domestic violence – they can at least get temporary housing when they tell the council they are facing homelessness. The idea of temporary housing was that it was a stop-gap, a short stay, while a more permanent housing solution was arranged. But now London has left these people with no permanent housing option, so 'temporary housing' has become permanent.

By 2024, there were 65,280 households in temporary accommodation in London – the highest figure on record. This represents a 14.5 per cent rise since before the pandemic and a staggering 82.3 per cent rise since 2011. The households include 86,810 children – also a record. It means one in every fifty London households and one in every twenty-one children is now homeless and living in temporary accommodation.[4] Many of these children are babies and toddlers. The city had an estimated 17,800 households with a child under five in temporary housing, 74 per cent of whom had been in temporary housing for more than six months. This is roughly the same number of preschoolers as you would find in Newcastle or other cities its size.[5]

It was the aftermath of Covid-19 which pushed the long-simmering homelessness crisis to boiling point. A lot of factors coalesced: evictions were banned by law during the pandemic, and when this was lifted, a lot of people were evicted all at once. They started arriving at town halls just as rents were soaring and landlords of the cheapest homes were selling up. The Home Office, under political pressure to move asylum seekers out of hotels, grabbed the cheap accommodation that was available. Councils had little choice but to find emergency housing charged at a nightly rate, which is the most expensive. In Waltham Forest, an east London borough, spending on this type of housing went from £35,000 annually in 2022 (a few last-resort cases), to £3.9 million by 2024. 'We knew it was going to get worse, but no one thought it would get this bad,' councillor Grace Williams, cabinet member for housing in the borough, told me.

And the conditions for these families were miserable. In summer 2024, I visited a small playground in Newham with the Magpie Project – an east London charity which supports homeless mothers in temporary accommodation with very young children. Jane and her colleagues at the project (many of them homeless mothers themselves) face the realities of London's housing crisis every day. The mums who come here live in hotels, converted office blocks or tiny rooms in shared homes. Most of them share beds with their children and have no cooking facilities. I watched the children play in paddling pools, having the time of their lives. Jane told me they had to be careful about the children's clothes getting wet, because their mums might not have anywhere to dry them.

'It's getting much, much worse,' says Jane. 'We had one homeless family who couldn't get a permanent place and were being shunted between boroughs and were homeless every morning for ten days. Every morning they sat in a children's service office and either got housed for a single night, or we paid for a hotel. Our staff training used to be "Don't worry, we're part of a network, there are services we can direct people to", but we just can't say that anymore and that is really, really scary.'

The mums struggle with the toll it takes on their ability to be a parent. 'It's a form of torture for a mum,' says Jane. 'It is thwarting your ability to put your child to sleep, to bathe them, to potty-train or feed them. These are just basic human rights which are not happening for the majority of our families and it is taking a physical toll. We see children with flat heads because they are lying in the same position all the time, children with no experience of play because their mums are just trying to keep them alive, delayed walking and crawling because there is no space for tummy time or literally no floor space at all. Children have gastrointestinal problems because they can't have a proper diet and they're being medicated with laxatives or nutritional supplements instead of their mums being given access to a kitchen. And this is happening from birth. It's cumulative and chronic.'

At the centre, I sit and talk to Chantelle, a mum of two children now aged seven and seventeen, both of whom have autism and other medical conditions. She had been working full-time as a cover supervisor at a secondary school, but became homeless after losing her job shortly after the birth of her second child. She was put in a tiny room, covered in mould. She was an hour from her son's school, so she would get the children up at six, give her son breakfast on the train and then walk the streets with her daughter in a pushchair until it was time to take him home again.

In just under two years, the family moved four times – with her oldest son being thrown out of his routine every time. One of the properties they were moved into had such a poor standard of electrical safety you could get electric shocks from the mouldy, wet walls or water coming out of the bathroom taps. An assessment from social services said it was unsuitable for human habitation, but it still took eight months for her to be moved on. Chantelle then found herself in a Travelodge with no cooking facilities and nowhere to store food or her children's medication, which had to be kept refrigerated. She had to feed her children chicken and chips every day and wash their clothes in the bath. 'You're in survival mode, you're doing whatever is possible to keep your kids alive,' she tells me. 'But you feel like no child should be living like this, so you feel like you are failing them, like you can't provide for them. And that makes you feel very, very low.'

Chantelle remains wounded by the way she has been treated and spoken to by the council's support workers. In one instance she was shown around a flat and found a large, unflushed turd in the toilet. 'If the estate agent was going to show the flat to someone else, they would make sure it was beautiful. For us, they wouldn't even flush the toilet. It's like you're nothing, like you don't matter and they don't care. It is dehumanising.'

Another mum, Baby, has been in a one-bedroom flat in Redbridge with her five-year-old son for more than three years. 'It was like a rubbish dump when they first showed it to me,' she tells me. 'It was smelly, the walls were dirty, the carpet was greasy, there were live cockroaches everywhere, the windows were black with mould. I told the agent it was not suitable for a baby, but the agent said he was sorry, there was nothing he could do. If I refused it, I would be made intentionally homeless.'

She came back the next day with two friends and they did their best to clean it. But the mould was very hard to shift, despite Baby opening her window every day – even when it was freezing cold in winter – and constantly scrubbing it with bleach or mould remover. 'You can't get rid of it,' she says. 'There was one morning I woke up and I remember my son's cot was full of mould.' She brought dehumidifiers, put him to sleep in the part of the flat with the least mould, and cleaned every day. But he still suffers from the damage his little lungs have taken from the spores: his sinuses are constantly blocked and he has hayfever-like symptoms all year round.

After several months, pest control arrived to work on the cockroach infestation. 'The pest control guy approached me and suggested that the reason for the infestation was because I'm dirty,' she explains. 'I was so angry, I had moved into this property in this condition and done my best to make it better. But when they investigated, they found the whole building was infested. When they eventually took the oven out, the number of cockroaches behind it was thousands, countless. You could just see a swarm of their heads.'

Jane, who sees dozens of families in circumstances like this pass through the doors of her project every year, is troubled by fears for their future lives. 'We know that the first two years set up a child's brain chemistry for the rest of their life. So this is really a life sentence. It's not just about under-fives, it's about future adults. We are in danger of breaking them before they get built.'

Many, if not most, of the children she supports suffer from housing conditions like those described above. A report by City Hall found that more than half the 'nightly let' temporary accommodation units they inspect receive a D-grade or lower for quality, on a scale which runs from A to E. 'Many Londoners living in TA encounter extremely poor or unsafe conditions, and a lack of safety, privacy and amenities,' the report said.[6] One in four suffer from problems as basic as a lack of running water, the report said. Researchers have described serious malnutrition – families living off meals of Pot Noodles and biscuits because they had nowhere to cook or store food. Basic cleanliness was a problem, with no washing machines and some accommodation giving fourteen families access to one bathroom. Older children were using their baby siblings' potty in a cupboard because they could not get to the shared toilet. Children arrive at school covered in bites from bedbugs. Particularly in the converted office blocks, the threat of a major fire disaster also looms large. There have been near misses – most notably in a major fire in Croydon in October 2022.

The health impacts of this sort of housing are very direct. As Dr Amaran Uthayakumar-Cumarasamy, a children's A&E doctor and a volunteer at the charity Medact, told me in 2024: 'You've got people living in homes that have fundamentally not been designed to accommodate people in good health. We end up prescribing inhalers, but that's a medical solution to a very deep-seated social problem. I had a ten-day-old baby come in with respiratory issues last week, who was in temporary accommodation. The chances are we'll be seeing that child again and again in the months ahead.'

Because of the length of stays in 'temporary housing' entire childhoods will take place in this type of accommodation. Mums will start off sharing a bed with their toddlers, and will still be sharing it with them when they have grown into teenagers. In 2022, I spoke to one mum who was sharing a bed with her fifteen-year-old son, a situation which had persisted since they had first entered the temporary accommodation system when he was eleven. 'It's a large chunk of his teenage years just gone,' she told me. 'He has missed out on so much: birthdays and Christmas were just miserable.' London has 20,430 families who have been in 'temporary accommodation' for more than five years – fourteen times as many as in the rest of England combined (1,460).

People have found ways to profit from this suffering. Research I carried out with the housing journalist Vicky Spratt in 2024 revealed some of the biggest beneficiaries of this money were effectively middle-men: rent to rent companies who sublet properties from private landlords, guarantee their rent and then fill the homes with homeless families who have applied to the local authority and bank profit paid for by the taxpayer. Companies like Theori and Elliott Leigh had turned over in excess of £50 million each in five years from these deals – handing over free rent to the landlords and banking a fee for themselves. In summer 2024 Newham announced it faced bankruptcy due to its temporary housing costs. Local authority sources I've spoken to suggest it will be far from the last in London.

This level of homelessness is something which should not be happening in a country as rich as the UK. The country has 51.2 people per 10,000 homeless – either rough sleepers or in temporary accommodation. This figure vastly exceeds that of any other developed country – the next closest is Belgium with a shade over 30. In Finland it is 0.4, meaning homelessness in the UK is 125 times more prevalent. Even in the US – a country known for its homelessness problems – the figure is 19.3 people in every 10,000, less than half the rate of homelessness in the UK. The US has more rough sleepers, but far fewer in temporary accommodation. We are hiding the scale of our problem inside hotels and converted offices.[7]

The brutal logic of our housing crisis ultimately leads to the deaths of children. Analysis by the National Child Mortality Database shows that seventy-nine children died between 2019 and 2024 with temporary accommodation listed as a factor in their deaths, most of them babies.[8] Children in temporary accommodation are three times as likely to die in childhood, compared to the general population.

The deaths of these tiny babies – malnourished, abandoned, left to cough and freeze in atrocious housing, from which a faceless landlord extracts a tidy profit at the public expense, is the final result of all the policy failures I have set out since the 1980s. At every juncture, we could have chosen a different path. At every juncture, we kept going, buying into the lie that rising house prices were good for everyone, no matter how many were left behind. And so far things look to continue as they are: a flourishing property market for those at the top and the avoidable deaths of children for those at the bottom.

FUTURE

Exodus

'WE NEVER THOUGHT WE WOULD LEAVE LONDON': OPTING OUT

'I think the assumption was that we would never leave London,' says Gavriel. 'Because we are from here, it's home. The thought just never entered my head.'

Gav is talking to me on the phone from his home in Bristol. He did, in the end, chose to do what just a few years earlier he regarded as unthinkable. He traded packed Tube trains, soaring house prices and the dysfunctions of London's increasingly fractured community for a four-bed in Bristol where his two young daughters now have a garden to play in.

To Gav, though, the decision remains a wrench. He grew up in a big basement flat with his parents, brother and sister in Belsize Park. His parents came to the UK from Tel Aviv in the 1970s.

'I wasn't English, I wasn't Israeli; I was Jewish, but not like the other Jewish kids at school. London was a place where you could have that weird sort of mongrel identity, which suited me as I got older. Now when someone asks where I'm from, I always say London – not England or Britain,' he says.

Gav and his siblings had friends across race and class lines. They had an interesting childhood and a lively adolescence – which encompassed football matches, independent cinema and the music scene of Camden and north London. 'I kind of felt sorry for people who weren't from London,' he explains.

'Because it felt more exciting and cooler, but I also felt we were a bit more worldly and saw more of a range of things and had a richer culture around us. Outside of London, England felt like this weird, confusing place and I could sense my parents were a bit scared of it.'

Post-university, in the early 2000s, he bounced around – living with his parents, renting with friends, working as a temp, moving to Spain for a period and then settling into some poorly paid local journalism gigs. 'It was doable,' he says. 'So long as you had a job, you could afford to live.'

As his journalism career progressed, he moved into a very small ex-council two-bedroom flat which he bought with his long-term girlfriend in Hackney. The couple were happy in the property, but then in 2020, two things changed. The first was the arrival of Covid-19, the lockdowns and the switch to home working, which massively impacted both of their industries (his partner works in publishing). The second was the arrival of their first daughter, Rosa, who was born in the middle of the first lockdown.

'We started to feel that sort of cooped-up-ness,' says Gav. 'I remember going for a walk with Lucy when she was heavily pregnant in the middle of lockdown and seeing all the ridiculous developments – all these office blocks, the Cheesegrater, the Shard – all empty, and just feeling like the city had died.'

Being young in Hackney and London Fields was suddenly less attractive as a new parent. 'We were in a different phase of life suddenly,' he recalls. 'One evening I walked round to our local Turkish corner shop to get nappies and there was a queue outside like a festival, with everyone buying massive bottles of beer and music pumping, and [I was] thinking, "Great for them, but I don't want to be around this anymore."'

The plan was to rent out their flat in Hackney, and use the proceeds to rent somewhere else in a quieter bit of the capital with a bit more space. But as they looked into it, the maths just didn't add up. Private rents – especially for family-sized homes – were shooting up in the aftermath of the pandemic. Gav was taking more time off work for childcare, with a consequence for his income, and the gap couldn't be breached.

But in Bristol, where they had friends, they found a house where the garden alone was four times the size of their entire flat in Hackney, which they could rent with the proceeds from letting out the flat in Hackney combined with their salaries.

'The thoughts and feelings on leaving were incredibly mixed,' says Gav. 'It was hard, but London was also starting to feel more and more like it was going to be a place only for the very rich and very poor and I didn't like that feeling. It wasn't somewhere I wanted to be anymore.'

His mum's health deteriorated quite quickly after they left. It is hard to keep an eye on her and his dad as her condition gets worse. 'They understand us leaving on an intellectual level,' says Gav, of his parents. 'But really, it was never on their radar. Ideally, they'd want us to be living next door, but these days we'd need a couple of million quid to do that.'

Being in Bristol is also strange. 'I like Bristol, but it's never going to be home,' he says. 'Not because of anything wrong with it, but because I spent forty years living somewhere that I got to know intimately, and I'm never going to have that here.'

Bristol itself is also not entirely welcoming of the influx of middle-class Londoners it has seen, particularly since the pandemic, and the rise in rents that their arrival has arguably exacerbated. Stickers – well shared on social media – started to appear in areas popular with ex-Londoners saying 'Refugees welcome, Londoners piss off', accompanied by a picture of a man in a suit being hit in the head with a rock. 'That got me,' says Gav. 'On the one hand I think "Don't hate the player, hate the game", but at the same time I can see that we've become a symbol of the gentrification of the place where we are now.'

As it is, Gav now has space for his family. He has a garden for his daughters and has even started to raise chickens. He can see the stars when he looks up at night. But he isn't home.

*

There is nothing inherently tragic or surprising about Gav's story. In some ways, it's the story of someone who has done quite well out of London's housing market – buying a flat and moving on to a more spacious property elsewhere. The outward movement of people who have found some money through the work available in the city and then traded it in for a nicer house in greener surroundings is almost as old as the story of London itself.

London's expat communities increasingly define the surrounding counties, from cockney Essex to the north London Jews who have swapped the capital for the Hertfordshire towns of Bushey, Borehamwood and Radlett. The millennials currently departing east London flats for Bristol, Brighton and the Kentish seaside towns are just the latest in that well-worn trend.

But what is currently happening is subtly different from the departures of decades past, with bigger consequences for the future of London as a place. During the pandemic, the moves out of London peaked – domestic migration to and from London produced a net loss of 186,000 citizens, a record for the modern era.[1] This included 93,600 people aged between thirty and forty-five – almost double the number for a normal year.[2]

In the years since, this has returned to a more normal trend. Despite the predictions of the pandemic creating an 'urban doom loop', where remote working and a desire for more open space would shatter the population growth of major cities, London has instead returned to population growth. Its trends remain below what was predicted before the pandemic, but birth rates exceeding death rates and migration from outside the UK have seen the city recover its lost population numbers and pass its pre-pandemic peak population by 2024.[3]

But that isn't to say there is nothing going on. In some boroughs – Lambeth, Lewisham, Haringey, Waltham Forest – population remains stubbornly below the pre-pandemic high. And viewed with a longer-term lens, the population of younger Londoners is declining, while the older population is increasing.[4]

As the *FT*'s data journalist John Burns Murdoch puts it, London has always represented something of a conveyor belt for young professionals – a large cohort move in post-university, and then move out again at some point in their forties as they seek more space to raise families. But the capital's dysfunctional housing market has caused that conveyor belt to shorten and accelerate. Since 2015, London's population of 25–39-year-olds has fallen 4 per cent, after steadily rising for decades. It is a demographic which has not declined in any other region of the UK and is, Burns Murdoch writes, 'made up of those who would historically have managed to stay in London, but have been forced to move elsewhere'.[5]

This is a problem which London needs to engage with if it is concerned about its future viability as a city. Those who are leaving in this particular way – looking for a bigger house with more space for the stage in their life when they start to settle down – probably share several demographic characteristics. They will be doing more senior jobs, maybe at a middle management level, or having worked their way up to department leader. As they leave, they take their experience and seniority with them, as well as taking their wages and spending power out of the local economy. As rents continue to rise, you might see the conveyor belt stop entirely. Will young graduates still move to the city, when such a large chunk of their starting salary will be handed over to a landlord? Recent anecdotal evidence from the recruitment industry has shown an increasing number of graduates turning down London firms to take up opportunities in more affordable cities.[6]

There may be something else lost, beyond the tangible, dry economic statistics on productivity, recruitment and retention. Often, it is when you have a permanent place to live and investment in a community by way of children in a local school that you start to engage in the neighbourhood around you. This is the stage in life when people become school governors, volunteer at local food banks and join gardening and litter-picking charities. As London is drained of more affluent, more permanent residents, it also risks losing a lot of its civic society. If the only housing options that London offers in the future are temporary and transient, then the city will feel that way too. A community needs people who know their neighbours' names, who know they are there to stay and so have a stake in a place improving.

As London's residents leave, they are also taking London's rent rises with them – bringing higher spending power into markets with traditionally lower rents. There aren't good figures on internal migration, so it is hard to know exactly where relatively affluent ex-Londoners are ending up. There are some positives for the anecdotally popular destinations. Deal, a Kentish coastal town of small, attractive seaside houses, has recently been dubbed Hackney-on-Sea due to the influx of homebuyers leaving London. Its organic butchers, independent shops and restaurants are now thriving. But the rising rents and shortages of properties to let, as Londoners snap them up to live in and Airbnb investors take the rest, mean young people in Deal increasingly need to move out of their hometown when they grow up. It is like a penny drop machine: those pushed out of London tumble down and push the next group down a rung as well in the place where they land.

But the departure of those who want to buy a larger house outside the city is just one facet of London's current exodus. For many it is less of a choice and more the only option left.

'WE WERE ALWAYS GOING TO REACH A STAGE WHEN ONLY WEALTHIER PEOPLE COULD LIVE IN THE CITY': PRICED OUT

Wael moved house in 2020. He and his wife had a fourth child on the way, and the family needed an extra bedroom. The place they moved to was nice: a house on a small, purpose-built estate of family-sized homes and low-rise flats, with gardens, garages and communal areas. Next to West Ham station in east London, it is the kind of development which was fairly common in parts of London like this in the late 1990s and early 2000s, but has since been rendered impossible by the increase in land values driven by the speculative development model.

Nonetheless, Wael and his family found a good home here. They got to know their neighbours, and their teenage children could play out after school. The rent was not cheap – £1,800 a month, but they could afford it. Wael works as a night manager at a hotel in Canary Wharf. He is experienced; it is a difficult job and he makes a reasonable wage. The family aren't poor; they have just never had the cash to put down a deposit on a home of their own.

In 2021, after a year in the property, the landlord increased the rent to £1,900 a month. This was a jump, but a bearable one. It just meant a slight tightening of family budgets, a bit less saved every month, a bit closer to the wire if something went wrong. But a year later, in 2022, the landlord told them the rent was going up much further, to £2,400 a month.

Wael was stunned. 'I said, "There is no way, I have four kids and I have to feed them. If I give you this money, you have to feed the kids – not me." I said the rent should just increase by a per cent – three or four or seven per cent. But he said, "No, we are in a free market, this is what we need now."'

Wael told him the family would not be able to pay. He phoned the council, who told him to look for an alternative home in the private rental sector. There was no chance his family would get social housing, with 34,000 families already on Newham Council's waiting list.

There were simply no properties available at anything like the rates Wael could reasonably afford. The four-bedroom properties were even more expensive than the £2,400 he had been asked for by his current landlord. Three-bedroom properties were also out of reach, and landlords refused to let a house of this size to a family of six. He stayed in the property as he searched, and the landlord went to court to get an eviction order, which was finally approved in 2024.

Finally, the family found a place on the city's boundary in the north west. The rent was just about affordable. The trouble was, Wael's three older children – all teenagers – desperately did not want to leave their schools in east London. So they began commuting to and from school – a journey of one hour twenty minutes through the London Underground system every morning and every afternoon.

'My daughter was crying, because she said, "Dad, how can I do it every day?"' he says. 'But I said, "Look, there is no other option. We have to go." The children go out at 7 a.m. in the morning from here to get to school at 8.30 a.m.,' he says. 'They are very tired when they get home, they just eat and go straight to bed. They find it hard to be active and to study.

'I tried to put them in a school around here, but it didn't work,' he adds. 'My daughter heard me talking to a friend about it, and she walked in and said there was no way she would leave her school. I will try to convince her to find a place here, but she is fourteen – her school friends are her life.

'At least we have a place to stay,' he reflects. 'The council said if we couldn't find somewhere, we would have to stay in a hotel and share a toilet and a shower. The kids would not accept that, so I was very afraid. I'm lucky, to be honest. It's a little bit far away, but at least we have a home.'

*

A city of London's size needs a vast army of key workers to function. These range from the lower-paid employees in the private sector – shop attendants, cleaners, delivery drivers, receptionists, security staff, nursery workers – through to skilled professions like plumbers, electricians and mechanics, and public sector jobs from refuse collectors, street sweepers, housing maintenance staff and healthcare assistants through to teachers, nurses and junior doctors. No city can survive without people like this making it liveable.

The trouble is, they can't afford to live in London anymore. Analysis by campaign group Generation Rent in 2024 showed average London rents would take up 106 per cent of a teaching assistant's salary, 90 per cent of a pharmacy assistant's, 76 per cent of a chef's and 49 per cent of a primary school teacher's. Not a single one of the thirty-two London boroughs would be considered affordable for cleaners, community nurses, hairdressers, hospital porters, kitchen assistants, painters and decorators, receptionists and a range of other essential professions.

The impact of austerity on public sector wages, combined with capped housing benefit and rising rent, means the maths simply no longer add up for far too many essential workers, especially those who need space to raise children, who are forced to live elsewhere. Analysis by the Greater London Authority (GLA) showed that an entry-level police constable in London would spend half their salary on housing costs, compared to just a fifth in an area representing the median UK house prices.[7]

With these economics at play, why would any key workers stay? London's growth in public sector recruitment is already lower than in the rest of the UK. 'With public-sector nominal wage growth in London being slower, this situation is likely to get worse, further harming public-sector employee retention at a time when most public services are based in the capital and when public-sector organisations are in greater need to hire and retain talent than ever before,' the report by the GLA said.[8]

This is a problem which is already severely worrying local authority leaders. One source explained to me that the lower-paid roles in particular – street sweepers and refuse collectors – are filled by older staff members, who typically live in social housing and have been doing the job for decades and there is no succession planning for their retirement. Meanwhile, in white collar roles, London boroughs are full of building control officers, planning officers and managers who live in Hertfordshire, Buckinghamshire or Kent. 'Local authorities are finding it really difficult to fill key roles,' councillor Grace Williams, housing lead for the umbrella group London Councils, told me. 'Occupational therapist roles in particular are a really difficult role to fill, and – anecdotally at least – that is to do with the unaffordability of the city.'

In education, London's housing crisis is at the heart of the sector's recruitment and retention struggles. Teachers have seen a real-terms pay cut of 16 per cent since 2010, at the same time as house prices and rents have soared in excess of inflation. Research by teachers' union NASUWT found that 71 per cent of teachers aged under thirty were considering leaving the profession due to housing costs. One in five teachers live at home with their parents, and 42 per cent apply for jobs based on local housing costs.[9] Teachers in London schools commute in from the Home Counties, marking schoolwork on the early trains in and the late trains out. 'We see it in teacher recruitment right now,' says Manny Hothi, chief executive of Trust for London. 'The teachers

London schools recruit are young, most of them are living with their parents and very few of them stay in the school beyond the very early stages of their career.'

Michael grew up in east London, trained as a teacher and got a job at the secondary school he had attended as a teenager. At the start of his career in 2013, he had been able to rent a room in east London for around £400 a month. But seven years later, he was paying £900 for a room in a similar area, and he couldn't justify the cost anymore. By this time, he was head of science, and – as a young Black man who had grown up in the deprived area in which the school was located – able to connect with its students in a way that graduates from outside the area could not do so naturally. But the city was unable to find a house for him. He moved out and eventually got a job at a school in Kent.

'It will be a big, big problem for London schools going forward,' he tells me. 'You have one generation of teachers nearing retirement who got mortgages when things were a lot cheaper, and then you have new graduates moving in who don't mind spending a big chunk of their salary on rent for a few years. But in that middle bracket, when people are settling down a bit, no one is staying. And teachers like that are the engine of a school, you can't make it work without them.'

Then there is the NHS. You could make an argument that recruitment and retention of staff is the heart of the health service's well-reported crisis. The most recent numbers at the time of writing showed 154,000 unfilled vacancies across the NHS – close to 10 per cent of the entire workforce. This is projected to rise to 570,000 by 2036, when it will resemble an astonishing third of today's entire staff headcount.[10] The result is extraordinary sums of money being wasted in hiring agency staff, which then bleeds money out of frontline healthcare. It also places a punishing burden on the staff who are employed, as they move mountains to make an understaffed team workable.

At the heart of this recruitment crisis is cost of living. 'Housing is a critical part of this staffing crisis – specifically, the lack of quality, available, affordable homes close to work for staff and their families,' said the introduction to a white paper on the crisis published in 2023.[11] Analysis by the property agency Savills in 2024 showed there was nowhere in London and only one borough in the entire south east (the Isle of Wight) where a nurse's starting salary could comfortably cover the rent.[12] In 2020, research by the Royal College of Nursing showed 57 per cent of the capital's nurses were planning on leaving either London or the profession altogether due to the cost of living.[13] In 2024, Rachel, a full-time nurse at a London hospital, described her situation to the *Guardian*. Like many of her colleagues, she was taking overtime to make ends meet. 'You have exhausted nurses trying to do their best for patients, but inevitably it can end up in mistakes,' she said. She spent nine years working in London hospitals, living in flatshares with no savings and hardly any disposable income. In the end, she quit and moved back home with her mum in Berkshire.[14]

And the same problem is experienced in the private sector too, which is just as reliant on low-income labour as the public sector. Soaring vacancies in the hospitality industry have driven some businesses to close. In 2022, a survey of staff working in hospitality showed that their mental health was worse than it had been at the height of the pandemic due to the pressure of working on teams with reduced capacity.[15]

What impact will all this have on a future London? In the private sector, the answer is probably an increase in the pace of closures of small businesses we have seen in the years since the pandemic, and a rise in prices in the places that do survive. 'Maybe in time, you will just have a smaller workforce that's paid a little bit better, and it costs more for people like us to use these services,' says Hothi. 'I don't see a future where these services don't exist. I just think there's probably one where there are fewer restaurants and they cost more.' So once again, we move towards a city that is catering only to the upper echelons. This adaptation will be easier for the larger chains, who can shut poorly performing branches and keep their focus on the more profitable outlets. For independent operators it is far harder, a trend which will leave London more homogeneous, less vibrant and more exclusive.

But in the public sector, it is harder to see a viable solution. There is no such flexibility to lift prices and close unviable outlets. There will be the same need for bin collections, buses, planning decisions and nursing, regardless of whether or not we can afford the staff. While it is hard to imagine how this could completely collapse, it is also hard to envision a way out of it without change.

The departure of London's lower-paid workforce is also changing the character of the city. Any observer of London can see that areas like Islington and parts of Hackney are no longer the working-class communities they once were. But on a more granular level, these trends have been accelerating recently and reaching into areas they didn't previously touch. London is starting to empty of poorer people.

'I think we are fairly certain that it's now happening on a scale which we haven't seen before. A lot of people in our team are starting to use the phrase "tipping point" to describe what's going on,' says Hothi. 'We were always going to reach a stage when only wealthier people could live in the city. And I think we are at that point now.'

The metric which has led Hothi and his colleagues to this conclusion is a sustained fall in London's poverty rate. After the mid-1990s this figure barely budged. But since 2018, it has been dropping to what is now its lowest level on record. There are no indicators to suggest this is thanks to people being lifted out of poverty. So the conclusion that Trust for London has reached is that many poor people simply don't live here anymore.

'For the people who are leaving, maybe that's the right choice. It's a hard thing to say, but we aren't anywhere near getting the level of housing costs down in London, and if that's the only way for them to find a better life, then fair play to them for that decision,' says Hothi. 'But it isn't the kind of city we want to see, one that's homogeneous and where only people of a certain income bracket can afford to be.'

The charity has backed up this hunch with new research which has looked at the micro-data on the areas of London which – until recently – did house lower-income and working-class communities. The results are profoundly depressing.

Their statistics take two points in time – 2012 and 2022. They use small-area data from the Office for National Statistics to home in on the areas which – in 2012 – housed people on the lowest incomes. These are dotted all over the city, with some significant patches in south London areas like Peckham, Bermondsey and Camberwell. But the main cluster is around the River Lea and the Thames in north and east London – a band starting in Edmonton and Enfield and moving south towards Stratford and Tower Hamlets and then east into Newham and Barking.

These areas are significant, because they are the places where, in 2012, the Olympic Games arrived, with their promise to improve the fortunes of the poorest and most deprived communities in London. But what the Trust for London data shows is that while the areas may have improved, this improvement has not been for the people who were living there in 2012. Instead, they have been forced out.

There are now far fewer people in these areas on lower incomes. Professions have changed too. There are now more people of 'lower managerial, administrative and professional occupations' in these areas and a big drop in the number of those doing 'routine occupations, long-term unemployed or students'. The changes in these formerly low-income areas have been much faster than in the rest of London over this period. There are also fewer children. The number of children has dropped across the whole of London, but in these areas it has declined much faster.

In broad terms then, what the data seems to show is lower-income people with children moving out, and people in their thirties or forties on higher incomes without children moving in. Ethnically these areas have changed too. In particular, the number of Black people in these areas has dropped sharply, despite staying almost exactly the same across the rest of London.

From these numbers, then, we can deduce that in the last ten years, poorer Londoners have been priced out of the areas they could once afford. And this has been most extreme for young, Black families. Whatever legacy was promised as a result of the 2012 Olympic Games, it wasn't this.

But as well as those lower earners realising with a heavy heart that they can no longer afford London, there is another contingent of even poorer citizens who do not get to choose where they end up.

'THE COUNCIL DOESN'T CARE ABOUT YOUR BABY': FORCED OUT

Sara came to the UK as an asylum seeker, and spent eighteen months living with her four-year-old daughter in hotel accommodation in northeast London. The hotel had no kitchen facilities, and the room was extremely small for mother and daughter to share for such a long time. She was able to build up a small community in the area: there was a local support charity where she volunteered and made friends with mums in similar positions. There was a school for her daughter, who has a speech impediment and was offered additional support from a speech therapist. Her daughter settled into the school, made friends, liked her teacher and was finding that her speech was improving. Sara was encouraged. After a difficult journey from a country riven by war, through refugee camps and finally into somewhere safe, it felt like she finally had some stability in her life.

But then she was granted refugee status. In some ways, this was a good thing: it meant she could stay in the country and she would have the right to work and support her family. But it also changed her housing status. She was no longer an asylum seeker in housing provided by the Home Office. She was now a permanent resident in need of private housing.

The local council in the area of London in which she had been placed by the Home Office told her she had to find a home herself. But private landlords demanded three months' worth of bank statements, cash deposits and guarantors, which she simply could not provide. 'We were new in this country, so we just didn't have these things,' Sara says. 'We received a letter [from the Home Office] saying we would be evicted from the hotel in seven days.'

She sent the letter to the council, who told her to make a homelessness application. Eventually, she was evicted from the hotel – out onto the streets on a January morning with all her possessions in bags and suitcases and nowhere to go. 'We sent emails to the council, phoned the council, but no one was replying to us,' she says. 'We thought we would just be sleeping on the street.'

At five o'clock in the evening, she received an email telling her the council had found her temporary accommodation. But the address was in Chatham, in Kent. It was dark. She had no idea where Chatham was or how to get there. The council said it would not help her with transport. She phoned someone from the charity which had been supporting her and told them she was on the street with her daughter and her bags. They managed to arrange for a car to pick her up and drive her out.

'When we arrived at the flat, it was without furniture,' Sara says. 'The weather was very cold on that day. There was a gap in the window, so the wind was coming in. Every shop was closed. There was not even a pillow I could get for my daughter. I just put my jacket on the floor and put my daughter on the floor to sleep, and I stayed awake until the next day.'

In the morning, she tried to call her housing officer to try and understand where she was, what was around her and where to get support in terms of registering for schools or local healthcare. She did not even know which local authority area she was in. But she could not get through to anyone who could offer her any help.

In the building where Sara and her daughter had been placed, there are eighty-five flats. All of the residents have been placed there by London boroughs, and most of them have children. Every school she phoned told her there was a waiting list, and that there was no space for her daughter. It took more than five months to get a school place.

'My daughter had nothing to do. She was asking for my phone and she was crying, so I gave her my phone,' says Sara. 'This was making the situation worse, with her speaking, but I didn't know what else to do.'

Eventually, she was offered a place at a school a long way from her accommodation. She explained about her daughter's needs, showing them the reports from her previous school. But no support has been put in place and no speech therapy has been offered. And the steady progress her daughter had been making diminished.

Now that her refugee status is confirmed, Sara has found work. She is a qualified paediatric nurse with an agency. But the job is not in Chatham. Instead, it is in London, at the end of a train ride which can take over an hour, with a ticket costing £53 in peak time and £37 off peak. 'The money that comes from work goes on travel,' she says.

She hopes to move back to London, but knows she can't afford it.

'I came here because the situation was very difficult with the war back home,' she says. 'I did not expect things to be so hard here.'

You might remember Carolyn, the civil servant in her early seventies, who was facing being shipped off to County

Durham. It doesn't matter whether you are a new arrival or someone who has been here for fifty years. If you aren't rich, the city simply can't accommodate you.

*

The phenomenon of London boroughs sending their poorer families to other parts of the country is not new. But it does seem to be accelerating.

Steve Iafrati, assistant professor of social policy at the University of Nottingham, has studied the impact of this for almost a decade. His interest in the subject came from an earlier stage in his career when he was a neighbourhood manager for Wolverhampton Council. 'I remember coaches of people, all clearly from London by their accents, who would arrive in the city,' he says. 'When I asked my managers at the council, they said "Oh, yeah, these are households that London can't accommodate, and we've agreed to take them on".' As he progressed into academia, he realised that although many people knew this was going on, no one was collecting good data.

People can find themselves forcibly moved out of area in two ways. The first is where a borough does provide temporary accommodation, but provides it somewhere else.[16] With London boroughs under so much pressure to find the cheapest possible temporary housing, it is often no longer within their own council boundaries, or even the city's. These actions hit the headlines in 2016, when Redbridge Council purchased a 200-home former military barracks in Canterbury, Kent. One of the organisations it outbid for the site was Canterbury City Council.[17] In 2024, almost 29,000 London households were in this position, an extraordinary rise from a shade over 5,000 in 2010.[18] This is what happened to Sara.

The other means is when a council accepts a 'relief' duty to someone threatened with homelessness. This means it has to find them a suitable home. But, for London boroughs, this increasingly means the offer of somewhere out of London – sometimes as far away as County Durham. If these offers are declined, the person or family risks being considered 'voluntarily homeless' and losing all rights to support. This was the position Carolyn found herself in, and it is not uncommon.

Recent research by housing campaigners found Enfield Council sent families the furthest afield – 94 per cent of its offers of accommodation were outside London and 59 per cent were to the north east of England. Enfield has expressly adopted a 'national placement policy' due to the difficulty of finding accommodation in the capital.[19] A local newspaper investigation in Waltham Forest, meanwhile, found the council was paying a private company – self-styled 'relocation experts' Reloc8 UK – to broker private rented units in towns around the UK to rehouse homeless residents.[20] The firm boasts on its website that within the last six months of 2024 it increased its business from London boroughs by more than 70 per cent, with a projected 500 lets for 2024/25. It contains glowing endorsements from private landlords, who have been able to buy up whole blocks in towns such as Luton, on the strength of demand from the firm.[21] The *Echo* found that Waltham Forest had worked with the firm to offer 316 households out-of-London accommodation between 2019 and 2023. Of these, 188 families had refused, the rest had departed. The most common destination was Stoke-on-Trent.[22]

For families who make these moves, the situation is bleak. Dr Iafrati has carried out qualitative research looking at their experiences and describes the findings as 'utterly heartbreaking'. He tells one story of a woman placed out of area after the breakdown of her marriage. She had lost count of the number of different addresses she had been moved to – at least ten in just a couple of years. She never stayed long enough to make friends or social connections and her son missed months of schooling. Her mental health began to deteriorate, though the frequent moves meant she had no regular GP. The hostels they were housed in were unsafe for children: full of single men, some of whom were recovering addicts or drug users. At one hostel, one of the residents killed himself. Afraid for her son, she stopped going out of the room and stopped eating – feeling unsafe in the communal kitchen.

'This sort of thing is really common,' says Dr Iafrati. 'These are not places that are suitable for children. You have single men sharing bathrooms with young kids. They are places where you see sex work, drug dealing, violence. The safeguarding risks are immense.'

The data gathered by Dr Iafrati also shows a racial imbalance. Across the country, 30 per cent of the families placed out of area by local authorities were white, 16 per cent had not had their ethnicity recorded by the local authority and 54 per cent were Black and minority ethnic.

'What's really cruel is that a lot of the mothers start to blame themselves. We'd hear it so much in our research – mums saying they felt ashamed of not being good enough parents to their children, because they'd allowed them to be housed in situations like this,' he says.

Many of the people who find themselves in this situation struggle against a bureaucracy which can be blunt to the point of callous. Jackson Caines, who works at a law centre in Harrow, recalls an instance where a pregnant woman told the council she needed a home big enough for the child she was expecting. 'The council officer was making a dry technical point, which is that our housing allocations policy doesn't consider unborn children,' he says. 'But what she said was "The council doesn't care about your baby", which was a horrible thing for this mother to hear.'

Council bureaucracy is also failing in this area. Councils are supposed to notify the receiving local authority when they place a household outside of London – a process known as a Section 208 notice – but frequently this does not happen, which means no support is put in place when a family arrives.

The child services team at the local authority where they arrive may well not know that the family is even living in their area. This, Dr Iafrati says, is likely to be partly caused by the long-term impact of austerity cuts on local authority teams.

> If you think about the process of sending thousands of notifications, that becomes essentially a full-time job. And in the context of local authority budgets, shrinking headcounts, overworked staff, it just isn't surprising that it gets missed. There should be some sort of minimum package. Everyone placed out of area should have access to the internet. Children should have access to a primary school. There should be automatic enrolment with a new GP. The homes people are moved into should be meeting basic standards of liveability.
>
> But really, this process can never be made trauma free. The disruption involved in uprooting someone from their home and placing them hundreds of miles away in an area they don't know is always going to be extremely difficult, especially for families.

'The councils are not the cause of this,' adds Caines. 'They're just playing the cards they've been dealt. Really, this is a total, catastrophic failure of policy that comes from central government.'

THE PIED PIPER

In the story of the Pied Piper of Hamelin, the titular piper takes revenge on the villagers who refused to pay him by luring away their children with a tune, into a mountainous cave from which they never emerge.

What people might not know is that it has at least some historical basis. German manuscripts dating to the Middle Ages recount a brightly dressed piper who led 130 children from the town of Hamelin on 26 June 1284. An entry from 1384 glumly records that 'it is 100 years since our children left'. Theories abound as to what really happened – from a massacre at a pagan ceremony by Christians, to a mass emigration to eastern Germany, to an outbreak of fever. What does appear to be clear, though, is that the town of Hamelin lost its children and suffered a trauma so deep that the legend is still told as a cautionary tale today all over the world.

All of London's housing-driven patterns of migrations out of the city – the middle classes seeking space, the lower-income workers searching for somewhere they can afford, and the poorest being brutally cleared away – have a common thread: children. London is emptying of its young. A friend of mine who serves as a governor at a local primary school says the issue occupies a huge amount of time at meetings. The academy trust which runs the school is rapidly losing money as pupil numbers drop by dozens each year, their grant dictated by attendance numbers. The board instituted one strategy after another to turn the tide, but nothing works. There are simply fewer children around.

This is a trend which is increasing: the 2021 census showed 62,412 fewer under-fours across London than in 2011, while at the same time the overall population grew by 625,000.[23] Analysis in 2025 predicted city-wide drops in demand of 3.6 per cent for reception places, and 2.9 per cent for Year 7s. Inner London borough numbers will decline much faster. The average decline in southeast London will be 8.2 per cent.[24]

It is not just parents moving out, but people choosing not to have children. Inner London boroughs have seen a 25 per cent fall in birth rates since 2008 – far faster than the national average and still dropping. This reflects broader social changes, but housing is undoubtedly part of the picture. Research from 2020 found that 13 per cent of adults under forty-five in a couple had delayed or decided not to have children due to the pressures of housing costs – including their inability to afford an extra bedroom.[25] This was national research, and in London, where the costs are at the most extreme, the figure will undoubtedly be higher.

This is tarnishing one of our few undeniable public sector success stories of recent years: in London, 94 per cent of schools are currently judged to be good or outstanding by Ofsted, the highest percentage of any region in England. In 2023, London's schools helped 60.9 per cent of pupils to achieve five A★ to C GCSEs, including maths and English, the top rate for any region and above the national average of 57.3 per cent.[26] But because of the way school grants operate, every unfilled desk represents a funding cut – and a cut not reflected in the overall costs of paying the teachers and maintaining the building. It's a financial death spiral that can only end in school closure. The damage is particularly acute after years of austerity, and rising demand for mental health and special educational needs support. School budgets are being devastated. A quarter of local authority schools in London were in budget deficit by autumn 2024, and most of those that weren't had a funding surplus of just 8 per cent, and falling. Schools across London will have a deficit of £500 million by 2025/26 on current trends. The only route out is to cut staff numbers, which will trash educational standards and leave disabled children without support. 'The majority of a school's budget is spent on staff,' a report by London Councils said. 'Increasing financial pressures have left some schools unable to create a sufficiently supportive environment for all pupils. To manage budgets, many schools have had to cut pastoral care and investment in inclusive practice and activities aimed at reducing attainment gaps. This has left them struggling to provide adequate support for children with additional needs.'[27]

And in some cases, they are closing altogether. Randall Cremer, in Hackney, had seen generations of East End children pass through its doors since 1875. 'Pupils like coming to this school,' said its most recent Ofsted report. 'They feel happy, safe and well cared for. Pupils are kind to each other and helpful to visitors. Pupils generally play well together and are sensible in lessons.' The report described how much children liked the school's small wildlife garden and regular trips to the local museum and theatres. 'Staff support pupils and their families well. There is a community feel in this school.' But in 2023, it closed its doors for good. Hackney Council's press release announcing the closure of this school and three others was blunt. 'There are simply not enough children,' it said.[28] And Hackney is not alone. Camden, Southwark and Lambeth have already announced primary school closures and other boroughs will follow.

What should worry us is that there is nothing coming over the hill to reverse this trend. Rents are more expensive than they have ever been. We are building less social and affordable housing than ever before. And benefits remain frozen at a level well below what it would take to house families in the city, the new Labour government having quietly continued with the austerity-era caps on overall benefits and local housing allowance put in place by its predecessors.

It may be, then, that what we are seeing now is merely the trickle before the flood. It is so hard to remain in London on a low income, so hard to remain in the city when you need space for a family, that it is difficult to see how anyone will do it in the future. Beyond those who occupy the remaining family-sized social homes, the current housing market in London does not have an offer for families except to leave, or be pushed to the very outskirts.

London's overall population may still grow, but it will no longer be a city where people come to start families or build communities. Larger homes will no longer be for families, but either short-term lets for tourists, or broken up into rooms to house workers on six-month rental contracts. This change is already well underway, but it is easy to see how it could accelerate. With no family housing options, how can we expect families to form or stay? And the departures risk becoming contagious. Families stay in London for their friends, and their kids' friends. But as more families leave, others will follow. As schools start to decline through lost funding and dwindling pupil numbers, the only reasons for parents to stay in the city will drop away. The pull of more space for less money will be hard to ignore, the push of ever-rising housing costs hard to resist.

What future then for the city? How will a place with no or very few families feel? London will become a place where people pass through, but don't live. It will be a 'hometown' to no one but the very rich, and the social housing tenants who cling on. What will it mean for the London of the future to have hardly anyone who grew up here? If my generation was the last to be born into a London which offered affordable housing, will my children belong to the last generation to grow up in London at all?

Generation rent growing old

Renting makes Chris feel insecure. He is never quite sure when his rent might increase to a point when he can't pay it, and will have to move. He and his partner live day by day – the classic 'just about managing' family: rent, bills and food take up all their income and they have nothing left at the end of the week. Any unexpected costs mean cutting back on food or heating – the only two variables they have financially.

Sue's landlord originally told her she could stay for two years, but ended her tenancy out of the blue after six months, saying she wanted the property back. Sue approached the council, who told her there was a shortage of social housing, and she should consider renting privately. But there is nowhere local that she can afford and she is not considered to be in 'priority need' so does not qualify for temporary accommodation.

After struggling to find somewhere he could afford to live, Michael found himself crashing on a friend's sofa. He has been there for a few months and the friend is now asking him to move out. But he doesn't know what to do. Letting agents locally have told him that there are forty to fifty applicants for every flat and he 'doesn't have a prayer' unless he can show he has a net income of more than £2,500 a month, which is well beyond his means.

For Abigail, the property she rents would be fine if it were properly maintained – but it is not. The walls are covered in black mould and the washing machine doesn't work. She has to wash her clothes at the local launderette, which eats into her already-stretched finances, and the mould spores are increasingly impacting her health. Her landlord 'doesn't do repairs', she says. 'She just wants to take the money and not do anything.'[1]

What do all these renters have in common? One answer might be the precarity and powerlessness inherent in their housing situation. Another would be that they are all pensioners.

While the discourse around the struggle of private renting remains slanted to younger people, the world has changed. Year on year, the number of older people finding a home in the rented sector grows. In 2012/13 there were 304,000 private renters in England aged over sixty-five and by 2022/23, this number had grown to 444,000 – a 50 per cent rise in a decade.[2]

And the growth of this cohort will accelerate from here on out. There are 1.2 million private renters aged between forty-five and sixty-four. This means the population of older private renters – already larger than many imagine – will balloon over the coming decades. This is particularly true in London where estimates suggest the population of pensioners in the private rental sector will double between 2014 and 2039.[3] The housing fiasco will drastically challenge our concept of what growing older means.

TIMEBOMB

The housing and pensions crises have grown together in an odd sort of lockstep through the decades we have considered in this book. Low interest rates in the late 1990s triggered the rush to invest in property, but also a simultaneous and related collapse in the expected returns on pension schemes. Savers responded by switching their investments to property in the buy-to-let boom, the only route they saw to a reasonably secure retirement, which saw us enter an ever-increasing cycle of rising rents and house prices. This in turn meant a younger generation was unable to save enough for their pensions. Even now, the big institutional investors in property who drive escalating rents and service charges are often ultimately pension funds – placing many renters and leaseholders in the absurd position of being pushed out by a landlord who is also administering their retirement fund.

The interwoven nature of these crises is not a coincidence. The model of retirement in the UK relies heavily on what property ownership was meant to achieve – you take a mortgage out early in your working life and use the rising wages of your career to pay it off, ideally before retirement, which means you can invest in a wider portfolio of assets which will sustain you through retirement where your lower income will be offset by the absence of the housing costs. This model, known as 'asset-based welfare', has been central to our vision of retirement for decades.

But it has always been flawed. The model would forever favour those whose lives gave them the means to gain a mortgage and pay it off, while leaving those who couldn't in the wind. As such, it has always entrenched inequalities and extended them into later life. But the bigger problem is that in converting houses into assets which are designed to provide a return later in life, we financialise them, cause their value to rise and ultimately shatter the model on which asset-based welfare relies, because the next generation coming up do not have access to an affordable home. The big price rise which happened between the 1990s and 2007 can only occur once.

'Current gains from housing in the UK are the result of a unique set of political and economic circumstances that cannot be repeated; therefore, current gains from residential housing are a one-off wealth windfall to particular (lucky) groups within society,' writes the political economist Johnna Montgomerie. 'The same conditions cannot be repeated in the way required for residential housing to provide a generalizable welfare function.'[4]

The trouble is, this has neither been recognised nor talked about enough, despite the looming societal crisis that comes with an ageing population who will not have the financial means to look after themselves in retirement, even as a cohort of those who were unable to get on the property ladder in time start to retire. 'I wonder if part of the reason we don't talk about it is because we don't really want to think about it. As a species we are just not good at thinking about the long-term future and we are not good at thinking about the scary aspects of the future,' says Helen Barnard, director of policy, research and impact at the Trussell Trust. 'People do not seem to realise that the two crises – housing and an ageing population – are going to collide and the human cost of that collision is going to be – potentially – really appalling.'[5]

The collision is rapidly approaching. It has always been hard to get onto the property ladder after forty, but the recent rise in mortgage rates since 2021 has made it even harder. This means that many of the renters currently in their forties and fifties will retire as renters. The number of private renters in the 55–64 age group has increased faster than any other group, growing at six times the rate of that of the population as a whole in the last ten years.[6] Average earnings typically fall after the age of fifty, which leaves this immediately pre-retirement cohort with no real option but to carry on renting. The estate agent Hamptons projects that the number of older renters will pass one million by 2030, noting that this 'trend has the potential to shape the country socially, economically and politically'.[7] This will see the total amount in annual rent paid by over-65s rise from £5.1 billion in 2023 to £12.7 billion by 2033 – with no corresponding increase in the state pension or housing benefit currently budgeted to fill this gaping hole. Should rents rise faster than anticipated, then the figure will be even higher.

And it is an issue which will keep growing from there on out. The swelling number of private renters in the generations coming up behind the current set facing retirement will mean more and more people retiring in private rented accommodation or – at best – with years still to go on their mortgage. In order to pay off a mortgage by retirement, you need to have started paying it off by midlife. In 2012/13, the number of households led by a private renter aged over thirty-five was 1.6 million. Ten years later it had reached 2.1 million. The number will keep going up. Even if this cohort does manage to buy, many will still be paying off their mortgage at retirement age. And it is London – with a higher proportion of renters and lower proportion of homeowners than any other region of the country – that is most exposed to this trend.

Not only will these renters have higher costs, they will also retire with less money. Auto-enrolment into workplace pensions has been a success, but only 19 per cent of workers, and just 1 per cent of lower earners, are saving enough for a decent income in retirement.[8] Among self-employed workers, only 16 per cent are saving for a pension at all – a collapse from 48 per cent in 1992[9] – a major concern as the number of 'gig economy' jobs rises. Worryingly, the demographic groups most likely to be private renters (certain ethnic minorities and lower-income workers) are also the least likely to have pension savings.[10] Most workplace pensions have switched from being 'defined benefit' (where you get a guaranteed sum, regardless of how well the investments perform) to 'defined contribution' (where your payouts simply reflect the amount paid in and the value of the investments). This means, in almost all circumstances, that private pensions will be lower on retirement for the current generation of workers, and they personally carry the risk of the investments underperforming and leaving them in poverty. The shift has been described as 'perhaps the most striking de-collectivisation of risk of modern times'.[11]

So we are saving less into schemes which will pay out less, just as the cost of our retirement is going through the roof. The maths is obvious and unforgiving. The full state pension of £11,500 in 2023 is almost totally exhausted by the average private rent for a two-bedroom flat, which was £11,200 per year. In London, where the average rent in 2023 was £22,300, the state pension leaves you £10,000 in arrears every year. Research suggests that without housing costs, a pension pot needs to reach £260,000 by retirement to maintain living standards through retirement. But with housing costs, that increases to £445,000, a figure which increases the longer you live.[12] I don't need to tell you how few private renters have savings of that kind. If they did, they wouldn't be renting.

And so we stand on the verge of a major crisis of housing-induced pensioner poverty. Since 2015, pensioner poverty has been slowly but surely creeping upwards, and current housing trends offer a bleak warning that it will keep doing so. By 2050, one in four people in Britain will be aged over 65 and the number of over-85s in Britain will have more than doubled compared to today.[13] A very large proportion of them will still be paying rent to keep a roof over their heads. What will their lives be like? To get a glimpse of the future, we can look at the lives of retired private renters today.

COLD, LONELY, POOR

It is the start of winter when I meet Edmund, the weather has recently taken a bitter turn and the first storm of the year has just stripped the trees of their autumn canopy of leaves.

Edmund is seventy-four, but looks older. His face is drawn and gaunt and his skin papery thin with blue veins visible on his forehead and neck. I'm pushed to ask him – out of a sense of concern as much as journalistic inquiry – whether his rent leaves him with enough money to eat. He insists that it does.

But he looks down at his hands as he says it. The rent is due tomorrow, he adds. He thinks he has enough to pay it but hasn't dared yet to check his bank balance to make sure. He will find out tomorrow. I ask what he thinks his landlord will do if he can't find the money.

'Oh, he's a very decent guy, very decent,' Edmund says. 'But I don't know what he'd say if I couldn't pay. I don't think he'd like that.'

Edmund spent his working life as a bookseller and teaching English as a second language. He moved around various bedsits in London, never really thinking about buying. 'I just didn't really know what I was doing, to be honest,' he says. 'I was just living. I didn't really think too much about the future, or what was going to happen when I got old.'

He eventually settled into a rented flat in West Hampstead in 2002, where he stayed until he reached retirement age in 2015. But at this point things took a turn for the worse. He'd never missed the rent, but the landlord called in pest control claiming there was an infestation of bedbugs and blaming Edmund for it – despite them apparently coming in from next door. The eviction which followed was illegal and unjustified, but Edmund didn't know this. He was made homeless, went to Camden Council for help and was placed in temporary accommodation. With the case worker at the council overstretched, he was left to find his own property.

'There's a website, you might have heard of it, spareroom. com?' he says. 'I found a place on there, which was OK, but I was sharing with a group of twenty-somethings.'

Edmund got on with his new housemates, but eventually wanted to find a place of own. Now he has a bedsit in Kilburn – one room, with a bed in the middle, a large chair and cooking facilities. He has a small bookshelf (he's put the rest of his books into storage) and a picture of two Spanish musicians resting on the top of it (it was given to him by a friend decades ago and he's attached to it, but he can't fix it to the wall under the terms of his tenancy). The room has an en-suite toilet, and altogether isn't much bigger than a master bedroom in a normal terraced house. His state pension, pension credit and housing benefit barely cover the rent. He has hardly any money left over and lives hand to mouth.

Dwelling in the property comes with its challenges. On one occasion, an upstairs neighbour was making noise into the early hours and Edmund knocked on his door to ask him to keep it down. 'He just started shouting and swearing at me,' says Edmund. 'He was using the F-word over and over again. It was really unpleasant.'

He can't afford to travel out of London anymore. He had a routine which involved eating in a local cafe, but he has had to stop that. And he has no security. If his landlord increases the rent any further, he'll have to move out. His tenancy has ended, and all he has is a rolling monthly statutory tenancy, which could end at any point. He says he'd like sheltered housing, but hasn't been able to find any.

'I'd like some security and to be able to take my things out of storage,' he says. 'I don't think people realise how difficult it is for the older generation renting. It isn't something which is talked about enough.'

Many of the problems inherent in the private rented sector are intensified in older age. Rents for older private renters rise in just the same way as the rest of the market – once the short fixed term ends, the landlord has complete carte blanche to up the rent. According to polling commissioned by Independent Age, 45 per cent of all older people who rent experienced a rent rise in 2023, two-thirds of these hikes were by more than £50 a month and 16 per cent were by more than £100 a month.[14]

Once retired, the options to cope with this are much more limited. For younger renters, it can be possible to increase their earnings – taking on some extra shifts, or even moonlighting a second job. But for older people, once they have left the workforce their earnings are fixed. Even if they were physically capable of embarking on casual work into their seventies to keep the rent paid, the harsh reality is that the job market discriminates against older applicants, so vacancies are scarce. The only financial variables are heating, food and new clothes – with more than 40 per cent of older private renters going without to make sure they make the rent, decisions with serious health impacts in old age.[15] An estimated 37 per cent of older private renters experience poverty, compared with 13 per cent of those who own their home, and for 25 per cent of older private renters this poverty is long-term, compared to 6 per cent of the whole pensioner population.[16]

But cost is just one of the problems older people face. Security becomes increasingly important as we age. A place in a community, familiar faces and neighbours you are comfortable with are all important factors in determining wellbeing for older people. But private renting strips all of these things away. When Age UK surveyed older renters, they found a lack of security was the biggest issue – dwarfing even the poverty inherent in their situations.

'The prospect of a Section 21 "no fault" eviction was a constant threat hanging over their heads,' the report said. 'Older private tenants were unable to really make the place in which they lived their home.'[17] This had various knock-on effects. Moving house is an increasingly physically difficult experience with the effects of age, so many were limiting the number of possessions they owned in order to make moving possible. Others were reluctant to ask landlords for repairs or invest in the property themselves, in case they were kicked out. Anyone who has ever raised a complaint with a landlord will know that it takes a degree of stamina. 'There's an energy required to push a complaint through a system, and often as you get older you become resigned,' says Lisabel Miles, housing policy manager at Age UK.[18]

This extends to necessary adaptations to make a home liveable for an older person – grab rails, walk-in showers, low-pressure door handles and so on. These are changes which should be paid for through a disabled facilities grant, but this is not widely known by either pensioners or landlords, which makes pensioners reluctant to request them and landlords reluctant to say yes. Inappropriate homes have many consequences. Older people may adapt by limiting themselves to a single room or by going out a lot less if they struggle with entry and exit. The social stigma associated with not having facilities which allow them to wash properly may force them to isolate. An oven which they need to bend down to use may result in the quality of the diet declining. Steadily, their homes will be closing them in, narrowing their world.

The problem of adaptations is a factor not just for pensioners renting privately, but for those in the social sector too. The current average age of a social housing resident is fifty-six. The population of social housing residents is ageing rapidly: there are already 1.1 million lead tenants aged over sixty-five in social homes and, with 1.5 million aged between forty-five and sixty-four, this number will grow sharply in the coming decades.[19] Particularly in London, many of these people live in blocks of flats, reliant on lifts to enter and exit. But with social housing maintenance struggling, this can transform a home into a prison. In 2024, I met Malcolm, a wheelchair user and tenant at a block in Hackney where the lift has been out of service for a total of 600 days across the last three years, during which time he has effectively been rendered a prisoner in his own home. At times he has been out and come back to find it broken – leaving him trapped outside. 'It affects every day of my life,' he says. 'I don't know if it's going to be working when I go out, or if it will still be working when I come back. So there is this constant anxiety that I might be trapped.'

For those that are evicted or have to move because of rent rises, the situation is miserable. 'Your environment becomes more and more important as you age – your community, maybe that next door neighbour who keeps an eye on you, or someone who might go and buy you a pint of milk. Having to move frequently and move out of that community exacerbates loneliness and dependence on social care for help rather than your community,' says Miles.

There is also the question of where they will live next. Getting around to viewings, responding rapidly to internet listings and convincing a landlord or letting agent to take you on are all simply more difficult for older people, even if they can find somewhere they can afford. 'I look at the case notes, and I'm really struck by the amount of people who have no solution,' adds Miles. 'The advisers can suggest a benefits check to see if people are entitled to more income, they can signpost people to local authorities for social housing, people can look at smaller homes or different areas but so often you are reading the cases thinking, "None of those routes are going to provide a solution." There is nowhere for them to go. And then you end up with stories of people sleeping on their friends' sofa in their eighties or staying with children, if they have them.'

For some, the only realistic choice will be to leave the city for the cheapest rental markets in the country – which may begin to become hubs of poor, older people – with a massive strain on local care services as a result. Figures are hard to track, but an analysis of census data by Independent Age in 2024 showed a flow of older private renters out of London and a corresponding increase in numbers in some of the most deprived areas of the country. 'The research suggests that the housing crisis is forcing older people on a low income to move away from their friends and family, their GP and other local services due to high rents. This will likely lead to increased loneliness and poorer health outcomes for people in this situation,' the charity said.[20]

What we desperately need are more social rent homes – or at least homes which are affordable on a state pension and housing benefits – which are adapted to old age. But we have a long way to go in this regard. The 2020 English Housing Survey suggests 91 per cent of homes in the country do not even reach a standard where they are 'visitable' for a wheelchair user, let alone usable.[21] Research suggests almost 70 per cent of new builds will not meet basic accessibility standards between now and 2030.[22] In London, the overarching planning rules published by the mayor demand a level of accessibility in all new-build homes. But just as affordable housing is argued away by developers under the cloak of viability, so too is accessibility. House builder profits come before any policy objective. There is also going to be an increasing shortage of care homes for older people. The city is developing less than half the specialist housing it needs, with the problem most acute in inner London,[23] where it is in competition with more profitable developments.

These experiences, already being lived out by tens of thousands of older private renters, are coming for a much wider proportion of the population unless there is radical change to the housing market, shattering the ideas we might previously have held about what it will be like to retire. 'I read the evidence about older private renters, and I see these accounts of people sitting in cold, damp houses, socially isolated, and their health is getting worse,' says Helen Barnard. 'And I'm reading it thinking, "This is a window into the future for enormous numbers of people if we don't do something about it."'

LEFT BEHIND

London's ageing population will soon run up against the departure of its young. An odd little statistical nugget in the 2021 census showed something strange and unexpected about inner London: the population in late middle age was booming. The number of 55–59-year-olds rose by more than

40 per cent since the 2011 census, in some inner London boroughs by 60 per cent. This compares with a nationwide rise of 27 per cent among this age group. The news website that spotted it, *On London*, branded the areas a mini 'grey belt' in the capital.[24]

We can only speculate about what is happening here, but a compelling argument would be that this is the generation who picked up cheap or cheap-ish homes in the 1980s and 1990s. Now they are securely housed, their mortgages paid off, sitting pretty in a home they have no desire to leave. This is fine while this generation sits in their current age category, but fast forward twenty years and they will be in a very different state. London remains a young city, but it is ageing. The population in the city aged in their sixties has grown at above the UK average. By 2030, projections suggest the number of over-65s will have grown by around 350,000, or 29 per cent. The number aged over ninety will have grown by around 37 per cent.[25] This is going to sharply increase expenditure on adult social care, following a decade when these local authority budgets have been cut, by almost 15 per cent across the city. As younger people leave the city it means that the unpaid care family members provide in older life will be much harder to deliver, increasing the burden on local authority provision.

When I write about this, I can't help but think of Sheila Seleoane, the resident of Peabody housing association, who lay dead in her flat for two years, as the landlord sent bills to her decaying body. When we looked into this at *Inside Housing*, we found several other grisly examples of residents dying and being forgotten for months or years behind the closed door of their flat – so isolated that no one even knew they had perished.

Is this the future we should expect in London? The elderly dying alone in their homes unnoticed, their children and relatives uprooted?

UNEQUAL

A few years ago, I went to dinner at a friend-of-a-friend's house. He lived not far from where my family lived, in one of the nice, spacious terraced houses which have become prize possessions of the area's middle-class families and landlord investors. He wasn't much older than me, and I assumed he rented a room in it.

Instead, he had the place to himself. A beautiful, modern kitchen with an island work surface, an extension, French windows providing glorious natural light and a loft extension offering several spare bedrooms.

'Does he own this place?' I whispered to my friend when the host went to fetch some wine.

She nodded, and glanced to the door to make sure he wouldn't overhear. 'He inherited some money when his parents died,' she said. 'I think he paid £750,000 for it.'

The previous, miserable descriptions of a generation locked out of home ownership, growing old in poverty, will not happen to all of us. The outlook for my generation is distinctly two-tiered. In our twenties, we were largely in the same boat: everyone was renting, no one could afford anywhere particularly nice, we were all in it together. But as we moved into our thirties, some people had better luck than others. Some married, got promotions, got a bit of help from their parents and scrabbled their way onto the property ladder. Others were stuck renting. A division started to open up between people who had once been the same.

But as our thirties have progressed, this is changing again. For some people, the challenge of housing costs, which has been the defining economic factor of their lives so far, is disappearing overnight. Put bluntly, this is because our parents have started to die. And for those of us whose parents got onto the property ladder, that now means more than simply grief and loss but a complete transformation of financial circumstances.

The UK currently has what is sometimes called an inheritance economy. In the next thirty years, £5.5 trillion will pass from one generation to the next.[26] This is a staggering, unprecedented sum of money – more than double the country's entire GDP. It is bounty from the extraordinary growth in property values between the late 1990s and today. Household net worth rose from £2.8 trillion in 1995 to £10.2 trillion in 2015 – largely due to house prices simply going up. With 70 per cent of this wealth held by the over-fifties, as this century progresses, it will increasingly be passed down to the next generation.

The most obvious point here is that this will entrench existing inequality. At present, those of us whose parents bought see big advantages – particularly if it happened to be a home in London. We have had the backdrop security of a parental home to retreat to if our careers or relationships hit a bump, and the potential opportunity to save on rent by staying under our parents' roofs while we work. For many young people I know who grew up in London (including me), it is this rather than being given cash directly which allows people to finally buy.

But if your parents live outside London and your job is here, you don't have such a financial cushion in their lifetimes. And if your parents rent, it's unlikely that your inheritance will enable you to get on the housing ladder. What is currently intergenerational inequality will be converted into intragenerational inequality by the potluck of inheritance.

Those who inherit this wealth will not always be the children of the rich. As we've seen, the opportunity to buy a home in the 1980s was much more widely available than it is now. You could have been a Malaysian nurse or an Irish builder and purchased what was an affordable home in the 1980s or early 1990s. The intervening decades have converted it into an asset now worth a small fortune, and this is the wealth the adult children of these families will ultimately inherit. It means some children of working-class families will find their lives transformed by the inherited wealth from a council home sold under Right to Buy which happens to be in a London borough where property prices have ballooned. One family lawyer told the *Guardian* in 2022 about clients of hers who were receiving seven-figure inheritances who had grown up in 'unimaginable poverty – broken windows, not enough shoes for all the children to go to school every day'. 'Someone who came over on the Windrush could have a secure blue-collar job and afford a mortgage on what would then have been a run-down house in Brixton or Tottenham,' she told the paper.[27] But broadly speaking, the looming great inheritance will – in the words of *New York* magazine – be a 'deeply regressive' change which 'exacerbates all existing inequalities'.[28]

How will this manifest? It is impossible to say. One hopeful conclusion might be that a generation who have endured a working life of crap rental properties and exploitative landlords may not be that keen to become landlords themselves as they inherit money in their fifties – and perhaps even sixties, given increasing life expectancy. Might the wealth be invested somewhere else, in something more productive, damping the overheated property market?

This is likely to be wishful thinking. The truth is that being a landlord in a country with high house prices and rising demand makes great financial sense and my generation will probably prove just as keen to get a slice of that as the one that came before us. But it does offer a chance from a policy perspective. Schemes should be set up now to encourage other routes for inheritance investment – into productive, green areas of the economy and away from simply restoking the fires of the property market. Could those who are inheriting a house be encouraged to sell it to a social landlord for social housing, rather than cashing out the maximum possible market value? It is possible to do this now, but it is a fringe activity. Perhaps with a tax incentive and a marketing push, it could become more mainstream.

There are also opportunities for raising taxes from this wealth transfer. There has been a lot of talk in housing policy circles for decades about some form of 'land value tax' – a means to secure some of the enormous growing wealth in property to fund our public services. These ideas are hard to implement. If a house increases in value, the people living inside it don't necessarily feel any richer and they certainly don't have spare cash in their bank account to give to the taxman. Even when the house is sold, the money usually goes straight into the purchase of the next property, which has also inflated in value.

But when it is inherited? Well, then, all of that accumulated wealth suddenly becomes liquid, a sum in a bank balance that can be taxed. There is a fairness argument here. This increased wealth is an economic accident. No one worked for it. It just happened because of a variety of local and global economic factors which have now split the country into a deeply divided place of haves and have-nots. We could use the tax system to fix that, and take even a small percentage of that £5.5 trillion to repair our public sector and adapt it to a hotter world. But doing so requires brave politicians. Labour's inheritance tax rise on farmers saw tractors occupying the streets outside Parliament. How would a generation of homeowners react if the same mechanism was applied to them?

TONIC

I genuinely thought I was lost looking for the home of a retirement village for older LGBT people in south London. I was walking along the banks of the River Thames. The Houses of Parliament were visible behind me, I'd just walked past Lambeth Palace, the London home of the Archbishop of Canterbury. I checked the blue dot on my phone app, and then checked it again. Surely this was not the home of an affordable housing development.

I was wrong. Nestled in between the skyscrapers was a pink and white sign: Tonic Housing. I was greeted at reception by Bob Green, a softly spoken Northern Irish man in a smart black coat and chinos, a large, swirly tribal tattoo visible through his short silver hair on the right side of his head. Bob is head of operations at Tonic, which provides twenty-six flats for older LGBT residents inside this fourteen-storey riverside apartment block.

He explains that there is a huge demand for specific older people's housing in the LGBT community. Mainstream retirement housing is not always an easy place to be gay. 'Our residents don't want to have to come out every day to each new member of staff, or to have to hide who they are,' says Bob. 'Loneliness is a real problem for LGBT people. They might not have children. Their families might not have accepted who they are and their partners might have died. We wanted to create a community where people could just be out and comfortable and happy.'

Tonic has a bar, which opens up on Thursday nights, and local drag acts come and perform (it is located close to Vauxhall and its world-famous gay bars). The community room on the first floor functions as a mini-cinema, a living area where the residents have built up what Bob calls a family. On the top floor, there is a veranda – a garden with an extraordinary view over central and south London, from St Paul's Cathedral to the Crystal Palace television transmitter. The residents have planted herbs and pumpkins and set up garden furniture, which makes this a discreet spot in the middle of a busy city for this ageing community to laugh, drink and share the sunsets over the city.

Flats with Tonic – despite being categorised as affordable housing – are not cheap. The properties were made available as part of the planning requirements with private developer St James (part of the Berkeley Group), which completed a luxury development here in 2021. Lambeth Council pushed for older people's housing and were impressed by Tonic's vision for an LGBT community. Lambeth has the third largest proportion of LGBT residents in the country, after Brighton and Hove and the City of London.[29] A £5.7 million loan from the mayor of London enabled Tonic to buy the flats from St James at a discount and open its retirement scheme.

But the flats are sold as shared ownership properties. Getting one requires a cash sum of between £500,000 and £750,000, with rent and service charges to pay on top. The scheme is designed for those who want to sell an existing property and move into a retirement community. Not all older people want retirement housing, they want to continue living in their existing homes in their communities. So a scheme like this isn't for everyone. But it may point the way to a solution.

As I stand with Bob and look out over the city, I reflect how incredible it feels that this little space in the midst of all the exclusive and gated property wealth that has popped up on the River Thames has been made available for this purpose. But maybe we shouldn't be surprised. Maybe we should ask why this feels so unusual. It would be perfectly possible to use the planning system to demand that within the new-build blocks which go up in the future we make proper space for the many older people who will need to be housed. If Berkeley had been ordered to sell the homes to Tonic more cheaply, the discounts given to residents would in turn have been bigger. The only cost would have been a small dent in profits, which reach into the hundreds of millions every year.

The London of the future needs to make space for its older people. Not just because there are many more of them, but because of what they add. Like children, our elders can be the life of our communities. Go anywhere which relies on volunteers and you will find older people. My parents' retirement has been full of litter picking, running clubs, cricket coaching, homelessness charities and much more. If London fails to care for its old, it is not just the old who will suffer.

Housing in the Anthropocene

While we can never know much about the shape of the future, we do have one certainty: it is going to get hotter. Whether we meet our international pledges on climate change or blow straight through them, the London that we occupy in mid-century will exist in a hotter, less stable climate than the one which exists as I write this book.

This has major implications for housing. A home won't simply need to be secure, warm and affordable in the era of climate breakdown, but also a safe haven from the heat, floods and fires which will become an increasingly large part of life. Housing today can feel like a battle for survival and as we progress further into the Anthropocene era that will only become more literal.

FLOOD

It was a Sunday in the middle of July 2021, a week after the complete lifting of the longest restrictions on socialising in the pandemic. We took the children to visit my mother-in-law in Canning Town, east London.

The weather had been warm but not unusual – higher than 25 degrees Celsius for a few weeks running and sticky at night. Rain was now forecast. But we had nothing planned other than time inside with our extended family – a pleasure you had learned to appreciate during those strange months of isolation, fear and disease.

The rain started at around five o'clock. First it was heavy, with thunderclaps loud enough to make our three-year-old son cry. Then suddenly it was biblical. Sheets of water were pouring from the sky and the noise of water on the roof was deafening.

Outside the window, something strange was happening. The water was no longer flowing away down the drains, but rising in the street. Before long, we were all staring out of the living room window as we watched puddles form into streams and the street turn into a river. The flood waters lapped into the front garden and my son excitedly asked if we were going to get home in a boat. In the end, driving five miles home through east London's side streets meant tackling a labyrinth of standing water and stranded cars. What we were seeing was a vision of the future.

Surface water flooding – which happens when so much rain falls in such a short period of time that the sewers are overwhelmed – is a growing hazard to the whole of the UK. But London, with its high population, Victorian drainage system and streets of concrete paving slabs and tarmac, is at particularly high risk. These are flooding events which are hard to predict and can happen anywhere at any time of year. They are the number one risk in London's risk register.[1] Water can flow at high speeds, and the floods can appear with little warning. One minute, the rain is pouring down the drains, the next it is backing up and flooding. The water is deeply unpleasant: filthy, fetid and swimming with sewage. In serious incidents, water can back up from toilets and showers, spraying sewage directly into homes.

The July 2021 floods which I witnessed in Canning Town were serious: at least 1,000 homes were impacted, and this is believed to be a major undercount. Eight Underground lines were suspended and multiple stations closed as they began

Housing in the Anthropocene

to fill up with water. Across the several days of flooding that month, insurers received thousands of claims and lost almost £100 million.[2] The floods came from what seems like a freak weather event: a narrow swathe of London saw 80 millimetres of rainfall in a few hours, almost double the 46.8 millimetres average for the entirety of July.[3] But anyone who knows the basics of climate change will not need to be told that this will get worse. A hotter climate means more water held in the atmosphere, which means more instances of freak rainfall.

Flooding will undoubtedly be harder for people who are already in housing stress. Building insurance is provided by landlords, but renters face the additional burden of chasing their landlord to chase the insurer to get the work done. Being flooded out means temporary accommodation, which is a frequently unpleasant and traumatic experience.

And while building insurance will pay for the repairs to the building, it doesn't cover the contents. The insurance industry estimates that more than half of renters have no contents insurance, so a flood would leave them destitute.[4] My own anecdotal experience would suggest the number is actually far higher than that. I never considered contents insurance when I was renting, and I'm sure most others don't either.

The aftermath of a flood is deeply unpleasant. Properties stink of raw sewage and mildew. Damp and mould take hold. For tenants this will mean a battle with their private or social landlord over repairs – at a time when thousands of other tenants may be making exactly the same requests. 'There is a link between flooding and poverty,' flooding expert Paul Cobbing told me. 'Poorer people are less likely to have contents insurance and will struggle much more to get back on their feet. They might not have a landlord who supports them, and they can get driven into a cycle of problems.'[5]

There is also greater direct danger for those in precarious housing. 'When the last hurricane hit New York it drowned people who lived in unlicensed basement dwellings. So anyone living in those circumstances in London needs protection. Flash flooding can happen in the middle of the night with no warning,' Professor Bob Ward, chair of London Climate Change Partnership, points out.

There are things we can do about this. Properties can be adapted to be more resistant to flood water. Defences can be added to developments and estates. Homes might need specific adaptations: plug sockets placed higher up, carpets replaced with ceramic tiles. More importantly, the entire fabric of the city needs to change to allow it to absorb more water: permeable surfaces, ponds and natural drainage should be added wherever we can find the space for them. Pavements should be as permeable as possible: small bricks with many gaps between them soak in water. There are porous asphalt and concrete substitutes, which allow water to percolate through. Some of this work is happening, but it is slow and piecemeal – an occasional add-on to pre-planned work. 'It is recognised that funding pressures mean there will not be funds specifically for a large-scale drainage improvement programme,' London's Sustainable Drainage Action Plan says.[6] 'What we need is a major restructuring and re-engineering of a city which is not designed to deal with the levels of rainfall we are starting to see,' says Ward.

A new mega-sewer – the £4.5 billion Thames Tideway Tunnel – was recently completed, having first been started in 2016. It is a giant infrastructure project – 15 miles of cavernous pipes running east to west under the city. This has been an enormous engineering success, but its main contribution will be to lessen the amount of sewage pouring into the river network in and around London; it won't stop flash flooding, which occurs when smaller sewers in a hyper-local area are temporarily overwhelmed by rain.[7]

We have made this problem much worse in recent decades by concreting over the city in the name of new development, which we never needed to do. Sustainable drainage systems, including ponds and permeable surfaces, can allow new developments to soak up water instead of being inundated by it – meaning building work can actually improve the position with regard to flooding on some brownfield sites.

But these features were only made mandatory in 2024. No developments up to this point had to take heed of them. And even when the rules do come into force, they may not be properly applied. A planning consultant – speaking under the condition of anonymity – told me how his firm was able to get away with adding a simple ditch to a development and writing an 'expert' report insisting it would be enough to mitigate any flood water. Developers would not accept any mitigation that reduced the overall number of homes on a site. 'That cuts straight into their profit,' the consultant told me.

New homes are also being built in areas at major risk of flooding. For example, a 475-home conversion of a recycling depot in east London's Olympic Park was given permission in 2016, despite the Environment Agency warning it had 'a high probability of flooding' with 'unacceptable' risk to life. But it did not stop the development going ahead, and this is one of many homes built in contravention of Environment Agency advice. The same consultant told me developers are often able to pressure planning authorities to accept new homes in high-flood-risk areas – with consultant reports used in similar ways to those which argue down affordable housing contributions.

All of this means London is desperately exposed to the threat of surface water flooding, and we confront the growing reality of the scenario predicted by then Environment Agency chief executive James Bevan in a speech in 2018: 'The clouds burst with astonishing intensity. Within minutes, water is overwhelming the drainage system. The underpasses start to fill up and the roads become impassable. The city starts to grind to a halt. Then the power goes out. It's dark, and water starts coming into thousands of homes. It is inches, not feet, in most places. But in parts of the city it pours into basements, where it's several feet deep, and people start to drown.'

And this is just surface water flooding. For most of London's long history, one of its biggest threats has come from its rivers. London is built on a web of tributary rivers which flow into the Thames. This means there are an estimated 24,000 London properties at risk from river flooding.

It is also not just excess rain that could cause London's rivers to overflow but the sea. The Thames is a tidal river – meaning that its level rises at high tide. London is one of the largest cities in the world built on such a river, putting it at particular risk from rising sea levels. What we should fear is the dreaded east coast storm surge. In this weather event, a combination of low atmospheric pressure over the North Sea and strong northerly winds increases the amount of water along our eastern coastline. The narrow gap at the Strait of Dover cannot allow all this water to flow past, and instead it 'surges' up through the nearest gap – the River Thames estuary and then London.

If this coincides with a seasonal spring tide, you will find a mass of water up to 11 feet high suddenly surging up the river towards the city. As sea levels rise with climate change and London – built on a bed of clay – slowly sinks, this danger rises year on year. In January 1953, this surge happened – bringing devastating flooding along England's east coast. More than 300 people died and 200,000 acres of agricultural land were lost, severely damaging the country's precarious post-war food supply.[8] While the worst damage was to the east coast and Essex, London was severely hit. The flooding washed out homes in Silvertown and Whitechapel, with families evacuated in cattle trucks from the East End. There were floods along London's tributary rivers all around the city: the Lea, the Roding, the Wandle.[9] There is less memory of 1928, when a storm surge combined with high tide, gale-force winds and weeks of rainfall to send the river crashing over its embankment walls in the centre of London. The water 'swept away inner walls and ripped through windows' of houses near the river.

We have forgotten these risks partly because of the flood barrier built in 1982. This has kept us safe as we have slept, the Thames becoming a gentle companion to city life. But have we become dangerously complacent? Because the water is rising and the barrier we built to keep it out will not hold forever.

The barrier was only closed ten times in the first decade after it was built. But in the last ten years it has been closed eighty-five times, including fifty in 2013/14.[10] This frequent usage puts it at risk of failure – according to its own guidance.[11] Some estimates are that it could reach the end of its life by the 2030s if the frequency of its closures increases.[12] An impact report into the 2013/14 closures said the lunar and solar conditions which caused the exceptionally high tides were rare, but could reoccur in 2032. If that happens to be a year when climate change delivers extreme rainfall, we will be pushing the ageing barrier to its limit. One of the largest storm surges recorded in London came in the 1940s, and was measured at 3.66 metres. The only reason this didn't devastate the city was because it struck at low tide. If it had come at the highest tide of the year, it would have measured 6.86 metres – just 14 centimetres shy of the top of the flood barrier.[13] And this was before the polar ice caps started melting and sea levels began to rise.

Yet there are currently no plans to renew or enhance the barrier. The Environment Agency expects it to keep protecting the city until 2070, and conversations on replacing it won't even open until 2040.[14] 'We're absolutely not ready,' Professor Hannah Cloke, an environmental modeller and forecaster at the University of Reading told the *Guardian* in 2023. 'Evidence shows sea levels rising faster than we thought... We should be preparing for that and we're not.' In fact, we are not renewing many of our flood defences and are allowing them to deteriorate even as we face a bigger risk: inflation and underfunding have led the Environment Agency to cancel 40 per cent of its planned projects and upgrades.

Writing in 1982, science writer Antony Milne said a major flood in modern London would 'be the greatest natural disaster this country is likely to experience'. It is hard to dispute this. Water breaching the banks of the Thames would pour into the Underground system, wrecking its electrics, and trapping any commuters who happened to be in its bowels at the time. The Houses of Parliament, Canary Wharf and the O2 Arena are all at risk, as are 400 schools, 16 hospitals and half a million homes. If the Thames Flood Barrier failed, an extreme tidal flood today would impact 1.25 million people and £200 billion of property.[15] The damage alone would transform the city forever, not to mention the enormous potential for loss of life. The aftermath would be crippling: flood water would 'pond' and stagnate in areas with poor drainage. Parks and gardens in the flooded area would be irrevocably damaged, never again able to grow the same sort of plants and trees as they had before. Power would be lost for days. The slime and filth coating the city would take months to clean.

HEAT

The North Lodge student housing building in Tottenham is pretty forgettable. It looks a bit imposing: densely packed, almost prison-like, but as the recent trend for pile-'em-high student blocks in the capital goes, it is pretty ordinary.

What is less ordinary is how hot it can get. The block houses more than 500 students from various London universities in poky little bedrooms, with kitchens shared by up to ten and long windowless corridors between the different apartments. The units were built in a factory and bolted together on site. The bedrooms are single aspect – meaning they have only one external wall – and the windows only open a crack, barely past the edge of the external wall of the building. This means it is nigh-on impossible for the residents to create a breeze. In

Housing in the Anthropocene 241

the summer of 2013, the heat in this building was monitored by academics at the University of Loughborough. What they found was alarming.

Flats on the upper floors were consistently above the temperature outside. Night-time temperatures of more than 26 degrees Celsius for 1 per cent of the night hours are considered to be uncomfortable – detrimental to a restful night's sleep. Temperatures in these flats broke this threshold for more than 44 per cent of night-time. Some reached highs of almost 35 degrees, a threshold at which the human body starts to experience serious, threatening heat stress. They remained so hot that they were considered to cause 'some discomfort' for almost all of the three-week period they were monitored, regularly rising into the 'great discomfort' category.

This research should be a major worry for the London of the future. The researchers described the building as 'emblematic of a type that has raised concern about overheating within the building research and construction community' and said that it was 'unlikely to be an isolated example'. 'It might just be that the early twenty-first century has seen the construction in the UK of a stock of apartment buildings that will be uninhabitable by the mid-century,' they warned.[16]

The whole of the UK's housing stock is at risk from overheating: around 90 per cent of the country's homes will be at risk if temperatures rise by 2°C, and all of them will be at risk if we see 4°C of warming.[17] A major study in 2018 found that the unusually hot summer of that year had severe impacts on overheating in homes. It estimated that 4.6 million English bedrooms (one in every five) overheated. While this was – at the time – the UK's hottest summer, that record has already been broken multiple times. And by the 2050s, what are unusually hot summers today will be the mild ones.[18]

'London is the most vulnerable part of the UK to overheating,' says the building physicist Professor Kevin Lomas. 'The south east has the warmest weather, and the urban conditions create a heat island which exacerbates this.' This is particularly true at night, when temperatures stay four or five degrees higher in London than they do in rural areas. This makes it much harder to cool homes down by opening windows and trapping cool air inside. London is also at risk because so many of its homes are in blocks of flats. 'Blocks of flats are also much more likely to be impacted by overheating, and these are more common in London than elsewhere,' explains Lomas.

People in the UK are also less adapted to coping with high heat. 'As a nation we don't respond as well as we might to warm summer conditions,' adds Lomas. 'People living in southern Europe have understood for years that you need to bring down the shades in the day and ventilate in the evenings and night. If you look at the temperatures we're likely to see in the UK towards the end of this century, it's going to be much more like Lisbon and southern Europe than the summers we are used to in London now.'

As with flooding, it is poorer people who are most severely at risk. The converted office blocks which house many homeless Londoners are incredibly vulnerable to overheating. Dr Amaran Uthayakumar-Cumarasamy, who carried out research on homelessness quoted earlier, explains: 'The residents in those office blocks are going to be at the most risk of being threatened with the health consequences of the climate crisis because those buildings were not designed to keep them safe. Younger children, babies and those in older age are most at risk.'

The engineering firm Arup, in its models for the Climate Change Commission, was confident that we could act. A package of measures – blinds, roof insulation, solar reflective walls and window replacement – would take the proportion of homes at risk of overheating across the UK down to 22 per cent under a 2°C heating scenario. But as with the adaptations required for flooding, this is a difficult and expensive shopping list of changes to a country where the built environment is very slow to change. And under a 4°C rise, even these interventions would leave 91 per cent of homes at risk of overheating.[19] The 2022 heatwave resulted in an estimated 3,000 excess deaths across the summer – mostly of older people.

It might be tempting to think that we could mitigate this problem with air-conditioning. But this would rely on a huge increase in electricity capacity, especially given other pressures as we decarbonise the grid. It would be hugely expensive for consumers and make the city hotter as the units pumped warmer air into the surrounding atmosphere. Some homes will be fitted with air conditioning. But it will likely remain a luxury.

Heat breaks much of our critical infrastructure. On the 40 degree day, London's trains stopped running as the metal rails buckled and bent. Hospital procedures were cancelled and data centres overheated causing IT outages. We may start running out of water. 'Water levels in London have been gradually going down and down and down, which is mainly an increase in demand due to an increase in population, but as climate change increases periods of dryness we will face a new challenge,' says Professor Ward. There have been discussions about building new reservoirs, but these get tied up in the usual planning delays.[20] And as the city gets hotter, London's homes will start to sink. The clay bed on which the city is built will shrink and swell during periods of extreme heat and extreme rainfall. A staggering 57.3% of the city's homes are projected to be at risk of subsidence by 2070 under a high emissions scenario, compared to 10.9% for the country as a whole. And heat is not the end of the perils of a warmer world for London. Because with more heat comes more fire.

FIRE

Chris is one of my oldest friends. We went to school together in east London. As an adult, like many of us, he moved to the outskirts of the city: a small village called Wennington, which is just on the border between London and Essex. I remember him proudly showing me the grassland that backed directly onto his house – an incredible expanse of space for someone who had grown up in the city, somewhere he walked his dog and took his young son to play.

On 19 July 2022, when news began to break of a wildfire in Essex, I recognised the fields from the news coverage and was immediately grateful that Chris and his family had moved out just weeks previously. Because the short row of squat, cottage-style terrace houses where they'd lived, and where I'd only recently taken my own children to play, were being gutted by flame.

The Wennington wildfire started at around 1 p.m. in a back garden. Victoria Schafer was at home with her husband and father-in-law when she smelled smoke, and ran outside to see white smoke rising from near a willow tree in the neighbours' garden, which then turned to flame. It looked like a compost bin had caught fire. The residents called the fire brigade, while her husband and father-in-law tried to extinguish the blaze with a hose pipe. The flames were crackling through the grass and stretching out into the marshland at the rear of the properties. 'It caught so quickly it ran out of control in minutes. It was terrifying,' Victoria recalled.[21]

What happened next was fast and devastating. A caravan ignited and burst into flames. The fire spread rapidly through the grass behind the properties, igniting fences, burning gardens and then ripping into the windows of homes and setting furniture on fire. 'It was like something out of a film,' one resident told the local paper.[22] 'Neighbours were running, people were crying with their belongings on their shoulders. At first, residents gathered in the village church, but flames licked from the fields, burned through the graveyard and came up to the walls of the church. They fled again.

Firefighters arrived after thirteen minutes and poured gallons of water onto the blaze, but the flames were too fierce.

The homes were gutted. In some instances, all that was left were three walls, rubble and holes where the windows and doors used to be. It took until nearly 10 p.m. to get the fire under control. By the evening, ninety residents had been evacuated and seventeen homes were destroyed. Pet cats were killed and residents lost all their possessions. Aerial pictures show a black stain of scorched grassland stretching for acres.

And it was not just Wennington. On 19 July 2022, when London recorded its first ever temperatures of more than 40 degrees Celsius, the London Fire Brigade (LFB) had its busiest day since the Blitz.[23] It received nearly 2,500 calls about more than a dozen fires burning simultaneously in different parts of the city. The service struggled to respond. And this day is a grim portent of what future summers in London will look like.

Wildfire is something most of us would probably associate with the hills of Spain and Portugal, or the forests of southern California – not London. But Wennington was not the first time flames have ripped through grasslands in or around London. In 2018, Wanstead Flats, an area of grass fields, trees, lakes and municipal football pitches between Newham and Redbridge in the east of the city, was transformed into black grass, bare scorched earth, and charred remains of trees. That blaze ripped through an area equivalent to about 150 football pitches and would burn again in 2020. One of the best things about London is its parks and open spaces: from Hyde Park to Walthamstow Marshes, Wimbledon Common to Epping Forest, London remains a very green city. But all of these areas are so close to such densely populated areas that they may become deadly threats as the years tick by and the summer temperature rises. In 2025, climate change had already made wildfire conditions six times as likely to occur in the UK.

Urban wildfires are not always huge headline-grabbing blazes which burn acres of land. Sometimes they start in a back garden and burn into a single house, but the risk to life is still serious. Guillermo Rein, professor of fire science at the

Department of Mechanical Engineering of Imperial College London, and his colleagues recently found a way to isolate all these wildfires in London (starting outside with natural fuel) in LFB data. The data shows regular spikes in the summer months – July and the first half of August. Overlaying this data with weather reports showed a striking correlation. Periods where the air was dryer (the vapour pressure deficit) and hot for ten days in a row produced a startling increase in both the number of outdoor fires and the number of hours fire engines were deployed to fight them. Professor Rein and his team termed these events 'fire waves'. In data going back to 2009 they found five such events, one in 2018 and four in 2022. It is early data, but it clearly suggests we have entered the start of regular, serious wildfires in and around London.

The city is very poorly prepared for this. 'The city of London has a structural problem with its green spaces,' says Rein. 'You would not see the kinds of parks and green spaces […] in the Mediterranean cities, because on the day of the fire they will not make it. Other cities are not doing it on purpose, but they have learned by trial and error the species of trees and plants that are more fire resistant. In other cities, you won't see so many trees connected at the top, or bushes connected to trees. In Spanish cities there is much less grass around houses, because the grass only stays green for about eight days and it costs so much to water it.'

London, with its green gardens, parks and tree-lined streets is different. But as it gets hotter and dryer, it places itself further at risk of catastrophe. 'It's not just the heat, it's the dryness. That's the problem. It takes the moisture out of everything, which massively increases the availability of fuel. Don't just think about this in terms of vegetation, think about the sheds, combustible materials in people's gardens, everything's available,' says Rob Harvey, an experienced firefighter and wildfire expert. 'In the past, there would still be moisture in things, but we're not seeing that in more recent times.'

Wildfires are a risk London desperately needs to prepare for. We have to put layers of protection in place. People need to start becoming aware of the risks: once the prolonged hot, dry conditions take hold, we need to know that there are enormous risks associated with smoking in a park, having a barbeque or dropping a glass bottle through which light can refract and ignite. Homeowners and landlords should think about the interface between combustible materials outside and their homes. We may also need to prepare by adapting the green spaces we love. Tactical burns can put effective firebreaks in place ahead of a wildfire taking hold. But these tactics are not widely understood in the UK.

The LFB is gearing up. After Wennington, it purchased equipment such as a 'holey hose', which can create a curtain of water up to 2 metres high, and hired ten wildfire officers and thirty wildfire tactical advisers.[24] But the challenges will be huge when they come. 'I saw stuff this week that I had not expected to see as a London firefighter,' said commissioner Andy Roe in the aftermath of Wennington and the fires which came on the same day. The conditions the firefighters faced were hellish: sixteen suffered heat-related injuries, two were hospitalised.[25] What happens when these conditions persist for weeks? What happens when one comes in the midst of a drought, limiting the water pressure firefighters have to combat the blaze?

Epping Forest, Wanstead Flats and Walthamstow Marshes are among my favourite parts of London. They are beautiful, natural oases within a harsh urban environment. But over the coming decades, I will probably see them burn. And when they do, the consequences for London could be unspeakable. It may not reach the scale of Los Angeles in January 2025, but London is very vulnerable to fire.

'On 19 July 2022 we were very lucky,' adds Rein. 'We were very lucky that on that day there was no wind. We were very lucky that day ended with rain. When there is wind, the fires become unstoppable. The embers fly hundreds, thousands of metres ahead until they find something that can burn. The embers will shower buildings until they find a hole, and then they will ignite the timber in the roof. They will enter through a vent, they will break a window, they will accumulate in the gutters. In a scenario with wind, the embers go everywhere. These fires will ignite cars. They will ignite ships in harbours. They will ignite anything in their path.'

A HOTTER WORLD

London needs to be physically re-engineered to cope well with the pressures of extreme weather events, be they unprecedented heat or heavy rainfall. This is what climate scientists mean when they talk about the costs of not cutting carbon emissions and allowing the planet to warm. According to Professor Bob Ward, 'This is the trade-off we have made. We didn't want to act quicker to cut greenhouse gas emissions, now we're having to pick up the bill to deal with the impacts.'

Of course there is uncertainty in all of these risks. We don't know precisely what climate we will face in thirty years, let alone the next hundred, and much depends on the emissions reductions which happen in the next few decades. We don't know exactly how sensitive the systems are – how much wetter, hotter and drier it will get, by exactly how much London's rivers will rise as a result. But we know things will get worse.

'Doing nothing is certainly not an option,' says Ward. 'If we don't adapt, we're going to end up with a lot of buildings which will be frankly useless to provide the services they are designed for. London's success is absolutely intertwined with its ability to adapt to the new climate. The alternative is a city where no one wants to live, or can live, because it's this hellish environment where people face the constant threat of flooding and overheating and fire.'

Housing in the Anthropocene also raises the question of insurance. Building insurance in general has been steadily creeping up in the UK in recent years, with the industry directly linking this rise to climate change. Some of those living in the highest-risk areas are already being refused cover.[26] Tenants and leaseholders will see these costs passed on in higher service charges, homeowners will discover them when they renew policies. For many it may be the final straw that forces them out of an increasingly unaffordable (and uncomfortable) city. And will 'air-conditioning poverty' in summer replace today's fuel poverty in winter as a topic of concern?

And what about the question of property prices full stop? Research on the American market suggests that properties in flood-risk areas are overvalued to the tune of $237 billion. What about London? How will overheating flats be valued in the future? How about homes at severe risk of flooding, or already damaged by it?

And what about the experience of those displaced by floods and fire? Even today, families displaced by events such as gas explosions can find themselves bounced from hotel to hotel, reliant on food vouchers to feed their children, unsure where they will come back to at night. What will we do if tens of thousands need rehousing at once? This country does not have a culture of temporary housing units, the sort of mobile homes that pop up in the aftermath of big US floods and New Zealand earthquakes. But it is something we must learn.

There will be other impacts from climate change on the demand for housing in London. Will the estimated 400,000 British expats in Spain want to stay there as the country desertifies? How about the 240,000 in Dubai? As the world gets hotter, will the very wealthy and mobile from around the world choose the cooler cities to place their wealth and their apartments? London, hot as it may become, will be far cooler than Qatar, Mexico City or Mumbai. Could a boom of wealthy climate refugees drive a fresh wave of super-prime housing – this time sold on the basis of their state of the art flood defences and air conditioning?

'I went to Hobart in Tasmania, Australia, recently [an island which is cooler than the mainland],' says Rowland Atkinson, who has studied the impact of super-prime investment on London. 'And all the houses are worth a million dollars, because you've got all this migration from mainland Australia where people are sick of the 40-degree summers and can't insure their homes due to wildfire and flooding. So what are the rich people in hotter cities going to do? How is Dubai going to survive? Will they choose New Zealand or London? All of these things are interconnected – London has never just been its own market, it's one bowl in the fountain with cash pouring down from elsewhere and then pouring out into the rest of the UK.'

In the end, just as climate change might lower some London prices, it might push others up – if it becomes a place the rich see as a sanctuary for their money from even worse chaos elsewhere. But more broadly, the collapse in community driven by the housing crisis has made London even less resilient to disasters than it might otherwise have been. 'We've always lived alongside disasters and come through them,' says Professor Lucy Easthope, an expert in post-disaster recovery. 'But what we've done is lost all the other things that make life bearable when these things happen: the lifescape, brief moments of joy that get you through. For too many people the aftermath of a disaster now means isolation in a hotel room.'

These are things the next century demands we rebuild. 'If the Thames floods what will get us through is the community laundry that opens up down the road, the community kitchens, and all those things,' she says. 'Your parents and grandparents lived alongside disaster and uncertainty. They survived these things and still enjoyed their lives. We can too, but we need to build that resilience.'

As housing becomes less secure, as communities are broken up and dispersed, as neighbours become strangers, these bonds have loosened. We do not have much time left to rebuild them.

Another way

THE CURRENT PATH

Predictions of the future are rarely accurate, the reality being more complex and nuanced than any prediction can manage. But there can be little doubt that London has a tough path ahead.

In 2016, the government commissioned papers looking into the future challenges and opportunities for UK cities across a range of policy areas. The paper on housing painted a fairly optimistic picture of London in 2060, with house prices rising at no more than inflation, density increased in the suburbs to meet housing demand and reductions in housing benefit due to rising wages being transferred to a 'great expansion in social housing production'.

In 2024, I spoke to the report's author, Michael Edwards, a lecturer at the Bartlett School of Planning at University College London. 'When I look back on that report, I do sometimes think "Oh my God, you were very naive",' he says. 'I think I attached too much importance to just building more homes, which has really just resulted in land prices being driven up. Speculation on land value growth and housing price growth has become one of the main driving forces of the whole economy. So I do think it will continue to get worse,' he says.

It is possible to envision London's housing crisis getting worse across all tenures. We have seen the financial difficulties facing social housing. Without more state money, the options will be reduced to a mass sell-off of the most affordable social homes, increased rents and the rise of for-profit providers with deeper pockets. Eventually we would look around and realise that social housing really isn't social housing at all anymore. It could be argued – and often is – that we're already several steps along that path.

Private renting will likely change too. If no-fault evictions are finally banned and new targets are introduced for environmental performance, we may see the 'small-time side-hustler' type of landlord pushed out of the market. Already, analysts are noting the change – with rising interest rates and tax changes squeezing smaller-scale landlords, who also feel incapable of meeting forthcoming environmental requirements and increased regulatory requirements. But this will have less of an impact on big, portfolio investors. 'Buy-to-let now involves so much legislation, the "mom-and-pop" buyer, purchasing one or two to bolster a pension, are gone, replaced by larger, corporate landlords, usually running as a limited company,' property expert Jonathan Rolande told the *i Paper*.[1] Bigger investors, like Blackstone, the world's largest real estate investor, are increasingly interested in what they call 'single family units' and ordinary people call homes. Blackstone has a legacy of rental hikes and 'aggressive evictions' which led the UN's then housing adviser to accuse them in 2019 of exploiting tenants, 'wreaking havoc' in communities and helping to fuel a global housing crisis.[2]

And as companies start to struggle to attract a workforce, we may also move towards more employer-owned housing – something which was familiar in London's private rental market in the past. Ryanair recently bought up most of the housing on a newly built estate near Dublin Airport, to protect its operations from the rising cost of renting in the city.[3] But while this may provide some employees in lower-paid jobs with a place in the city, there are obvious downsides to having your employer as a landlord, and the extraordinary power that they would wield over your life as a result. In Chinese cities, investors have got rich providing cheap dormitory accommodation for low-paid, mostly migrant workers – four beds in a small room, often subsidised by employers. Will this be the future of London's housing too?[4]

The future of buying a home is much harder to predict. Someone, somewhere has been predicting an imminent property price crash in the capital since I first started writing about housing in 2013. But while house price growth has softened and sometimes flatlined, the trend always seems to be upwards eventually. The game-changing crash which is regularly, hyperbolically predicted never arrives.

We may – perhaps – be on the verge of a new era in this regard. If the defining force which drove high house prices from the 1980s onwards was low interest rates, we have now left that era. Interest rates have always mirrored house prices – when one goes up the other goes down. We are yet to see that happen, but it may be a matter of time. 'There's just huge uncertainty,' says the economist Ian Mulheirn. 'You could end up with this whole situation getting much worse, and going back to even higher multiples with house prices up to fourteen or fifteen times earnings in London. Or you could get it gradually dropping to around five or six times income, which is much closer to the twentieth-century norm – at which point we could look back and say, well, the early twenty first century was a real aberration.'

The latter seems, to me at least, less likely. In a world where investors want a piece of real estate in big cities, there is almost no natural cap on prices. What will this mean for people? Some – due to the great wealth transfer – will likely plug inherited money straight back into housing, along with their own savings, another driver to keep the high-house-price party on the road. For others, the idea of really 'owning' a home – as in, having it without owing a mortgage to a bank – may simply disappear. 'The financial sector will have to innovate and provide people with products where they don't pay their mortgage off, and they're effectively part renting from the bank for the rest of their lives,' says Mulheirn.

The future is unpredictable and chaotic. Perhaps the most likely is a simple, miserable continuation of the status quo: those with money buy a house, those without suffer and those who have found a way to make money out of both get extraordinarily rich.

'I think it's quite unlikely we're going to get into a world that's much worse than the one we've already been in with regard to housing, which, let's face it, has been extraordinarily bad,' says Mulheirn. 'But I think it's just worth realising that a much worse world is not off the table. And we do have to work out as a society how you enable people to do what they need to have the security and affordability they need, given those trends. Because in the twenty-first century so far, our response has been to just sit back and watch while this stuff blew apart the social deal that we used to have.'

But a negative vision of the future is never a prophecy. It is, at best, a warning. Whatever future city we do live in will be made by human choices. It remains in our gift. So let's consider what can be done.

ANOTHER WAY

By 2023, mother-of-three Amanda had spent twelve years in a one-bedroom council flat. She bid every week for a bigger home, but there were simply no vacancies in the south London borough of Southwark where she lived and worked and where her children went to school.

'Our old flat had condensation because it was overcrowded and my back was breaking from having to move things around constantly,' she recalled, when I spoke to her in 2024. 'It was such a tight area, so there was hardly any space for the children to play and my son couldn't get homework done – he went backwards at school quite quickly. Really and truly, he just needed some space and a good night's sleep, but it's impossible when the baby's crying, it was just chaotic.'

At this point, you might think the housing system will proceed to chew her family up, spit them out and compound their trauma in the process. Except that isn't the story I'm going to tell this time.

In June 2023, Southwark Council completed a scheme of twenty-one new council homes in Woodham Court, just off the Old Kent Road. Based on what was previously a disused garage site, the scheme provided seventeen flats and four three-bedroom homes at social rents, as well as a new community hall. Aesthetically, they are functional – brick facades, square windows with heavy black frames and flat roofs. But to Amanda they are life-changing. 'When I got here, I was just really in shock because it is absolutely beautiful. I've never been as happy,' she tells me. 'I was just so glad to get my teenager his own room, and to have my own room. It just gave me the headspace I really needed.'

While the social housing renaissance initiated under Sadiq Khan's mayoralty has been small, and is threatened by economic pressure, it has resulted in 32,000 council homes being started around London and thousands more at social rents started by housing associations. Even though some may ultimately not be built due to the changing economic circumstances, that is still thousands of families like Amanda's finally relieved of the pressure housing has placed on them for so long.

'It's such a weird feeling, like I can breathe again,' she told me of her new home. This feeling is the outcome housing policy should be working towards. And there are ways to get there.

First, though, we need a change in thinking. Housing needs to be seen as a fundamental part of welfare provision, in the same way as we think of education and health. If this theory became embedded, solutions would become available to us, things which are already in place around the world, things those fighting for change elsewhere are pushing for and things that have worked in the past here.

MUNICIPALISATION

There is a slight wistfulness when housing policy enthusiasts in the UK talk about Germany. It is a country, we hear, where renting is *normal*. In 2023, more than half of the German population lived in rental accommodation (52.4 per cent), the largest percentage in the EU.[5] People are happy to rent for their whole lives, tenancies are long and rents are relatively stable. The lack of a desperate focus to get everyone on the housing ladder produces a more sensible, progressive housing market.

Or so we are told. But scratch a little beneath the surface and the picture looks less rosy: housing is still extremely unaffordable, with 13 per cent of Germany's population spending 40 per cent or more of their income on housing, only a shade below the 15.1 per cent who do so in the UK, and well above the EU average of 8.8 per cent.[6]

In Berlin, as in London, there is a serious housing crisis. Rents doubled between 2009 and 2019 and continue to rise, a major social problem in a city where 85 per cent of inhabitants rent. The city has rent controls – known as the *Mietpreisbremse* – which hold rents to within 10 per cent of a regionally set rent index. But these indices do rise, and an attempt to convert the controls into a rent freeze in 2020 proved a disaster: properties were rapidly withdrawn from the market, forcing new renters out into the satellite cities, where prices soared due to exploding demand. Within thirteen months, the constitutional court declared the policy unconstitutional and many tenants were required to pay back the difference to their landlords.

Four years on, the situation for renters in Berlin is described as 'suffocatingly tight' in the media. Any vacant apartments are flooded with hundreds of applications mere hours after they are posted and students moving to the city spend months sleeping on sofas while they wait for a permanent home.

Amid this chaos, campaigners have begun to call for a more radical solution. Even after the sell offs and demolitions described in prior chapters, London still has far more social housing than Berlin. There are 90,000 social homes in the German capital, mostly owned by six state-owned housing corporations. This amounts to 4.5 per cent of the total housing stock, compared to 23.1 per cent in London. And building more has not proved successful, amid similar economic pressures to those here. In 2022, there were no applications to build new public housing at all in Berlin. 'There are no adequate [housing] offers or support for the bus driver or the kindergarten teacher,' one senior member of a housing corporation told the *Berliner*. 'Neither the state nor the federal government has enough money for that.'[7]

Campaigners decided it was time for the size of the public housing sector to grow in another way. A grassroots campaign was launched to seize the assets of the city's largest landlords and convert them to public housing. The campaign, named Expropriate Deutsche Wohnen and Co.! (Deutsche Wohnen is Berlin's biggest landlord), has struck a chord with Berlin's frustrated renters. The proposal it set out, to effectively nationalise 240,000 apartments, was put to a city-wide referendum in September 2021, and passed 59 to 41 per cent.

This is not to say it will happen. The referendum is non-binding and the mayor of the city has spoken out against the idea. But there remains sustained pressure to implement it. The Left Party has threatened to leave Berlin's ruling coalition if it is not implemented. A commission was set up to investigate its practicality in 2022. After more than a year's work, the thirteen-member commission concluded that the proposal was 'legally permissible, proportionate, constitutionally appropriate, and suitable for containing the explosion of rents in the German capital'. Activists have now engaged a law firm to write a Socialisation Act, and are pushing for a second referendum which would be binding, after being frustrated by the lack of progress in the Senate.

The project is often described as 'radical' and 'innovative' in the media. But actually, the nationalisation of private housing is something which is decades old, and is a policy which London, as well as Berlin, could do well to return to.

Not all of London's social housing was built as such. Instead, a good deal of it was purchased by the state. This small scale, flat-by-flat, nationalisation is known in housing policy circles as municipalisation.

'There were two major phases of municipalisation in London. The first was up until the 1960s, which really had its roots in old-school socialism,' says historian John Boughton. 'There was a belief that private landlords were bad and that the whole model was exploitative and that all homes should really be treated as a public good.' During this period, the Labour Party was out of power nationally but had control over the London County Council (LCC). In 1954 a conference motion committed the party to municipalisation, and the LCC followed through with programmes of home purchase. Derek Jarman (not the film maker), who was then a postman in the area and later became a Camden councillor, recalled to me: 'When I did my rounds, if I saw blocks in a poor condition, I would go back and say "This needs buying".' On his advice, the council bought whole blocks, including mansion flats near Parliament Hill which would sell for millions today. Camden was an ambitious supporter of this drive for new council housing. In 1964, a policy document said, 'All residential properties or sites in the new borough which come on the market should be acquired by the… council.'[8]

'This was an era when the private rented sector was in terminal decline, and a lot of landlords were looking to sell. The returns on private rents were marginal and the effort required to repair the properties was not seen as worthwhile,' says Boughton.

Ruth Glass, the sociologist who famously coined the phrase 'gentrification' in the 1960s, reviewed Camden's housing policy in 1970 and felt that municipalisation should be expanded – to spread the reach of council housing to a wider demographic, particularly those who were priced out of private housing but not likely to qualify for a social home.

While the policy would fall out of favour in the 1960s, in favour of slum clearance through demolition and rebuild, it came back with a bang when Labour returned to power nationally in 1974 under Harold Wilson. It put forward municipalisation as part of its manifesto in the two elections it won that year, and found that it proved popular with a population struggling with housing costs.

The Budget of 1974 put an additional £350 million (about £3.2 billion in today's money) into a programme of 'new council house building, municipalisation, and the buying of unsold newly-built homes'. The last of those was taken as a direct response to the struggles of the private house-building market and was effectively a bail-out for private builders who faced enormous losses on homes they had built but could not sell in the difficult economic climate.[9]

The policy resulted in a major expansion of social housing. In the two years to April 1976, 60,000 properties were bought on the open market around the country for use as social housing. This process was led by Islington, which bought 4,000 by itself.[10] 'London boroughs like Camden and Islington were pretty zealous in making use of that finance,' says Boughton. Both boroughs acquired thousands of street properties, many of which remain part of their council housing stock today, albeit much reduced by Right to Buy.

There are obvious parallels with today. A moderate Labour government took power exactly fifty years before the current one, and was faced, as the current one is, with a difficult situation in the housing market: private building rates were teetering and housing affordability was a major issue. But the Labour Party of the 1970s responded not by tearing up planning rules in the hope that the private market would somehow ride to the rescue, as the current government plans to, but by expanding the state – buying up homes private builders were struggling to sell, building council housing and replacing struggling private landlords with public ownership.

There are rumbles of support for the same sort of policies today among the devolved Labour administrations. Andy Burnham, mayor of Greater Manchester, has set out plans to introduce standards for private landlords in the region and empower councils to compulsorily purchase homes which slip below the standard and re-let them as council housing.[11] In London, Sadiq Khan set up London's first major municipalisation programme since the 1970s, with his Council Homes Acquisition Programme, launched in 2023. The scheme allows councils to bid for money to buy homes on the open market, with a particular focus on those previously sold under Right to Buy.[12] But without major central government support – primarily new powers and funding – these schemes will only ever tinker at the edges of the housing crisis.

There are major advantages to municipalisation. The first is that the home is available immediately. There are no delays with the planning system, no problems with contractors failing to build properly, no new-build snagging defects. You simply acquire a home and house a family in need. Such a programme in the UK today would not necessarily need to be done via the direct 'expropriation' proposed by the Berlin campaigners. Instead, incentives could be introduced for sellers to offer their home to the public sector first – a reduction in capital gains tax if they sell to the council, for example. As Burnham has proposed, municipalisation could also be used as a stick – a penalty for the worst-performing landlords, or those convicted of crimes, who could be forced to sell at a discounted rate.

This is not to say municipalisation does not come with problems. The cost of housing in London means that it would be expensive to implement – more so than the construction of new homes. Buying homes in poor repair would also have consequences for maintenance spend. There are also challenges with supply. Turning an existing home into a council home does not increase the overall housing stock, which remains below what is required. 'What appears to be a ready solution does bring its own problems,' says Boughton.

But there are also reasons to do it. As we have seen, councils in London are going bankrupt spending money renting out units from private landlords to house homeless families. It would make far more sense from everyone's perspective for councils to club together and buy properties themselves to provide this housing. An attempt to do this through a venture called Capital Letters failed. Despite obtaining 6,500 homes and saving the taxpayer £240 million on temporary accommodation in the process, the company announced it was winding down in 2025, the extraordinary post-pandemic rent rises breaking its business model.[13] But with central government support it is still a model that could succeed.

'The area where I think that the economics do really, really stack up for municipalisation in London is temporary accommodation,' says Darren Baxter, principal policy adviser at the Joseph Rowntree Foundation. 'You would be reducing the cost of temporary accommodation on councils, as well as driving up the standards.'

There would also be scope for turning a profit from some the homes acquired, especially if they were purchased from private landlords with the tenants still there. If the social landlord reviewed the existing tenants' incomes on acquiring the home, they could set a rent which was far more affordable than the private landlord, but still enough to provide a return to the council, which would fund cheaper rents elsewhere. This would be a major shake-up of rent setting, but it would follow models which are common overseas. In fact, it happened on a small scale in 2014 at the New Era estate in Hackney, where tenants were threatened with a 10 per cent rent hike by a private investor. After a big public campaign, the estate was instead purchased by a housing charity, Dolphin Living, which introduced a pioneering model of 'personalised rents', set according to each household's income. There were plans to expand this model across other estates, although the ambitions were never realised.

Then there is the other part of municipalisation – buying homes which private builders are struggling to sell. It may come as a surprise to learn that this has already been taking place in London as the economy has stuttered. In 2023, Newham Council, for example, bought 102 homes from the private house builder Barratt when it feared it was set to make a loss on a development in East Ham, many of which were used to rehouse homeless families in the borough.[14] In 2020, there were calls from City Hall to provide central government funding to make social landlords in London 'buyers of last resort' on properties like these, where they would purchase them at cost and convert them to social housing – saving the private sector from crushing losses while also providing a social home.[15]

It cannot be glossed over, though – none of this is cheap. Buying up property like this would not happen without central government agreeing to borrow a large amount of money to finance it. With the government currently unwilling to turn on the public spending taps in that way, it will only ever be limited to small-scale initiatives.

But this is a result of our economic philosophy more than outright impossibility. In the 1970s, municipalisation of tens of thousands of private homes happened when the country was poorer and interest rates were a good deal higher. It was possible because investment in housing is not simply money down the drain for a government. Over a long period of time, homes let at social rents will pay back the debt taken out to build them through the rents, as well as generating long-term savings in housing benefit spend, as the millions currently claiming benefit to pay private rents move into lower-rent social housing units. The country is expected to spend close to £60 billion on housing benefit, which will go to private landlords, over the next five years. The government's own analysis shows that social housing pays back 69 per cent of the grant used to build it within thirty years, and 110 per cent within sixty years, through reduced housing benefit expenditure alone.[16] It also produces other benefits – reductions in the cost of homelessness services, healthcare savings and less tangible savings in education, mental health and criminal justice as people are relieved from housing stress. It is only our fiscal policy, which insists all state borrowing is treated the same, which stands in the way of us doing this again. 'Unlike other forms of infrastructure, [housing] pays for itself through rent,' Ken Gibb, director of the UK Collaborative Centre for Housing Evidence and a professor of housing economics at the University of Glasgow, told me in 2023. 'It should not be treated as or accounted for in the same way as other capital projects.'

But municipalisation would only ever be one piece of the solution. More Londoners rent from private landlords than social, and that is not going to change overnight. So to make London sustainable, we also need to grasp the nettle of unaffordable private rents.

RENT CONTROL

The uprising of ordinary Spanish people against austerity in the early 2010s has had a much more lasting political legacy than any similar movements in the UK. Spain's Indignados movement, which culminated in a mass sit-in in Madrid in

May 2011, was the catalyst for the creation of the new party Podemos, which formed a national government coalition in 2019. It was also the start of a new left-wing movement in Spain which continues to influence its politics today.

Housing sat at the heart of this movement. In the aftermath of the global financial crisis, Spain faced an evictions watershed. Spain's housing market is primarily focused on home ownership (around 80 per cent of the population own), and unlike other countries in Europe there is hardly any social housing. Some of this is a legacy of Franco-era politics that encouraged individual ownership. Under Franco, social housing was built by private developers in Spain and sold at rates greatly subsidised by the state, with buyers also benefiting from a state-subsidised loan. But after thirty years, these homes could be sold on the open market at full value, so were effectively only social homes for one generation. Though 6.5 million social homes have been built since 1955, only 400,000 of them are public housing today, just 2.5 per cent of the total stock and one of the lowest percentage figures among developed economies.[17]

In the years leading up to the financial crisis, Spain saw a huge house-building boom – driven in part by continuing state support for home ownership. Between 2001 and 2011 there were 4.2 million homes built, more than the combined total of France, Germany and Italy in the same period. But, with investors plunging in, the average cost of a home rose 232 per cent between 1997 and 2007. Individuals were simply taking on more debt, and investors, some of them from the UK, piled a fortune into second and holiday homes, further inflating values.[18]

Then, when the bubble burst in 2008, everything went wrong. The building boom collapsed, and people who had purchased at such inflated rates could no longer afford their mortgages. Evictions and foreclosures swept through the country. Between 2008 and 2013, there were 550,000 evictions – around 180 a day.

Direct resistance to evictions became a key battleground between protestors and the state. The Platform for People Affected by Mortgages, or PAH, became a national movement – with 250 nodes around the country. At the hub of the crisis was the city known internationally for its footballing success, its wide sandy beaches and the architecture of Antoni Gaudí: Barcelona.

For natives of Barcelona, the housing crisis was acute. Rents were sky high, evictions were a constant threat and the city's 1.7 million inhabitants faced competition for housing from 32 million visitors who passed through annually. Hailing from Barcelona was Ada Colau, a housing activist and the national spokesperson for PAH. In July 2013, she was on the literal frontlines of the activist movement – photographed being forcibly dragged out of a bank she was occupying by riot police. But in 2014, she switched tack, quit PAH, formed a new political party, Barcelona en Comú (Barcelona in Common), and stood for election as mayor of the city – and won.

Eduardo González de Molina, a European housing policy expert, joined her team as a policy adviser on housing. He helped design a new 'Right to Housing Mission' which set out to double the city's stock of publicly owned housing in ten years, through programmes of new build and municipalisation, with an overall goal of growing the public housing sector from 1.5 to 15 per cent over a longer period.

'We recognised this was not going to happen immediately, because nothing in housing does, so we set out a plan for the longer term,' he told me in 2024. New byelaws granted the city the right of first refusal to purchase certain classes of property – particularly those being targeted by larger rental investors – and allowed it to buy up homes left empty. The city zoned land for the construction of social housing only. By 2022, it had increased public housing stock 54 per cent to 11,737 and was on course to reach 15,000 by 2025. This included the purchase of fifty buildings with 1,600 apartments throughout the city, at a cost of €190 million, and 1,700 formerly empty homes from private owners.[19] When the homes purchased had tenants already living in them, rents were set according to income – similar to the New Era example cited above. But adding to the public housing stock was only ever going to be one part of the plan. 'We recognised that because our public housing sector is very small, most people will be renting from private landlords, and this will be true even if we manage to grow the number of social homes,' says González.

The city took action on short-term rentals, like Airbnb, which had grown from almost nothing to 11 per cent of the city's rented housing stock in just a few years. It first introduced zones where new Airbnb-style lets were permitted and zones where no more homes could be converted to short-term lets. And in June 2024, it announced an outright ban to take effect in November 2028, when short-term holiday lets will be outlawed completely – meaning the estimated 10,000 homes in the city used for this purpose will be forced to return to residential ownership or the long-term rental market.

But the new Barcelona government also wanted restrictions on the regular private rented sector. The city, with support from the regional Catalan government, therefore moved to implement a system of rent control. Despite the national dominance of home ownership, the percentage of Barcelona's population who rented their homes had risen sharply in the 2010s – from 30 per cent in 2011 to 42.3 per cent in 2019. Prices had shot up too – from €681.56 per month in 2013 to €978.81 per month in 2019. Colau's housing strategy set out a plan to put controls in place to 'avoid the substitution of resident populations with higher-income populations'.[20]

In 2020, the city introduced a policy which it said struck a balance 'between the duty to respect the interests of the landlord with recognition of the social function of urban property'. It was founded on two basic rules. First, the rent could not be more than 5 per cent above the index rate for similar properties in the area. And second, any rent rises were to be contained according to mechanisms set out in the law. It was applied across Catalonia by the regional government – although only to regions where there was believed to be a strain on housing affordability.

Views on the impact of this are mixed. One study by academics from the universities of Barcelona and Uppsala (in Sweden), published in July 2022, said it had been positive – resulting in a 6 per cent reduction in rental costs without a fall in available rental properties.[21] 'Our results suggest that rent control policies can be effective in reducing rental prices and do not necessarily shrink the rental market,' the academics concluded. However, a study by another group of academics came to almost the opposite conclusion – they found that while prices had decreased in the most expensive properties, cheaper homes had increased their rents to the limit of the cap. They also found a 10 per cent reduction in the number of rental agreements signed, concluding that rental prices were better addressed through policies to increase supply.[22]

Really, the impact needs to be assessed over a longer period. But this has not yet happened. Eighteen months after the rent control law came into effect, the city's policy was deemed unconstitutional by Spain's national constitutional court and revoked. But this only led the left-wing coalition, who now had power nationally, to change the law. In 2024, Barcelona reimposed rent controls, this time covering the whole of the city. There are early reports that this has reduced the availability of rental housing – but at the time of writing, the policy remained in its early days and the ultimate success or failure will only become clear over time.

Few housing policies divide opinion quite as much as rent controls. The decision on whether or not you support them seems to be determined much more by your political affiliation than any available evidence. To some on the left, they are the holy grail – and anyone who questions them is quickly branded a stooge for landlords and property investors. To some on the right, they are an unacceptable intervention in the free market and the very essence of property rights and are constantly shot down as something which 'never works'.

In fact, the UK sits in an extreme position with regard to rent control. The country, in the words of a review by academics at the London School of Economics, 'is at one end of the international spectrum of regulation' – the end which provides the most freedom to landlords. Elsewhere, rent control policies of varying degrees of restrictiveness are 'core elements in the movement towards sustainable private rental sectors, particularly in Europe'.[23]

The literature on rent controls identifies 'three generations' of control in order of how firmly the price is regulated – from the most straightforward control of setting an overall ceiling or freeze on rents across the market (first generation); to a system where rents can be set at any rate when a property is first let, but limits are placed on how much it can increase from one tenancy to the next (second generation); and finally to the least restrictive, where a free market approach is taken to the initial tenancy, but a limit (such as inflation) is placed on price increases during the tenancy (third generation).

Most of Europe has third- or second-generation rent control, with long or even unlimited tenancy length. The Netherlands has full first-generation rent control, which it has had in place for decades – a system where the government sets out a valuation system for each property, awarding points for quality, access to amenities and so on. Maximum rents are then set depending on how many points are scored, with only those at the very top of the market allowed to charge what they want. In North America, Canadian states have varying degrees of rent control. The US is mostly a free market, with controls in place in a handful of cities or states: New York, New Jersey, San Francisco and a few more. Longer tenancies than we see in the UK (effectively a form of third-generation rent control) are also common in the US.

To have none of these in place, and to have such limited security of tenure, which allows easy eviction and replacement with a richer tenant, therefore puts the UK market at the most radically liberal and deregulated end of the scale in the global North. For a sector that now houses families, pensioners and our vital but poorly paid key workers, this is plainly not good enough.

The trouble is, what to do about it? We have become reliant on private landlords to provide homes to those who cannot afford to buy to such an extent that policies which result in them leaving the market could be extremely dangerous for the tenants who need a home. The chaos in private rented housing post-pandemic was partly caused by a sudden drop in availability while demand spiked.

There is no point pretending this is not a risk. Many countries deregulated rents in the 1980s – although rarely to the same extent as the UK under Margaret Thatcher. But political pressure due to rising rents has seen restrictions tightened or reintroduced around Europe – especially in cities. In France, for example, the law allowed landlords to charge what they wanted at the outset of a three-year tenancy, with increases during this period limited only by a national index. But in 2014, this was toughened. When a home was re-let to a new tenant, the new rent was still limited by the index rate – and this was set by a government agency, rather than a simple assessment of 'the market' (second-generation rent control, as described above). Over the next few years major cities, including Paris, Lille, Lyon, Bordeaux and Montpellier, introduced overall rent ceilings (first-generation control). 'The new regulations seem to have eliminated, or almost eliminated, extreme rents,' the paper *Le Monde* said, in a major review in 2024. The kickback, however, has been a sharp fall in the amount of rental properties available.[24] In Ireland, the concept of 'rental pressure zones' was introduced in 2016 for areas such as Dublin, where rents could only rise by 4 per cent, reduced to 2 per cent in 2024. In the first few years, there was little impact, but now the availability of rental units in Dublin has fallen – with just over 2,000 homes available to rent in May 2024, well below half the 2015–19 average of almost 4,400.[25]

Cutting off rental supply is a disaster for those looking for a home. Long term, the best approach may be to build up the availability of social housing again so we are less reliant on private landlords – but that simply won't happen overnight, and until it does, decimating the supply of rental homes would leave people who can't afford to buy with nowhere to live.

This risk is the biggest argument against rent control, and there is no point pretending it isn't valid. But what critics of rent controls fail to see – but renters can – is the status quo bias in this sort of argument. There might be some difficulties with rent control, but there are also difficulties now being caused by a lack of rent control – the exodus of poor people and key workers from our major cities, the economic damage that comes from salaries being eaten up by housing costs, the transformation of homes into investment assets – in short, everything we're living through right now. So the best approach might be to try and design a rent control system which mitigates the risk of landlords selling up, rather than give up and leave things as they are.

The magic elixir would be a system of rent control which kept a lid on prices without killing off supply. 'Mainstream economists purport not to like price controls, but we accept price controls in a lot of the areas of the economy – such as the minimum wage,' Dr Beth Stratford, an economist at University College London, told me in 2024. She says that simply relying on supply and demand to lower prices does not work with regard to housing.

'Once you understand the macroeconomics of housing and land, you realise it is completely different from other goods in society. If we're talking about bikes, for example, if there are enough bikes in the market, the price will go down towards the production cost and it will reach a fair price. But we are never, ever, ever going to reach that point with land, especially in desirable locations, which is inherently limited in supply.'

The important aspect, Dr Stratford explains, would be to consider what we want rent control to achieve and what we don't. A successful system needs to avoid major competition for the most desirable properties. It also needs to avoid a mass exodus of landlords from the market, with a subsequent evictions crisis and a lack of available rental housing.

But it is possible to anticipate these problems and design a system which mitigates them. Rent control systems can be designed to consider the quality and attributes of the property – rather than a flat rate, which creates a mad rush for the best properties. Quality-based rent control would assess the value of the property – its location and amenities – and set the price accordingly.

'Part of the reason I didn't advocate for rent control in the past was because I couldn't see how it would be feasible to implement a rent control system that kept rents in proportion to the quality and attributes of the property, but I now realise that is totally feasible. There are at least six places in Europe where they do a version of quality-based rent control,' adds Dr Stratford. 'In the Netherlands the system involves the landlord filling out a form with details, applying the formula and there's your rent cap. The cost of running the system is tiny.'

And there are ways to avoid a mass exodus of landlords. Rent control does not necessarily make being a landlord unprofitable. In fact, HMRC data studied by Dr Stratford shows that letting a property in the UK would remain a profitable activity even with controls applied.

There are other levers the state can pull. Protection from eviction, with strong enforcement, would be a necessary part of any rent control regime. And the tax system could be used to encourage landlords to stay in the game – reducing tax on rental profits, while increasing it on the sale of investment properties. And if a municipalisation policy of the kind described above was implemented, landlords who really no longer wanted to let out the home could be incentivised to sell it, tenanted, to a social housing provider.

But what about the conditions in the private rental sector? As we have seen, renting privately is not only financially draining but frequently dangerous, as tenants wrestle with damp, mould, leaks and chronic maintenance problems. The problems here come down to a balance of power. With local authority enforcement teams stretched beyond their limits, tenants are basically on their own, armed only with the power to send an angry email, against a foe who can make them homeless.

But tenants can be given power over their landlord. It is the tenant who pays the rent. If they stop doing so, the landlord suffers very quickly. In the current system, that is very unwise – it will lead to eviction, homelessness and difficulty securing another tenancy. But the system can change. A statutory right to withhold rent due to disrepair sounds radical to people used only to the UK market, but it is normal elsewhere. 'Quite a lot of US states have repair and deduct laws,' says Siobhan Donnachie from the London Renters Union. 'Those allow the tenant to fix an issue themselves and take the money out of their rent. Other countries have systems where the rent is paid to a court in the event of a dispute, and the court only pays it out to the landlord if they are satisfied they have made the repairs.'

There are systems like this in place in the Netherlands, Germany and many other European countries. They are regulated and formal, but represent a very powerful bargaining chip for residents. So they constitute an excellent tool in community organising in areas where huge private equity investors dominate the rental market. The UK already has a system of 'rent repayment orders', which can be imposed on landlords for offences such as failing to license an HMO. An extension of these powers to deal with issues of serious disrepair would certainly gain the attention of rogue landlords.

It also shouldn't be underestimated how powerful campaigning can be in these areas. Renters are an increasingly important body of voters – particularly in major cities. While the Renters Rights Bill has its weaknesses, particularly around unlimited rent rises and a lack of enforcement, it will bring to an end the era of short tenancies and no-fault evictions, which have been the driving force of inequity in the rental market since 1988. That this legislation was first tabled by a Conservative government historically hostile to renters' rights shows the potential power of civil society campaigning in forcing change that can sometimes seem unlikely.

There is almost universal agreement among market economists that rent controls are a bad thing. But their theories are not the only way of looking at the world and are not always proved right. In the years before the introduction of the minimum wage in 1999 there was also 'almost near universal agreement in academia in opposition to [it], with around 80 per cent of academic economists agreeing that [it] would result in higher unemployment'.[26] But since its introduction, it has worked so well that revoking it now feels unthinkable. And if we can have a minimum wage, why not a maximum rent?

HOMES OF THE FUTURE

Louisville, Kentucky, is known to the world as the birthplace of boxer Muhammad Ali, the home of bourbon whiskey and the site of the Kentucky Derby, the world famous horse-racing meet.

The latter two of these mean the city attracts a lot of tourism – from whiskey enthusiasts seeking out the 'bourbon trail' and horse-racing enthusiasts who descend on the city each May for the fortnight-long derby festival. As such, it has focused a lot of its recent development and investment on catering for this lucrative crowd. 'The city invests a lot in passive economic development, where people are just coming here to experience the city for a weekend,' councillor Jecorey Arthur, who represents one of the city's most deprived neighbourhoods, told me in 2024. 'So there is a lot of investment in hotels, a lot of investment in our downtown district, a lot of investment in luxury and not a lot of prioritising of the people who live here and have struggled here.'

Louisville, particularly to its Black citizens, is about more than horse racing and whiskey. Situated on the Ohio River, it was one of the largest slave ports in the south, and the legacy of that dark history continues today. Black neighbourhoods in the city's west end trace their roots back to the Civil War, and suffered for decades as segregation and Jim Crow laws drove public and private investment away from their neighbourhoods.

But Louisville, like all major cities, has grown in the twenty-first century and higher earners have started to move into the formerly deprived neighbourhoods. This has had a racial edge. In 2010, the neighbourhood of Smoketown, which was one of the few places where Black communities were allowed to live after the Civil War, was 79.8 per cent Black and 16 per cent white. But by 2020, the Black community had shrunk to 65.5 per cent while the proportion of white residents had grown to 27.4 per cent.

'[Smoketown] has not gotten the same type of investment as other parts of the city, from public trash cans, to the sidewalks, to infrastructure. There has been a long-term disinvestment in the area,' Jessica Bellamy, a community organiser, housing activist and lifelong Smoketown resident, told me in 2024. But as money and development did finally arrive in Smoketown, it did not appear to be mobilised for the benefit of the existing community. In the USA, estate regeneration schemes are known as 'HOPE VI' projects, after the federal funding scheme which finances them. Like their cousins in London, these schemes have always been controversial, with accusations of forced gentrification and the deliberate displacement of Black communities from inner city areas. In 2012, one such scheme began in Shepherd Square in Smoketown, with city-funded non-profit developers receiving land at hugely discounted prices to demolish and redevelop. But the houses which were being built were priced way out of the reach of the local community. 'A number of folks including myself got really engaged, because here's all this money and resource coming into the neighbourhood, so why can't it be used to match the vision the community has for itself and support folks who have been here for years?' says Bellamy.

Meanwhile, poorer Black households struggled to get affordable contractors to restore homes in disrepair. These homes were ultimately purchased, retrofitted and resold by investors to wealthier, often white, residents. Steadily the community was being displaced.

Bellamy and other campaigners began organising a community fightback. 'For over a decade now, I've been organising in Smoketown – talking to people on couches, on their doorstep, conversations about what their problems are and what their vision of the future is,' she says. With the help of Councillor Arthur, then a Democrat and now an independent, this grassroots campaign came together to draft a globally unique piece of housing legislation.

This legislation put in place a new requirement to review proposed developments against their potential to displace the local community. The rules said that if developers were going to use city resources – whether land, grants, letters of support or tax benefits – then they should build for the benefit of the community. A matrix was developed, with the help of academics at Boston University and the University of Southern

California, to grade developments for the potential displacement they might cause. If they scored too highly, they would be denied support and would have to be resubmitted.

The proposal was rejected by the city's then mayor, but the campaigners were undeterred. The combination of a grassroots campaign and canny political organising by Arthur mobilised a vote in favour of the proposal. Despite the mayor's opposition, councillors of both parties supported it – listening to a wave of anger against developers from their constituents. It became law in 2024.

Now, in order to gain city support for a development project, developers will need to put their proposal through the anti-displacement metric. And they will need to make changes – such as boosting the proportion of affordable homes, changing densities or reserving homes for local people – if they fail. 'We just believe that public resources, limited as they are, should be reserved for projects which help people who need them the most, not simply for the greed and profit of developers whose only motivation is to make money,' says Arthur.

The success of community organising in Kentucky is a powerful reminder of why the planning process is an important part of democracy. What gets built in our cities has an impact on us all. And it is possible to use the political process to take some control of that. The solutions in London will be different from those in Louisville. But they will require us to engage in local democracy, from our neighbours upwards.

Even if municipalisation and rent control policies were implemented, London would still need new housing for a population which has been growing at a faster rate than new homes have been built for decades and will continue to grow for several decades yet. But we should be bold enough to retain control over what sort of housing is built, and who it is built for.

Let's start by turning to the past. In the decades between the wars, London sprawled outwards – with agricultural land on the fringes of the city converted into enormous housing estates, like Becontree on the boundary between Essex and east London. Then, after World War II, the imposition of green belts to prevent this kind of sprawl saw a new approach taken. The inner city Victorian-era slum housing, and the bomb-damaged areas of the city, were cleared and replaced with a new generation of social housing estates. And outside the city – beyond the green belt – new towns, including Stevenage, Harlow, Basildon and Crawley, were built from scratch to accommodate an exodus from the inner city. The current government says it wants to replicate this new-towns model. But the approach it is taking is very different from what led to success in the past.

The New Towns Act 1946 was a powerful piece of legislation, described by some commentators as 'perhaps the greatest single creation of planned urbanism ever undertaken anywhere'.[27] By 1952 10,000 homes a year were being built in these new towns, a level of delivery which was kept up for most of the next decade. But these were not triumphs of free market capitalism. Instead, they were mostly social housing projects, led by state-owned development corporations and funded by public borrowing.

The New Towns Act allowed for the creation of statutory bodies that were empowered to buy the land cheaply, given low-rate sixty-year loans by the Treasury to fund the development. The magic was that these corporations retained ownership of the land. And so, as the town was built, and the land increased in value, they were able to generate income streams to repay their debts, by selling plots to developers, leasing commercial buildings and collecting rents on the social homes.

This also gave them control over how the cities developed – ensuring a balance of open space, cultural facilities and new housing. They were able to pay back their loans early, making the Treasury a profit. 'A proper development corporation is a body with a responsibility to act on behalf of the community that it's building,' Katy Lock, director of communities at the Town and Country Planning Association, told me in 2023. 'So they can retain that huge uplift in value that results from development and reinvest it in the place to maintain it to a really high quality in the long term.'

But this vision was killed off. In the 1980s and 1990s, the corporations were wound up and the towns became just the same as anywhere else, with the land sold off and the social homes subject to Right to Buy.

The new towns did not just grow quickly because of the corporations. They also grew quickly because they were social housing. At Harlow, in Essex, built with the explicit aim of rehousing east Londoners made homeless by the Blitz, all of the homes were social rent until the mid-1950s. This meant they could be built immediately, and were filled immediately. In Basildon, also in Essex, 69 per cent of the new town was social rented housing until Right to Buy arrived in the 1980s to begin carving it up.

Keir Starmer is not the first politician to try and reignite the new-towns boom in the twenty-first century. But all of the previous efforts have floundered. Gordon Brown told his first conference as Labour leader in 2007 that he would oversee the creation of new towns 'in every region of the country'. But by 2009, just four of the fifty-seven sites his government had slated for possible new towns had been deemed suitable to proceed. Only one made it anywhere, Northstowe, which was to be built on an ex-army base in Cambridgeshire. But the progress was a far cry from the 1950s. By May 2020, just 550 of the 10,000 promised homes had been built.

To find out why, consider the case of Ebbsfleet in Kent. This development is home to the UK's only purpose-built high-speed rail line (at the time of writing), which connects it to Stratford in east London in twelve minutes, and to St Pancras in central London in nineteen minutes. This effectively makes it closer to central London for a commuter than much of London itself, and should make it a very easy sell to those who work in the city but want a bit more greenery and a bit more space. The planned development is attractive – full of water features, nature, beautiful views across the Thames estuary and cycling routes.

The trouble is, the homes are taking decades to build. The site was first slated as a new town in 2002 but when I visited in 2016, just 414 homes had been built and the area was mostly scrubland and building sites. Progress has picked up since – the 3,000th home was built in 2023 – but the full development won't be finished until at least 2035.

The problem is the volume house-building model. It takes a lot of money to turn the disused quarries and flood plains of Ebbsfleet into a garden city, and this makes the scheme highly reliant on big profits later down the line. In order for the volume house builders to get the returns they need to justify their involvement, they drip out homes slowly – trying to ensure there are multiple potential buyers for each new home, which allows them to get the best price. The last thing they want is more homes on the market than potential buyers.

This may be sensible business, but it is not conducive to building fast, or producing homes cheap enough for those locked out of the market to afford. In the end the only winners are the builders themselves, and Land Securities, the FTSE 100 company which packages up the land to sell to them.

None of this is unknown. A major government review into why it takes private developers so long to develop major sites was carried out in 2019. Led by Oliver Letwin – a former member of Margaret Thatcher's policy unit – it found builders take 15.5 years on average to complete large sites and longer in London, mostly due to the slow release of housing described above. To speed up delivery, Letwin said local authorities should be given powers to dictate a wider range of housing types: more affordable housing and more homes for rent. He said they should be empowered to enforce this through the planning process and even to compulsorily purchase land at lower than market rates.[28]

The report was genuinely extraordinary: one of the intellectual architects of Thatcherism calling for the state to requisition land and force private business to act in a way which reduced their overall profits. And it was correct. The fundamental problem Letwin uncovered has been repeated again and again in academic research and a review by the Competition and Markets Authority in 2024.

But such is the power of the house builder and landowner lobbying over the political process that lessons are never implemented. Instead, we keep asking large private house builders to do something they have no incentive to do (build homes rapidly and sell them in a way which lowers overall prices) and we reward their failure to do this by giving them more of what they ask for (state-backed finance, reduced planning restrictions, lower affordable housing requirements and more developable land).

The answer is to look to the past and to the lesson of Louisville. If we want our newly built housing to provide homes which people can afford, and communities which match our aspirations for the way we want to live in the future, we need to drive the system towards this outcome, not stand back and hope for the best. And this means using the planning process more proactively, to define what can and can't be done with a piece of land.

Land itself is worth nothing. Its value comes from its potential to provide something: agriculture, housing, retail space, renewable energy or even a car park. And it is land that could provide our answer to building up a new generation of social housing. In February 2025, the Royal Institute of British Architects (RIBA) published a report calling for major public land release for building social homes.[29] In recent years, vast swathes of public land have been sold to developers – from abandoned hospitals to entire airbases. The approach has been to gain the biggest receipt possible for the public purse by selling the land to the highest bidder. But this has locked us into a model where the land is simply used for the highest profit development possible. A report in 2020 revealed that of 131,000 homes to be built on previously public land, just 2.6 per cent would be for social rent. This has been a senseless privatisation of our public estate.[30]

Instead, RIBA said, the surplus public land should be transferred to councils for free. They would then build social homes and some 'market-sale' homes on the sites. With land costs eliminated and no need to pay developers' shareholders a dividend, the only cost would be construction. The councils would make a decent profit from the market-sale homes, which would pay for the social housing. Up to 65 per cent of the homes delivered could be social housing on some sites, according to RIBA's modelling.[31] This would be a one-off hit – public land would be exhausted eventually – but it would make a big dent in our housing crisis, and provide longer-term benefits than simply flogging the sites off to the highest bidders.

Even where public land is not involved, there are still ways to reform the system to produce better outcomes. People make money out of land by capitalising on its change of use. If you buy a site which is only allowed to be agriculture and gain planning permission for it to become residential, you can sell it at an enormous profit. This is how land speculators become wealthy.

Much of the land around London which sits in the area designated 'green belt' cannot be used for residential. If we are to house the population of London comfortably, we need to change that. Homes should be built in these areas, especially around railway stations where people can move out of the city and not be totally reliant on cars. If we change the law to allow new residential developments on these sites, as Starmer plans to, we will enrich the landowners at little public gain.

There is a huge opportunity to tax this unearned profit. We could mandate a certain level of affordable housing as a condition of the change of use – with no wiggle room for viability assessments. If builders knew they had to build a scheme with 50 per cent social housing, and the land would only ever be sold at a value which reflected this.

In many cities around the world this is precisely what happens. Whole areas are subject to zoning laws which mean new housing can only be developed if it meets thresholds for affordability. In Zurich, the local authority has set a target for subsidised housing to represent a third of the market. It provides land to community trusts and affordable housing providers at discounted rates to facilitate this. 'The quality of the accommodation is really high. It's fantastic. But when you look at what it costs people there, even in an expensive city, [the cost is] relatively low. And [the local authority] did this not with loads of cash but with land, which the city provided at the start,' David Ireland, chief executive of World Habitat, a group that works to share examples of successful housing policies from around the globe, told me in 2023.

A similar approach is taken in the Netherlands. 'In Amsterdam, the land for social housing will cost only one-tenth of the land for a private market flat,' explains Josta van Bockxmeer, a housing journalist at *De Correspondent*, a specialist publication. The land is sold by the city to the providers at a discount to allow affordable homes to be built.

And in Vienna – a global icon of social housing where 60 per cent of the population live in some degree of social housing and social developments have heated swimming pools and roof terraces – it is land again which is the key part of the puzzle. The city, with a population of two million, builds around 7,000 social housing units a year. Vienna has a land bank, Wohnfonds Wien, a body owned by the city authority that buys up land to build new neighbourhoods and dictates the amount of affordable housing that can be developed on it. The work is financed by a 1 per cent tax on all salaries in the city. Only 10 per cent of Austrians view housing costs as a major burden – the lowest percentage for any country in Europe.

Other European cities also show us how land can also be handed over directly to the community, rather than being sold to developers for the biggest possible profit. The community land trust (CLT) model involves a community group collectively buying a piece of land, and working together to develop housing on it. The ownership of the land is separated from the buildings, and the land is only ever owned by the trust. People buy homes at a discounted rate, or pay for them to be built, but they never own the land. The homes are resold at the same affordable rate they were bought for. 'This means the land cost is not shooting up in price. So you've stabilised the land price, and all you're doing is paying for the building itself – which means people can either afford to buy or build a house at a much lower price than they would in a private market,' explains Ireland.

Well structured, these models can allow slightly wealthier purchasers to pay a little more to fund subsidised rents for those who can't afford to. A community lives side by side in the development, with no landlord, no rapid house price growth or rental inflation and no gentrification. And it doesn't require vast sums of public money, just access to the land.

This might sound like a utopian pipe dream, but it isn't. Elsewhere in the world, CLTs are a much more mainstream proposition. There are thousands in the United States, where organisations such as the Champlain Housing Trust in Burlington, Vermont, houses around 20,000 people – none of them paying more than 30 per cent of their income for their home.

In Europe, one of the largest and most impressive recent examples is in Brussels, which was inspired directly by Burlington. 'Over ten years, they have developed a reasonably sized operation which has more than 1,000 residents,' says Ireland, who worked with the CLT in the early stages of its creation. 'They are providing homes for people on pretty low incomes, but ones who would fall through the gaps of the social housing system in Brussels.' The Brussels CLT mainly operates in Molenbeek, one of the poorest areas of the city, but one into which gentrification is slowly but steadily creeping. 'They have a lot of members now from the West African community, who would have got displaced, if it wasn't for what they've done,' says Ireland.

There is some history of this in London, and a movement which is trying to bring it back. Some of the most famous are those developed by Walter Segal, a pioneering architect and Jewish Hungarian refugee, who devised a means of turning old bombsites into community housing with an attractive and cheap timber-based house-building method. Two of his projects, Walters Way and Segal Close in Lewisham, are still thriving today, thirty years after they were completed.

Today, London has a CLT network which is small but growing. The story of the schemes built in recent years is genuinely hopeful. In Lewisham a community group which sprang up in 2014 to lobby for more affordable housing was able to pressure the council to commit to finding land for a community development. Campaigners literally walked the streets of the borough to make a list of potential sites. In March 2016, they were able to finally secure an abandoned garage site in Sydenham from the local authority. In 2019, they secured planning permission and in 2023, the development was finally completed.

Now, a small, smart block of flats provides eleven homes costing £272,500 for a two-bed and £215,000 for a one-bed, in a borough where the average property price is £520,000. 'Moving into the CLT has been completely transformative. Knowing that I'm part of a community, that I'm buying into something bigger than myself, rather than paying a landlord's mortgage, is great. It's also changed the way me and my partner have been able to think about our futures, our lives. We've never had such stability to rely on, to depend on, to have as a basis for our plans and dreams,' said Kes, one of the new residents, shortly after the scheme's completion.[32]

But achieving models like this at scale would mean taking on one of the most deeply vested interests in British politics – landowners. The Who Owns England project described land ownership in the UK as 'the most closely guarded secret in the thousand-year history of the country'. They found that almost half the land is owned by 1 per cent of the population: aristocrats and gentry own 30 per cent, oligarchs and bankers own 17 per cent. On top of this, a further 18 per cent is owned by corporations such as Land Securities. The compulsory purchases, zoning requirements and handovers to CLTs would be a direct threat to these interests.

And if we are to build new homes, we also need to make sure they are of good quality. It may be that technology helps here (building work on Britain's first 3D-printed housing development was due to start in Accrington as this book was being written), but it is dangerous to rely on this. The push towards factory-produced housing in the 2010s has now all but collapsed, despite enormous investment and political backing. It was plagued by the same quality issues that impact traditional house building – belying its promise of precision engineering.

But really, the problems here have been regulation, enforcement and economics. We can build a home so well insulated that opening and closing windows is all it takes to heat and cool it, and place solar panels on the roof which combine with battery storage to provide all its energy needs. But to do so, we need to challenge the model which focuses only on profits and cuts costs at every turn. Consumers need much stronger powers to hold developers to account if they are sold a shoddy home.

If politicians are not willing to take on these interests, there is something else they could do for London's housing crisis: leave. Despite its housing pressures, London continues to attract people from around Britain and the world because it is the country's capital of everything. It holds our financial district, our cultural hub, our political centre, the heart of our media establishment, our tech industry, our legal profession and many other areas of the economy. This creates employment opportunities not just in these industries, but in those which spring up due to the money spent by the people employed in them.

Other countries do not centralise their entire economy in one city in this way. In Switzerland, for example, the political centre is in Bern, the financial capital is in Zurich and Geneva is a hub for headquarters of international organisations. In Germany, the political capital is Berlin, the financial sector is based in Frankfurt and Munich is home to the country's powerful automobile and technology companies like BMW and Siemens, as well as being the hub of the country's life sciences. As a result, the pressure spreads across the country. But in the UK, almost everything centres on London.

The Houses of Parliament in Westminster need a refurbishment which will cost between £11 billion and £22 billion, and will almost certainly see MPs move out for a period of time. Why not send them to Leeds and leave them there, converting the venerable old buildings on the banks of the Thames into a museum of democracy? Were politicians to leave for Yorkshire, they would take an entire infrastructure of thinktanks, lobbyists and media with them. It may be that priorities in British politics would also shift, if politicians and opinion formers were regularly waiting for the TransPennine Express to get them into work.

REPAIR, REUSE

France, and Paris in particular, gets something of a bad rap for its social housing. Many people in the UK are familiar with the idea of *banlieues* – the large slab-style housing blocks on the outskirts of the city, synonymous with poverty, crime and riots. But while there is some truth in the idea that Paris failed to achieve what London did in the post-war decades, weaving social housing into the fabric of the city, it would be a big mistake to think the UK has nothing to learn from France when it comes to social housing.

In fact, France is probably one of the most progressive countries in the world when it comes to social housing provision. In 2000, the country implemented a law, *Solidarité et renouvellement urbain* (Solidarity and Urban Renewal), which requires each district in the country to rebalance its housing stock to ensure 25 per cent of the overall housing provision is social housing. Municipalities release land to a mixture of public and private companies to build this housing, and funding them is considered a major part of the country's social welfare system. Local administrations can face fines if they fail to meet their targets.

The country also brings private money into the system through the 'Livret A' – a financial service offered by French banks to regular savers, dating back to King Louis XVIII in 1818 to pay back debts incurred by the Napoleonic wars. It is essentially a savings account open to all French citizens, and the money saved is invested in publicly beneficial projects like social housing. It pays a modest, tax-free return and, as of September 2024, it had fifty-six million investors and €428.7 billion under investment. This bank provides loans of forty to fifty years in length, which means they can be paid back slowly and social housing can be built at low rents with relatively small direct grants from the state.

The result has been an extraordinary success. France has built approximately 1.8 million social housing units between 2001 and 2019 – an average of 100,000 per year.[33] This means there is enough social housing for it to be socially mixed. The French system of social housing involves four tiered levels of rent, catering for those on no income, low incomes, middle incomes and those who need extra care. Like Britain's old post-war estates, houses are inhabited by teachers, firefighters and train drivers, not only society's very poorest.

In recent years, there has been some regression, as President Emmanuel Macron has embraced a free market philosophy which is less friendly towards social housing, and the resurgent far right has weaponised the issue – claiming that the beneficiaries of social housing are immigrants, rather than society as a whole. Macron imposed cuts on the social housing sector in 2017 which directly mirrored George Osborne's policies in England. The political rhetoric regarding social housing has toughened. Recent elections involved discussions about limiting social housing to French citizens and a former Macron housing minister, Guillaume Kasbarian – known for his penchant for flat caps and a curly moustache he used to twirl during interviews – pushed for laws which made it much easier for people to be evicted, even for very small levels of rent arrears, and a change to the local targets to allow much more expensive 'intermediate rents' to count as social housing. The policies were described as 'a clear attack on social housing' and helped drive a wave of evictions in the build-up to the Paris Olympics.[34]

But the reality is that even within this changing political climate, social housing in France is in a far, far healthier state than it is in the UK. 'For us, it was seen as a crisis when the number of social homes built dropped to 92,000,' says Zoe Kenan, who works at the body which represents social landlords in France. The UK managed 34,000 in 2023/24 – just 9,500 of them at the low rents we would previously have described as social housing.

Having so much social housing creates a different challenge: how do you keep it in good condition? Just under two-thirds of the social housing in France was built before 1975, and the concrete tower blocks are starting to show their age, just as they are in London. In France we can find alternatives to the demolition-and-rebuild model we have all too frequently experienced in the UK. In fact, the French government has recently implemented a policy called Seconde Vie ('second life' in English), which is designed to encourage social housing providers to refurbish old buildings instead of demolishing them. The policy gives social housing providers fiscal incentives (reduced VAT and a temporary exemption from property tax for up to twenty-five years) for the refurbishment of buildings that are over forty years old, on the condition that the renovations give the building, at minimum, an additional forty years of life. The aim is to carry out 10,000 renovations a year.[35] This philosophy has led to some truly inspiring projects.

At first glance, the sixteen-storey Tour Bois le Prêtre looks like a classic example of urban gentrification. A large rectangular block, not far from the central ring road in northern Paris, it is clearly modern and high-end, with its glassy facade and large balconies, and stands out like a sore thumb in the midst of an ageing public housing estate. In fact, what this building represents is a model of hope for ageing social housing blocks around the world. The sixteen-storey tower was first built between 1959 and 1962, as part of the reconstruction of Paris after World War II, using slab concrete construction. By the early 2000s, like so many of these buildings, it was running into difficulties. The fabric of the building was decaying, it was getting cold in winter and social problems led to it being nicknamed 'Alcatraz'. In 2002, a nearby block, too close to the ring road to be comfortably habitable, was pulled down and it seemed this tower would suffer a similar fate.

But it did not. Instead, a contract was handed to the pioneering French architecture practice Lacaton & Vassal, who got to work on restoring the building. Their project utterly transformed it: the facade was re-formed to move the floorplates outwards, with conservatories and balconies added. Large windows were installed to let in more natural light. The conservatories were more than just an amenity: they provided a barrier between the outside and inside, making it less cold, which reduced the building's energy consumption by 50 per cent. It was an extraordinary and total transformation of the building, completed without moving residents out, without increasing rents and without the loss of a single home to demolition.

It also cost only €55,000 per unit, at a time when the French government was offering €167,000 per unit for demolition. And it was complete within two years, compared to the twenty years or more which demolition-and-rebuild projects soak up. The effect was described by one of the judges in an architecture competition as 'a clever and elegant solution' that is 'far from the usual cosmetic approach that fools no-one'.[36] More than a decade after the end of the refurbishment in 2013, the building remains a comfortable home to almost a hundred social housing households.

Anne Lacaton and Jean-Phillipe Vassal, the partners in the firm who carried out this refurbishment, have adopted this philosophy as the core of their architectural practice. Their attitude is to never demolish, but always to add, transform and reuse. They have repeated the work at several other social housing blocks around France, which would otherwise likely have been knocked down. The duo won the Pritzker Prize – effectively the Nobel Prize for architecture – in 2021. 'Demolishing is a decision of easiness and short term,' Lacaton told the *Guardian* after receiving the award. 'It is a waste of many things – a waste of energy, a waste of material, and a waste of history. Moreover, it has a very negative social impact. For us, it is an act of violence.'[37]

Even if we were to build a new generation of social and affordable housing in and around London, the reality is that the homes we have now will still be the homes most people are living in for the next 100 years or more. London therefore desperately needs a strategy for what to do to ensure these homes remain liveable, as they age and as the changing climate wreaks its havoc.

In a city as large as London, there will always be homes that need to be demolished. Some, like the 'large panel systems' buildings which are prone to collapse, are becoming increasingly dangerous over time. Asking people to keep living in these buildings because we are uncomfortable with the idea of demolition serves no one well. For buildings like this, the question is more about treating the residents equitably and ensuring their community is maintained during and after the demolition process.

But the truth is that buildings truly in this category are a fringe part of the overall number of social homes facing demolition. Instead, it is too often a lazy answer to housing that has fallen into decline, but could be given a new lease of life with refurbishment. The disruption, delay and cost associated with demolition, as well as the carbon emissions associated with new construction, mean demolition should be the absolute last resort.

'It is insane, from a straight-up scientific carbon point of view, to keep demolishing existing buildings because of the sheer amount of energy it takes to build anything new,' says Phineas Harper, the former chief executive of the charity Open City and former deputy director of the Architecture Foundation. 'The fact that we're just wasting buildings by building them, letting them fall apart, then knocking them down is not a serious way to treat the built environment during a climate emergency.

'But it's also insane because it takes so long for a community to mature, neighbours to make friends and for rituals and residents' associations to establish themselves. Every time you knock somewhere down, you destroy years of work developing community. So there's no wonder that these days, lots of people feel like they don't know their neighbours in London, and they feel socially isolated, because we're just constantly destroying our community.'

The philosophy of Lacaton & Vassal needs to become the twenty-first century's answer to ageing housing. Just as we now baulk at endlessly throwing away plastic bags, so we need to stop mindlessly destroying and rebuilding our housing when repair and reuse is available as an option. But achieving this would take strategy, finance and will.

One of the reasons why demolition has been favoured in the UK and elsewhere is its ability to attract private finance. If a housing developer thinks it is going to get its hands on prime real estate on which it can develop and sell as high-density housing, it is willing to contribute to the up-front cost of the demolition. Moving away from a demolition-based programme to refurbishment does raise a question about where the money will come from.

This question may not be as large as it first appears. The majority of estate demolition schemes involve direct government cash as well as private finance. If the cost savings of refurbishment compared to demolition that Lacaton & Vassal were projecting in Paris could be realised in schemes in London, then it may be that the government money which would have paid for demolition could simply be repurposed towards refurbishment.

A bigger problem might be know-how. The unique expertise of a firm of Pritzker Prize-winning architects will not be available to every council estate in the UK. Attempting to refurbish on a shoestring budget and getting it wrong can be catastrophic – as the Grenfell Tower refurbishment and the combustible cladding panels retrofitted to hundreds of other tower blocks around the country demonstrate. But this sort of knowledge does exist in this country. The Park Hill estate in Sheffield is a huge and famous 'streets in the sky' project, built out of brutalist concrete with balconies and walkways connecting its three blocks. It overlooks Sheffield city centre and has provided a backdrop to many films and TV shows. In 2002 it was falling into disrepair, but because of its architectural status it could not be demolished, and was put forward for retrofitting instead.

As a purely architectural intervention, the refurbishment that has taken place since has been a success. The project has been shortlisted for the prestigious Sterling Prize twice – once in 2013 for the first phase and once in 2024 for the second. The blocks, sold by the council to property developer Urban Splash, now feature larger windows, wooden flooring, colourful panels and glass lifts. 'The more we came, the more I fell in love with [the building],' one of the architects of the 2013 refurbishment told the BBC. 'The original architects really did a good job... It's the size of the rooms and the light, and the location.' Once written off as a troubled 'sink estate', Park Hill is now a desirable place to live.

The trouble is, the original residents didn't get to share in this success. They were evicted to make way for the refurbishment when the estates were sold by the council. Only a handful have been rehoused in the refurbished blocks. The rest have been scattered around Sheffield. Architecture writer Owen Hatherley has branded the scheme 'class cleansing'.

But this, as France shows us, does not need to be the case. The refurbishment can happen without the displacement. The idea that buildings should be seen as adaptable, that as they age and the world around them changes, they can be fixed up and repaired instead of bulldozed into the ground and transported to landfill, is increasingly gaining ground. Hundreds of architecture practices have signed up to the Retrofit First campaign led by the magazine *Architects' Journal* in recent years, and retrofitting has been increasingly recognised in architecture awards. A government consultation launched in September 2024 sought views from the profession on changing rules to prioritise retrofit over demolition.

As well as moving away from demolition-as-default for our ageing social housing, we also need to ensure social housing is kept in a decent condition on a day-to-day basis. While there is a long way to go in this regard, there are also some seeds of hope. In 2024, social housing providers in England spent more than they ever have in the past on routine maintenance – £8.8 billion.[38] New regulations as well as a recently revitalised housing ombudsman are forcing the managers of these homes to up their game on repairs, alongside the powerful resident campaigning from figures like Kwajo Tweneboa.

Financially at least, this is a problem which can be solved. Social housing rents should cover the cost of looking after the homes. In 2023/24, housing association tenants paid a collective £18.4 billion to their landlords in rent and service charges.[39] This money is more than enough to keep homes in decent condition, particularly given the fact that it is an income stream which can support long-term borrowing.

The trouble is that these rents fund all sorts of other things as well. They are the primary source of finance to build new social housing (or pay off the interest on the private loans we've taken out to do so). We use them to repair fire safety defects which have emerged since Grenfell, rather than mandate that those responsible pay. And we use them to fund decarbonisation schemes which – while utterly necessary – are part of a national objective to cut our carbon emissions, not the sole responsibility of the residents who live in social housing.

A sensible system of social housing should view rents as a mechanism for paying for the maintenance and management of the homes, and ringfence them for this purpose. In countries such as Denmark, social tenants pay 'cost-based rents' – rents which are set according to the cost of managing their home. These remain low enough for the poorest to afford. To make this work, new social housing and decarbonisation would have to be much more directly funded through central government investment (including through land release, as described above). If this was the case, the money tenants pay in rents each month could be targeted towards keeping our social housing stock in decent condition.

If we apply technology properly, the cost of keeping homes in a decent condition may also fall. I am intrinsically nervous of tech solutions to housing problems, but in basic maintenance, it is clear that a revolution is already underway. It is now common for drones to be used to assess properties and problems are assessed by video call before contractors are dispatched, and this may be the tip of the iceberg. Technology can allow regularly required checks which previously took a staff member a week to complete for a single building – like the functionality of self-closing devices on fire doors – to be monitored constantly on a single iPad. Smart ventilation systems can monitor humidity and extract moisture from the internal air if it gets too high, slashing the probability of damp and mould. In decades to come, nano robots will be deployed inside pipes to find and fix leaks – technology which is already being piloted in sewers. New solutions to keeping our housing stock in decent condition will become increasingly available. They just need to be implemented.

But repairs and maintenance will never truly be solved until we empower residents to fight back against neglectful landlords. We need tenants' associations to be given statutory rights and funding; legal aid should be reinstated and strong penalties enforced when homes are allowed to deteriorate into the terrible condition described earlier in this book. In a country as wealthy as ours, it is simply not right for people to live in the conditions residents have endured in recent years, and, as well as funding and technology, we also need accountability.

PUSH BACK

I'm not putting forward a manifesto here. I do not credit myself with the experience or originality of thought to bring truly new solutions to our problem of housing in the UK. Instead, the point I'm making is that it is simply obvious that other, better ways of doing things are possible, and already exist. It is natural, when things trend in a certain direction over a number of years, to believe in the inevitability of that continuation. We have arrived at the point of believing that the housing market is so dire, so unforgiving, that no better alternative exists. And that is not true.

With a new approach, the future of London could look very different. The challenges of a hotter world, an older population and all the other things the coming century will throw at us would still come. But as they did, people would have something the city currently does not offer: resilience, community and home.

So are any of these changes remotely realistic? On the one hand, the answer is yes. They are all things which are either being done elsewhere in the world or have been done before in Britain. They are not impossible. The obstacles would be political will and the options which our system of economics offers us.

There is no point offering false hope here. These obstacles are significant – changing the status quo brings much resistance, even when faced with the clearly failing current system. Our political ideology is wedded to land ownership and the promotion of home ownership as the only way out of the housing crisis. Our politicians see increased house building as a key tool to drive economic growth more than a way to genuinely meet housing needs. Any change which threatened the overall volume of homes built, or pushed money that would be used for new build towards refurbishment or municipalisation, would meet stiff political resistance.

Politicians from both major parties, encouraged by right-leaning thinktanks and property industry lobbyists, have come to believe that planning restrictions are the only barrier to the market solving our housing crisis by itself, based on a binary view of supply and demand that discounts the other factors which have made the housing crisis so severe. And so we remain firmly stuck to the broken, market-led approach which we adopted in the 1980s, even as almost unimaginable suffering proves it to be a mistake.

There is also the problem of economics. Investing in public housing in the way I've described above would require sensible state borrowing, which would be repaid over time. But this is no longer the way our government functions. This is not solely because of politicians, but the impact of international finance.

The UK is a country with a lot of debt, £2.8 trillion at the time of writing. And like anyone with a lot of debt, we are at the whim of our creditors. UK debts are held in 'bonds' which are bought and sold by investors and investment funds around the world. So we are reliant on the views of these investors, and the credit agencies which provide us with a national credit rating. If investors are less willing to buy our national bonds, they will offer a lower price. This means we have to offer them a better return to entice them to do so. This increase results in higher borrowing costs, which reverberate through the economy and translate directly into increased costs for individual mortgages. As a result, governments are terrified to do anything which might make us less attractive to the international money markets. Taking on lots of additional debt – even if we are clear about how to repay it – is the surest way to do this.

Therefore, even if we built a political movement that believed in major public housing investment, won elections and by-elections, and finally forced a shift in our domestic political ideology, we might still come unstuck due to this problem. When former prime minister Liz Truss decided to turn on the state's spending taps, both to offer relief on energy bills and to fund her enormous tax cuts, she found herself out of a job very quickly. This was not because these policies were unpopular, but because international investors were spooked by the increased level of borrowing she had committed to, and triggered an increase in the price of our national debt.

It resulted in increased borrowing rates for the government, which translated into increased mortgage and borrowing costs for everyday people, which translated into enough public anger to force her to resign within days.

It's easy for those on the left to laugh at this turn of events, but they shouldn't. What it tells us is that we are locked into a narrow economic pathway by the views of international money markets. A high-borrowing government – whether from the left or the right – would be threatened by this reality.

Even though the kind of borrowing I would like to see used to invest in a new generation of social housing is economically and socially responsible, if the investors who own our bonds didn't like it, the policy would fall apart in an instant. Even the small steps taken by Labour in its first Budget in 2024 caused wobbles when combined with broader fears about the impact of a Donald Trump presidency. An increase in the cost of government debt caused a mini-panic in January 2025. The government immediately responded by signalling it would borrow less and spend less to calm the nerves of investors. Our politicians do not have the freedom to make major public investments in the way they used to – even if they wanted to.

'One of the things politicians worry about is that gilt market investors will look at the gross amount of outstanding debt and that they will get spooked if that gets too high,' economist Ian Mulheirn told me in 2023. 'At the end of the day, international debt markets are a beauty parade, and if they look at you and think your government debt is consistently going up in an unsustainable manner, then the fear is that they're going to say, "No thanks."'

With all these forces stacked against change, I am not hopeful. My honest expectation is that we will merely continue to tinker at the edges of the housing crisis, as it continues to rip our communities and social fabric apart. Those who win will get richer. Those who lose face a century of increasing precarity, poverty and suffering as the intersecting crises caused by climate breakdown combine with their housing insecurity to leave them bereft.

But this fear mustn't stop us from trying. It is easy to forget when you are stuck inside the bowels of the city, but London is always changing and this change is within our control. Mostly, it has been for the better: a city wracked by disease and plague, with gutters swimming with shit, orphans roaming the streets and chronic rates of infant mortality has been confined to the past. Even in my lifetime, a lot of good has been done. London in the 1980s was not a utopia: it was an aching, broken and dirty city which needed to change. So yes, we still have housing pressures, but these have always been part of life here: inadequate, expensive and insufficient housing, and the struggle between newcomers and the existing population have been a feature of London's story from the medieval period onwards. In some ways, it was the post-war stability that came from high levels of social housing and strong regulation that was the exception.

If we lost that stability within one generation, perhaps it can be rebuilt by the next. We have been here before. My dad was born in 1944, when the city was hollowed out by the Blitz and still being subjected to V-2 bombing raids. It was a city of twisty little backstreets and tiny terraced houses, where whole families were packed into single rooms with outside toilets, no running water and livestock in the back gardens. By the time he was thirty-five, in 1979, an entire social democratic revolution had taken place – with more than a third of the city living in stable, secure and affordable social housing. We have a much stronger starting position now than the one the city was faced with at the end of World War II.

If we want this better future, we need to push for it. The left should pay attention to what was achieved in Spain, in particular. There, housing gave left-wing populism a voice and a connection with voters that saw it grow from a street movement to power in less than a decade. As the global left continues to struggle to find a populist voice, it should look more to housing. Where the populist right has its bogeymen of 'political elites' and immigrants, the populist left can define itself against the greedy property developers and landlords who are making people's lives miserable. Our anger about the cost of rent or mortgages, the lack of opportunities for our children and the destruction of our communities is very real and very powerful. And on housing, the left has better answers than the right. Bound by its economic ideology, the right can only call for lower immigration and lifting planning restrictions, but it will never support rent control or mass social housing.

These housing movements exist and they need fuel. The London Renters Union remains small compared to the number of tenants in the city, but it has made big strides in recent years. Other, similar groups under the 'ACORN' banner have popped up in other UK cities and are starting to build a movement of renters that can push for political change, as well as hold landlords to account. This is hard work – renters, by their nature, are tired, time poor, financially stretched and overworked – but it is driven by the unique determination of people who have had enough. The viral success of campaigners such as Kwajo Tweneboa shows the potential appetite for a housing campaign fronted by a talented communicator with an authentic voice. There is no reason to believe these movements will not get larger and more influential as the housing crisis gets worse – particularly given that Labour's relative feebleness on these issues will leave struggling renters feeling like they have no other choice. And even if the big changes we need prove too hard to achieve, there is much to be fought for on a smaller scale.

We need activists like those in Berlin and Louisville, and independently minded politicians willing to work with them to win as much change as the current system allows. We can find policy advisers and policy makers who work to produce creative, adaptable solutions that can at least be adopted locally or nudge the dial in the right direction. We can engage architects, like Lacaton & Vassal, who are willing to challenge the prevailing orthodoxy and prove that it can work. We can find community groups willing to walk through years of struggle to build a community land trust from the ground up and sustain it for the next generation. We can find housing professionals willing to roll up their sleeves and make the best of a difficult situation, and people and businesses in the built environment interested in creating communities rather than simply profits. And even when nothing else works, we can find people who set up charities, food banks, advice centres and support networks which help those struggling to survive.

We may not win the fight for a better city, or a more equitable housing market. But it is only in the struggle for one that such a future can be built. As the philosopher Slavoj Žižek writes, we live in a strange moment when multiple future possible worlds exist at once. 'Whichever form our present morass of possibilities collapses into, it will remain inscribed with all the ways it could have been different,' he says. On housing at least, we need to make those inscriptions, even if they ultimately stand only as reminders of the future we could have had. No one can see the future, but my hunch is that it will neither be completely dark, nor completely light. Instead it will be as the present is and the past was: shades of success and failure, victory and defeat, struggle and joy. Each new social home that is built, each eviction resisted and each homeless person supported into a stable home is a better outcome than we would have had without that effort. A future which is just a few shades brighter than it might otherwise have been is still one worth fighting for.

Acknowledgements

Any book is an act of collaboration more than an individual effort, so thank you first to the team who have made this one. Chiefly to Cecilia Stein at Oneworld, for working out how to turn my loose ideas into something like a workable book, and then for her typically smart, pointed and perceptive instructions throughout, especially after some shaky early attempts. Thanks also to Hannah Haseloff, Rida Vaquas and Jonathan Wadman for their excellent and diligent work on the manuscript – all of you left it in much better shape than you found it.

Thanks to John Boughton, Stuart Hodkinson and Paul Watt for reading early drafts. Thanks to the entire team at *Inside Housing*, on whose wider work I have once again leaned. Thanks to my agent Monica MacSwan for her great belief in the project, wise suggestions and support.

Thanks to the many experts who shared their time for interviews, especially those of you to whom I told my usual bare-faced lie that I would 'only take half an hour of your day'. I'm always amazed by people's generosity in sharing their knowledge, insight and personal libraries, and journalism of the sort I attempt would be impossible without people like you. Any mistakes or misunderstandings will, of course, be my own. A particular thanks to Newham Bookshop for help with the research – a true, surviving community institution.

Acknowledgements

Thank you – particularly – to all those who shared their personal stories with me. Listening to you all was a great privilege and I hope I have done justice to what you told me. So thanks to (deep breath) Pauline, Michael, Hannah, Andrew, Katy, Manju, Sharda, Derek, Meric, Dave, Carolyn, John, Peter, Jothi, Rosie, Patricia, Sean, Eli, Motiur, Dhillon, Lottie, Conall, Melanie, Chantelle, Baby, Gav, Wael, Sara, Edmund and Amanda. Those of you who I'm referring to by pseudonyms, please delete and replace with your real names in your minds. And those whose words I have used less of than expected, I am sorry. Cutting down is the hardest part of writing, and it is no reflection on the stories you told, but simply the balance of what better writers than me call 'narrative'.

Thanks to my sister, Lucy, who remains the better writer in the family and shared typically thoughtful and incisive comments throughout, as well as general encouragement. Your support remains invaluable (although I'm not going to put your name in bold here, as per your request). Thanks to my mum and dad for my existence, my interest in books and (particularly latterly and thematically) a house in which to write. Thanks to Samuel and Benjamin for being beautiful, joyful and silly in a world that is increasingly not. You remain my enduring reason to hope – against the mounting evidence – that there might indeed be a better future for us all.

And thanks – I suppose – to London, by which I really mean all the people within it who I have loved and who have made me who I am. There is nowhere else I will ever call home.

The Londoners

Andy – After growing up in Clapham, he moved to the Cressingham Gardens estate in Lambeth with his wife Ann.

Hannah – Born and raised with her mum on the Samuel Lewis estate in Hackney.

Andrew – The son of a postman, Andrew grew up on a council estate in Newham, east London.

Manju – A private tenant in a rent controlled flat in Kensington, west London.

Sharda – Daughter of Manju.

Dave – Came to London as a budding music journalist in the late 1970s.

Carolyn – Came to London as a budding actor in in the early 1970s

John – An east London school teacher, born in Clapton.

Su – Daughter of John.

The Londoners

Peter – Came to London as a graduate to work in Newham Council's housing department.

Jothi – Came to east London from Malaysia to work as a nurse.

Rosie – Daughter of Jothi.

Patricia – Born to Irish Catholic family in west London and grew up in Burnt Oak.

Sean – An Irish labourer who came to London in the 1980s.

Ruphina – A seamstress, secretary and child minder who moved to London from Dominica and settled in the east.

Eli – Son of Ruphina,

Dhillon – One of three brothers who spent their teenage years on the Robin Hood Gardens estate in east London.

Motiur – A neighbour of Dhillon on the Robin Hood Gardens estate.

Melanie – Grew up in social housing in west London and got a job working for a housing association.

Lottie – Moved to London from Kent and saved up to buy a flat.

Conall – Moved from Dublin to London to find work in the late 2010s.

Notes

Introduction

1 Newham Council, 'Regeneration Project: Canning Town and Custom House' [Online]. https://www.newham.gov.uk/regeneration-1/regeneration-project-canning-town-custom-house (accessed 5 March 2025).
2 Stewart, H., 'Whatever Jeremy Hunt thinks, £100k is by any measure a high income', *Guardian*, 24 March 2024 [Online]. https://www.theguardian.com/money/2024/mar/24/despite-what-jeremy-hunt-thinks-high-income-salary (accessed 5 March 2025).
3 'Unwind @ Canning Town Serviced Accommodation', Airbnb [Online]. https://www.airbnb.co.uk/rooms/822719207351843112 (accessed 8 March 2025).
4 de Botton, A., 'The idea of home', *Independent*, 7 June 2008 [Online]. https://www.independent.co.uk/arts-entertainment/books/features/where-the-heart-is-writers-invite-us-into-their-idea-of-home-841568.html (accessed 5 March 2025).
5 See for example Simmons, L., 'The "crisis of belonging" at the root of our political and social divides', *Stanford Business*, 22 November 2022 [Online]. https://www.gsb.stanford.edu/insights/crisis-belonging-root-political-social-divides (accessed 5 March 2025).
6 International Organisation for Migration, *World Migration Report 2024*, Chapter 2: 'Migration and Migrants: A Global Overview' [Online]. https://worldmigrationreport.iom.int/what-we-do/world-migration-report-2024-chapter-2/refugees-and-asylum-seekers (accessed 6 March 2025).
7 Simmons, 'The "crisis of belonging" at the root of our political and social divides'.
8 Göpffarth, J., 'Why did Heidegger emerge as the central philosopher of the far right?', openDemocracy, 23 June 2020 [Online]. https://www.opendemocracy.net/en/countering-radical-right/

why-did-heidegger-emerge-central-philosopher-far-right/ (accessed 6 March 2025).
9. Masterson, V., 'What has caused the global housing crisis – and how can we fix it?', World Economic Forum, 16 June 2022 [Online]. https://www.weforum.org/stories/2022/06/how-to-fix-global-housing-crisis/ (accessed 6 March 2025).

1980s

1. Porter, R., *London: A Social History*, 2nd edn (Penguin, 2000), p. 370.
2. Newham Monitoring Project, *Newham: The Forging of a Black Community* (Newham Monitoring Project/Campaign Against Racism and Fascism, 1991), p. 40.
3. *Hackney Gazette* interview quoted in O'Neill, G., *My East End: Memories of Life in Cockney London* (Penguin, 2000), p. 315.
4. Black, J., *A Brief History of London* (Postscript, 2022), p. 195.
5. From the transcript contained in the online archive of the Margaret Thatcher Foundation, 'Speech commencing construction of Broadgate', 31 July 1985 [Online]. https://www.margaretthatcher.org/document/106107 (accessed 6 March 2025).
6. Forshaw, A., *1980s London: Portrait of a Decade of Change* (Amberley, 2022), p. 60.
7. Office of Population Censuses and Surveys (OPCS): Census 1981, Great Britain.
8. Watt, P., *Estate Regeneration and Its Discontents: Public Housing, Place and Inequality in London* (Policy Press, 2021), p. 43.
9. Author interview.
10. Forrest, R. and Murie, A., *Selling the Welfare State: The Privatisation of Public Housing* (Routledge, 1988), p. 108.
11. See for example Boughton, J., *A History of Council Housing in 100 Estates* (RIBA Publishing, 2022), p. 102.
12. Hansard, HC Deb., 6 May 1981, vol. 4, cols 153–5.
13. Author interview with councillor Paul Dimoldenberg relating to Hermes and Chantry Point in Westminster.
14. Author interview.
15. 'Who Lives in Tower Hamlets? Where Do They Live?', Tower Hamlets Council, November 2012 [Online]. https://www.towerhamlets.gov.uk/Documents/One-TH/Communities-and-Housing-Evidence-Pack-FINAL.pdf (accessed 6 March 2025).

16 Transcript of interview between Margaret Thatcher and journalist Kenneth Harris, reproduced in the archive maintained by the Margaret Thatcher Foundation with the permission of the *Observer* newspaper. 'Interview for *Observer* (4th Anniversary as PM)', Margaret Thatcher Foundation, 11 April 1983 [Online]. https://www.margaretthatcher.org/document/105127 (accessed 6 March 2025).
17 Jones, C. and Murie, A., *The Right to Buy: Analysis and Evaluation of a Housing Policy* (Blackwell, 2006), p. 23.
18 Hansard, HC Deb., 15 January 1980, vol. 976, col. 1445.
19 Jones and Murie, *The Right to Buy*, p. 33.
20 Ministry of Housing, Communities and Local Government, Live Tables on Social Housing Sales series, Live Table 691.
21 Jones and Murie, *The Right to Buy*, p. 64.
22 'Average years in current home for social renters in England from 2010 to 2020', Statista [Online]. https://www.statista.com/statistics/786378/average-number-years-current-home-england/ (accessed 6 March 2025).
23 Jones and Murie, *The Right to Buy*, p. 86.
24 Ibid., p. 98.
25 Boughton, J., *Municipal Dreams: The Rise and Fall of Council Housing* (Verso, 2019), p. 214.
26 Ministry of Housing, Communities and Local Government, Live Tables on Housing Supply series, Live Table 244.
27 Hansard, HC Deb., vol. 980, col. 937, 10 March 1980.
28 McCabe, J., 'Thatcher's secrets', *Inside Housing*, 4 April 2014 [Online]. https://www.insidehousing.co.uk/insight/thatchers-secrets-39472 (accessed 6 March 2025).
29 Ibid.
30 Porter, *London: A Social History*, p. 367.
31 Watt, *Estate Regeneration and Its Discontents*, p. 45.
32 'Private finance in the social housing sector: how we got here', Housing Finance Corporation, 16 September 2022 [Online]. https://www.thfcorp.com/insight/private-finance-in-the-social-housing-sector-how-we-got-here/ (accessed 6 March 2025).
33 Partridge, S. and others, 'Shared ownership: a key piece in the housing puzzle', Savills UK, 26 June 2024 [Online], https://www.savills.co.uk/research_articles/229130/363354-0 (accessed 6 March 2025).

34 'Housing tenure over time', Trust for London, December 2024 [Online]. https://trustforlondon.org.uk/data/housing-tenure-over-time/ (accessed 6 March 2025).

35 Conservative Political Centre, *The Eclipse of the Private Landlord: A Study of the Consequences* (Conservative Political Centre, 1974).

36 Bano, N., 'Thatcher's landlords: rise and fall', *Legal Form* (blog), 21 December 2020 [Online]. https://legalform.blog/2020/12/21/thatchers-landlords-rise-and-fall-nick-bano/ (accessed 6 March 2025).

37 Hansard, HC Deb., vol. 123, col. 620, 30 November 1987.

38 Hansard, HC Deb., vol. 133, col. 35, 9 May 1988.

39 Delahunty, S., 'The housing act from 1988 that shaped the sector today', *Inside Housing*, 13 January 2025 [Online]. https://www.insidehousing.co.uk/insight/the-housing-act-from-1988-that-shaped-the-sector-today-89675 (accessed 6 March 2025).

40 'House Price Statistics', UK House Price Index [Online]. https://landregistry.data.gov.uk/app/ukhpi/browse?from=1977-06-01&location=http%3A%2F%2Flandregistry.data.gov.uk%2Fid%2Fregion%2Flondon&to=2018-06-01&lang=en (accessed 6 March 2025).

41 Author interview.

42 Ryan-Collins, J., *Why Can't You Afford a Home?* (Polity, 2018), p. 47.

43 'House Prices in Brock Road, Plaistow, East London, E13', Rightmove [Online]. https://www.rightmove.co.uk/house-prices/e13/brock-road.html (accessed 6 March 2025).

44 'New Earnings Survey (NES) – Age Group Gross Weekly and Hourly Excluding Overtime Data', Office for National Statistics, 21 March 2017 [Online]. https://www.ons.gov.uk/employmentandlabourmarket/peopleinwork/earningsandworkinghours/adhocs/006810newearningssurveynesagegroupgrossweeklyandhourlyexcludingovertimedata (accessed 6 March 2025).

45 Boléat, M., 'The 1985 to 1993 Housing Market in the United Kingdom: An Overview', *Housing Policy Debate*, 5.3 (1994), pp. 253–74, doi:10.1080/10511482.1994.9521165.

1990s

1 Office of Population Censuses and Surveys (OPCS): 1991 and 2001 Census aggregate data. UK Data Service.

2 Jowett, S., *Health and Wellbeing in the 1990s: A Study of Young People's Attitudes and Behaviours in the London Borough of Newham*, National

Foundation for Educational Research, January 1995 [Online]. https://www.nfer.ac.uk/media/y5nczu5j/91094summary.pdf (accessed 6 March 2025).

3 Author interviews with adults who recall attending the trips as children from schools in Hertfordshire.

4 MacInnes, T. and Kenway, P., *London's Poverty Profile*, New Policy Institute, 2009 [Online]. https://tfl.ams3.cdn.digitaloceanspaces.com/media/documents/LondonPovertyProfilefull.pdf (accessed 6 March 2025).

5 Ibid.

6 Jeraj, S., 'The legacy of Cardboard City, and Britain's grim renaissance of homeless encampments', *New Statesman*, 18 February 2020 [Online]. https://www.newstatesman.com/long-reads/2020/02/legacy-cardboard-city-bullring-britain-grim-renaissance-homeless-encampments-tent-cities (accessed 6 March 2025).

7 Gordon, D. and Pantazis, C., *Breadline Britain in the 1990s* (Summerleaze, 1997), p. 7.

8 Anderson, H. R. and others, '50 Years of Asthma: UK Trends from 1995 to 2004', *Thorax* 62.1 (2007), pp. 85–90, doi:10.1136/thx.2006.066407.

9 Anderson, H. R. and others, 'Health Effects of an Air Pollution Episode in London, December 1991', *Thorax* 50.11 (1995), pp. 1188–93, doi:10.1136/thx.50.11.1188.

10 Ritchie, H., 'What the history of London's air pollution can tell us about the future of today's growing megacities', Our World in Data, 20 June 2017 [Online]. https://ourworldindata.org/london-air-pollution (accessed 6 March 2025).

11 'Jubilee line raises property value by estimated £2.1bn at Canary Wharf and Southwark Tube stations', Transport for London, 7 June 2005 [Online]. https://tfl.gov.uk/info-for/media/press-releases/2005/june/jubilee-line-raises-property-value-by-estimated-andpound21bn-at-canary-wharf-and-southwark-tube-stations (accessed 7 March 2025).

12 Wilcox, S. (ed.), *UK Housing Review 2004/5*, University of York Centre for Housing Policy, October 2004.

13 Moody, G., *Council Housing: Financing the Future* (Chartered Institute of Housing, 1998).

14 See for example the Cambridge Road redevelopment in Waltham Forest, as described at 'Cambridge Road Redevelopment Area',

University of Edinburgh [Online]. https://www.towerblock.eca.ed.ac.uk/development/cambridge-road-redevelopment-area (accessed 4 April 2025).
15. Council papers accessed through Newham archive.
16. 'Kerrin Point blast: Lambeth to plead guilty', *News Shopper*, 28 November 1998 [Online]. https://www.newsshopper.co.uk/news/6490020.kerrin-point-blast-lambeth-to-plead-guilty/ (accessed 7 March 2025).
17. Hollamby, E., 'Cressingham Gardens', Architectuul [Online]. https://architectuul.com/architecture/cressingham-gardens (accessed 7 March 2025).
18. Birch, J., 'Taking the strain', *Inside Housing*, 30 January 2012 [Online]. https://www.insidehousing.co.uk/comment/taking-the-strain2-30333 (accessed 7 March 2025).
19. 'A brief history of buy-to-let', Paragon, 19 October 2021 [Online]. https://www.paragonbankinggroup.co.uk/news/insights/a-brief-history-of-buy-to-let (accessed 7 March 2025).
20. Stephens, M. and others, *UK Housing Review 2024* (Chartered Institute of Housing, 2024).
21. Boléat, M., 'The 1985–1993 Housing Market in the United Kingdom: An Overview', *Housing Policy Debate*, 5.3 (1994), pp. 253–74, doi:10.1080/10511482.1994.9521165.
22. Ibid.
23. Ibid.
24. Interview with author, 29 February 2024.
25. Ryan-Collins, J., *The Demand for Housing as an Investment: Drivers, Outcomes and Policy Interventions to Enhance Housing Affordability in the UK*, UCL Institute for Innovation and Public Purpose, October 2024 [Online]. https://www.ucl.ac.uk/bartlett/public-purpose/sites/bartlett_public_purpose/files/241009_iipp_policy_report_ukhousing_layout2.pdf (accessed 7 March 2025).
26. 'Blair's speech: single mothers won't be forced to take work', *Politics 97*, BBC [Online]. https://www.bbc.co.uk/news/special/politics97/news/06/0602/blair.shtml (accessed 7 March 2025).

2000s

1. Weaver, M., 'Livingstone's towering legacy', *Guardian*, 19 February 2008 [Online]. https://www.theguardian.com/politics/2008/feb/18/london08.london1 (accessed 7 March 2025).

2 'The Wet Autumn of 2000', Met Office, 6 November 2012 [Online]. https://www.metoffice.gov.uk/binaries/content/assets/metofficegovuk/pdf/weather/learn-about/uk-past-events/interesting/2000/the-wet-autumn-of-2000---met-office.pdf (accessed 7 March 2025).
3 'Freak storm batters south London', BBC News, 3 July 2007 [Online]. http://news.bbc.co.uk/1/hi/england/london/6267234.stm (accessed 31 March 2025)
4 'For a Rainy Day: The Mayor's Role in Managing London's Flood Risk in the Case of Severe Rainfall', London Assembly Environment Committee, July 2011 [Online]. https://www.london.gov.uk/media/77059/download (accessed 31 March 2025)
5 'People in poverty over time after housing costs (1996/97–2022/23)', Trust for London, May 2024 [Online]. https://trustforlondon.org.uk/data/poverty-over-time/ (accessed 7 March 2025).
6 Easton, M., 'Why have the white British left London?', BBC News, 20 February 2013 [Online]. https://www.bbc.co.uk/news/uk-21511904 (accessed 7 March 2025).
7 Ibid.
8 House of Commons, Committee of Public Accounts, *The Decent Homes Programme: Twenty-first Report of Session 2009–10*, HC 350, 18 March 2010 [Online]. https://publications.parliament.uk/pa/cm200910/cmselect/cmpubacc/350/350.pdf (accessed 7 March 2025).
9 'Planned maintenance works programme', Hackney Council, 26 February 2024 [Online]. https://hackney.gov.uk/planned-works (accessed 7 March 2025).
10 Hodkinson, S., *Safe as Houses: Private Greed, Political Negligence and Housing Policy after Grenfell* (Manchester University Press, 2019).
11 Memoli, M., *Investigation report on long-standing complaints of the Kensington and Chelsea TMO*, Local Governance Ltd (April 2009).
12 Author interview.
13 Author interview.
14 Greenhalgh, S. and Moss, J., *Principles for Social Housing Reform*, Localis, 2009 [Online]. https://www.localis.org.uk/wp-content/uploads/2009/04/localis-principles-for-social-housing-reform-web.pdf (accessed 7 March 2025).

15 'The Pepys Estate, Deptford: "a Tale of Two Cities"', *Municipal Dreams* (blog), 18 August 2015 [Online]. https://municipaldreams.wordpress.com/2015/08/18/a_tale_of_two_cities/ (accessed 7 March 2025).
16 Apps, P., 'A guide to the history of council housing in 100 estates', *Inside Housing*, 28 November 2022 [Online]. https://www.insidehousing.co.uk/insight/a-guide-to-the-history-of-council-housing-in-100-estates-78966 (accessed 7 March 2025).
17 Apps, P., '"They have swapped one unsafe building for another": the story of Kennington Park Square', *Inside Housing*, 10 June 2021 [Online]. https://www.insidehousing.co.uk/insight/they-have-swapped-one-unsafe-building-for-another-the-story-of-kennington-park-square-70965 (accessed 7 March 2025).
18 John, P., 'Cameron has much to learn on housing', *Progress*, 14 January 2016 [Online via Web Archive]. https://web.archive.org/web/20160503113339/https://progressonline.org.uk/2016/01/14/camerons-has-much-to-learn-on-housing/ (accessed 7 March 2025).
19 Bloomfield, R., 'Has the regeneration of Elephant and Castle been a success?', *Spectator*, 28 June 2023 [Online]. https://www.spectator.co.uk/article/has-the-regeneration-of-elephant-and-castle-been-a-success/ (accessed 7 March 2025).
20 'The Heygate Diaspora', 35% Campaign, 2022 [Online]. https://www.35percent.org/heygatepages/diaspora/ (accessed 10 March 2025).
21 *English House Condition Survey: 2001*, Office of the Deputy Prime Minister, December 2003 [Online]. https://doc.ukdataservice.ac.uk/doc/8004/mrdoc/pdf/2001/8004_private_landlords_survey_report_2001.pdf (accessed 7 March 2025).
22 Bano, N., *Against Landlords: How to Solve the Housing Crisis* (Verso, 2024), p. 74.
23 Scanlon, K. and Whitehead, C., *The Profile of UK Private Landlords*, Council of Mortgage Lenders, December 2016 [Online]. https://www.lse.ac.uk/business/consulting/assets/documents/The-Profile-of-UK-Private-Landlords.pdf (accessed 7 March 2025).
24 Hobson, F., 'Local Housing Allowance (LHA): Help with Rent for Private Tenants', House of Commons Library, 21 December 2023 [Online]. https://researchbriefings.files.parliament.uk/documents/SN04957/SN04957.pdf (accessed 7 March 2025).

25 'Everything you need to know about investing in a HMO', Shawbrook [Online]. https://www.shawbrook.co.uk/property-finance/insights-hub/insights/everything-you-need-to-know-about-investing-in-a-hmo/ (accessed 7 March 2025).
26 'History of Flat Conversions in London', London Flats & Apartments [Online]. https://www.londonflatsandapartments.com/history-of-flat-conversions-in-london/ (accessed 31 March 2025).
27 'UK Housing Review 2017', Chartered Institute of Housing, Table 95a [Online]. https://www.ukhousingreview.org.uk/ukhr17/compendium.html (accessed 6 March 2025).
28 McGreevy, R., 'End of an era for Irish in London as iconic Galtymore dance hall to close its doors', *Irish Times*, 28 April 2008 [Online]. https://www.irishtimes.com/news/end-of-an-era-for-irish-in-london-as-iconic-galtymore-dance-hall-to-close-its-doors-1.917589 (accessed 7 March 2025).
29 Office for National Statistics, 'Ratio of House Prices to Earnings, Borough', London Datastore [Online]. https://data.london.gov.uk/dataset/ratio-house-prices-earnings-borough (accessed 7 March 2025).
30 Ryan-Collins, J., *Why Can't You Afford a Home?* (Polity, 2018), p. 37.
31 *Britain's Housing Crisis: What Went Wrong?*, Episode 1, BBC 2, 17 October 2023 [Online]. Available at https://www.bbc.co.uk/iplayer/episodes/m001rkn5/britains-housing-crisis-what-went-wrong (accessed 7 March 2025).
32 Weaver, M., 'Government urged to keep home ownership scheme simple', *Guardian*, 23 June 2005 [Online]. https://www.theguardian.com/society/2005/jun/23/housingdemand.politics (accessed 7 March 2025).
33 'Just in time for the crash', *The Economist*, 27 January 2005 [Online]. https://www.economist.com/britain/2005/01/27/just-in-time-for-the-crash (accessed 7 March 2025).
34 Searle, R., *History of the Housing Crisis* (Rowman & Littlefield, 2022), p. 87.
35 Colenutt, B., *The Property Lobby: The Hidden Reality behind the Housing Crisis* (Policy Press, 2020), p. 57.
36 Ibid.
37 London Datastore, 'Dwellings by Property Build Period and Type, LSOA and MSOA', Valuations Office Agency [Online]. https://

data.london.gov.uk/dataset/property-build-period-lsoa (accessed 31 March 2025).
38 Bar-Hillel, M., 'Persimmon cheated flat-buyers', *Standard*, 13 April 2012 [Online]. https://www.standard.co.uk/hp/front/persimmon-cheated-flatbuyers-6967189.html (accessed 10 March 2025).
39 Haurant, S., 'Repossessions up 68% in 2008', *Guardian*, 17 March 2009 [Online]. https://www.theguardian.com/money/2009/mar/17/fsa-respossessions-arrears-rise (accessed 10 March 2025).
40 Story, C., 'Brown finds £2.1bn to build social housing', *Inside Housing*, 29 June 2009 [Online]. https://www.insidehousing.co.uk/news/brown-finds-21bn-to-build-social-housing-16015 (accessed 10 March 2025).

2010s

1 'London borough budgets fall a fifth in eight years, with inner London hardest hit', Centre for London, 13 May 2019 [Online]. https://centreforlondon.org/news/london-borough-budgets-fall-fifth-eight-years/ (accessed 10 March 2025).
2 'Austerity in London's local authorities', London Assembly [Online]. https://www.london.gov.uk/who-we-are/what-london-assembly-does/questions-mayor/find-an-answer/austerity-londons-local-authorities (accessed 10 March 2025).
3 'London's parks "could become inaccessible to the public"', BBC News, 21 June 2015 [Online]. https://www.bbc.co.uk/news/uk-england-london-33205239 (accessed 10 March 2025).
4 Stop School Cuts [Online]. https://schoolcuts.org.uk/schools/?coords=51.567911038571026%2C-0.02748046141425098&zoom=15 (accessed 10 March 2025).
5 'Libraries lose a quarter of staff as hundreds close', BBC News, 29 March 2016, https://www.bbc.co.uk/news/uk-england-35707956 (accessed 10 March 2025).
6 'MPS budget cuts', London Assembly [Online]. https://www.london.gov.uk/who-we-are/what-london-assembly-does/questions-mayor/find-an-answer/mps-budget-cuts-1 (accessed 10 March 2025).
7 Lister, J., 'Funding needed sooner not later: London mental health cuts', *Lowdown*, 15 September 2024 [Online]. https://lowdownnhs.info/mental-health/funding-needed-sooner-not-later-london-mental-health-cuts/ (accessed 10 March 2025).

8 Charles, S., 'London's coffee scene is booming – but can it afford it?', *Coffee Intelligence*, 25 September 2024 [Online]. https://intelligence.coffee/2024/09/londons-coffee-scene-is-booming (accessed 10 March 2025).

9 'Shocking data reveals number of pubs in London fell by 25% since 2001', Mayor of London, 19 April 2017 [Online]. https://www.london.gov.uk/press-releases/mayoral/number-of-pubs-in-london-fell-by-25-since-2001 (accessed 10 March 2025).

10 Press Association, 'Teenager sentenced to 18 years over fatal stabbing at Westfield Stratford', *Guardian*, 7 April 2014 [Online]. https://www.theguardian.com/uk-news/2014/apr/07/teenager-stabbing-westfield-stratford-kojo-smith-woodards (accessed 10 March 2025).

11 Author interview.

12 Author interview.

13 Colenutt, B., *The Property Lobby: The Hidden Reality behind the Housing Crisis* (Policy Press, 2020), p. 108.

14 Foye, C. and Shepherd, E., 'Why Have the Volume Housebuilders Been So Profitable?', UK Collaborative Centre for Housing Evidence, September 2023 [Online]. https://housingevidence.ac.uk/wp-content/uploads/2024/01/CaCHE-housebuilding-report-v9-25.09.pdf (accessed 10 March 2025).

15 Wainwright, O., 'Revealed: how developers exploit flawed planning system to minimise affordable housing', *Guardian*, 25 June 2015 [Online]. https://www.theguardian.com/cities/2015/jun/25/london-developers-viability-planning-affordable-social-housing-regeneration-oliver-wainwright (accessed 10 March 2025).

16 *Faulty Towers: Understanding the Impact of Overseas Corruption on the London Property Market*, Transparency International UK, March 2017 [Online]. Available at https://tfl.ams3.cdn.digitaloceanspaces.com/media/documents/TIUK_Faulty_Towers_Web.pdf (accessed 10 March 2025).

17 Ibid.

18 Ibid.

19 Hammond, G., 'Help to Buy has pushed up house prices in England says report', *Financial Times*, 10 January 2022 [Online]. https://www.ft.com/content/19236eef-abed-4401-a6b1-25c1035ab095 (accessed 31 March 2025).

20 Carozzi, F., Hilber, C. and Yu, X., 'On the Economic Impacts of Mortgage Credit Expansion Policies: Evidence from Help to Buy',

Centre for Economic Performance, March 2020 [Online]. https://cep.lse.ac.uk/pubs/download/dp1681.pdf (accessed 10 March 2025).
21. *Britain's Housing Crisis: What Went Wrong?*, Episode 1, BBC 2, 17 October 2023 [Online]. Available at https://www.bbc.co.uk/iplayer/episodes/m001rkn5/britains-housing-crisis-what-went-wrong (accessed 7 March 2025).
22. Foye and Shepherd, 'Why Have the Volume Housebuilders Been So Profitable?'.
23. Berkeley Group, Annual Reports and Accounts, 2010 to 2019. https://www.berkeleygroup.co.uk/investors/annual-report (accessed 11 June 2025).
24. 'The Changing Shape of the UK Mortgage Market: Emerging Themes', UK Finance, December 2019 [Online]. https://www.ukfinance.org.uk/system/files/The-changing-shape-of-the-UK-mortgage-market-FINAL-ONLINE-Jan-2020.pdf (accessed 10 March 2025).
25. Hill, D., 'London's booming: how the city's population surged past its post-war peak', *Guardian*, 9 January 2015 [Online]. https://www.theguardian.com/cities/2015/jan/09/london-booming-population-growth-success-challenges (accessed 31 March 2025).
26. 'Housing in London 2014', Greater London Authority, April 2014 [Online]. https://www.london.gov.uk/sites/default/files/housing_in_london_2014_-_final.pdf (accessed 31 March 2025).
27. Author interview.
28. 'No "Kosovo-style cleansing" of poor says Johnson', BBC News, 28 October 2010 [Online]. https://www.bbc.co.uk/news/uk-england-london-11642662 (accessed 10 March 2025).
29. 'Temporary accommodation types in London (2002–2024 Q2)', Trust for London [Online]. https://trustforlondon.org.uk/data/temporary-accommodation-over-time/ (accessed 10 March 2025).
30. Spurr, H., 'Clegg: Tories blocked social housing as it produced Labour votes', *Inside Housing*, 26 February 2016 [Online]. https://www.insidehousing.co.uk/news/clegg-tories-blocked-social-housing-as-it-produced-labour-votes-46324 (accessed 10 March 2025).
31. 'Affordable Housing Statistics: AHP Conversions', Mayor of London [Online]. https://www.london.gov.uk/programmes-strategies/housing-and-land/increasing-housing-supply/affordable-housing-statistics#ahp-conversions-26632-title (accessed 10 March 2025).

32 Apps, P., 'The fall and rise of social rent', *Inside Housing*, 13 July 2018 [Online]. https://www.insidehousing.co.uk/insight/insight/the-fall-and-rise-of-social-rent-57184 (accessed 10 March 2025).

33 *London Borough of Islington & Ors v The Mayor of London* [2014] EWHC 751 (Admin) [Online]. https://www.bailii.org/ew/cases/EWHC/Admin/2014/751.html (accessed 10 March 2025).

34 Robertson, G., 'Death of a watchdog', *Inside Housing*, 25 June 2010 [Online]. https://insidehousing.co.uk/insight/death-of-a-watchdog-20572 (accessed 10 March 2025).

35 Apps, P., 'Three landlords plan sector's biggest ever merger', *Inside Housing*, 6 April 2016 [Online]. https://www.insidehousing.co.uk/news/three-landlords-plan-sectors-biggest-ever-merger-46671 (accessed 10 March 2025).

36 Small, J., 'Housing Revenue Account financial pressures', London Councils, 15 December 2023 [Online]. https://archive.londoncouncils.gov.uk/members-area/member-briefings/housing-and-planning/housing-revenue-account-financial-pressures (accessed 10 March 2025).

37 Barnes, S., 'Less than half of RTB replacements are for social rent', *Inside Housing*, 26 May 2017 [Online]. https://www.insidehousing.co.uk/news/less-than-half-of-rtb-replacements-are-for-social-rent-49138 (accessed 11 March 2025).

38 Copley, T., 'Right to Buy, Wrong for London', London Assembly Labour, January 2019 [Online]. https://www.london.gov.uk/sites/default/files/rtb_report_feb_update.pdf (accessed 11 March 2025).

39 'Peter John', Terrapin Group [Online]. https://www.terrapingroup.co.uk/ourPeople/17 (accessed 11 March 2025).

40 Watt, P., *Estate Regeneration and Its Discontents: Public Housing, Place and Inequality in London* (Policy Press, 2021), p. 172.

41 'Woodberry Down', Berkeley Group [Online]. https://www.berkeleygroup.co.uk/developments/london/finsbury-park/woodberry-down (accessed 11 March 2025).

42 'Knock It Down or Do It Up? The Challenge of Estate Regeneration', Greater London Authority, February 2015 [Online]. https://www.london.gov.uk/sites/default/files/gla_migrate_files_destination/KnockItDownOrDoItUp_0.pdf (accessed 11 March 2025).

43 'A perfect storm of disadvantage: the history of Grenfell Tower', *i*, 26 July 2017 [Online]. https://inews.co.uk/news/

perfect-storm-disadvantage-history-grenfell-tower-80807 (accessed 11 March 2025).

Social housing

1. Butt, M., 'Girl suffering kidney failure forced to live without heating or hot water while awaiting transplant', *Independent*, 10 January 2024 [Online]. https://www.independent.co.uk/news/uk/home-news/kidney-transplant-girl-dialysis-southwark-b2475762.html (accessed 11 March 2025). This account is a description of the story as at January 2024. Southwark did fix the boiler following media coverage
2. Hewitt, D., 'Britain's housing shame: a story of shocking conditions and tenants' despair at a lack of action', ITV News, 12 September 2021 [Online]. https://www.itv.com/news/2021-09-12/britains-housing-shame-shocking-conditions-and-despair-at-a-lack-of-action (accessed 11 March 2025).
3. Hewitt, D., 'Collapsed ceilings, mice and mould: appalling conditions uncovered on housing estate of 500 homes', ITV News, 16 June 2021 [Online]. https://www.itv.com/news/2021-06-16/collapsed-ceilings-mice-and-mould-appalling-conditions-uncovered-across-an-entire-housing-estate-of-nearly-500-homes (accessed 11 March 2025).
4. Barker, N., 'The story of a neglected block', *Inside Housing*, 16 January 2020 [Online]. https://www.insidehousing.co.uk/insight/insight/the-story-of-a-neglected-block-64668 (accessed 11 March 2025).
5. English Housing Survey 2022/23, Annex Table 4.7 [Online]. https://www.gov.uk/government/statistics/annex-tables-for-english-housing-survey-headline-report-2022-to-2023 (accessed 11 March 2025).
6. Regulator of Social Housing, 'Four social landlords fail to meet RSH's standards', gov.uk, 9 August 2024 [Online]. https://www.gov.uk/government/news/four-social-landlords-fail-to-meet-rshs-standards (accessed 11 March 2025).
7. English Housing Survey 2022/23, Annex Table 4.7.
8. 'Housing Revenue Account financial pressures', London Councils, 15 December 2023 [Online]. https://www.londoncouncils.gov.uk/newsroom/2023/housing-revenue-account-financial-pressures (accessed 11 March 2025).
9. Delahunty, S., 'Lambeth Council ordered to pay out £13,000 after six severe maladministration findings', *Inside Housing*, 30

November 2023 [Online]. https://www.insidehousing.co.uk/news/lambeth-council-ordered-to-pay-out-13000-after-six-severe-maladministration-findings-84155 (accessed 11 March 2025).

10 Delahunty, S., 'Dead for two years: how Peabody missed the death of a tenant', *Inside Housing*, 24 August 2022 [Online]. https://www.insidehousing.co.uk/insight/dead-for-two-years-how-peabody-missed-the-death-of-a-tenant-76932 (accessed 11 March 2025).

11 Delahunty, S., 'Large patch sizes at Peabody contributed to failure that allowed resident's dead body to lie undiscovered for nearly two years', *Inside Housing*, 22 July 2022 [Online]. https://www.insidehousing.co.uk/news/large-patch-sizes-at-peabody-contributed-to-failure-that-allowed-residents-dead-body-to-lie-undiscovered-for-nearly-two-years-76620 (accessed 11 March 2025).

12 Jayanetti, C., 'Affordable rent costs double the equivalent social rent in parts of England', *Inside Housing*, 20 April 2023, https://www.insidehousing.co.uk/news/affordable-rent-costs-double-the-equivalent-social-rent-in-parts-of-england-81195 (accessed 11 March 2025).

13 'Housing Association Service Charge Issues and Impact: Initial Findings', Social Housing Action Campaign, January 2023 [Online]. https://shaction.org/wp-content/uploads/2023/01/SHAC-Initial-Findings-on-Housing-Association-Service-Charges-January-2023.pdf (accessed 11 March 2025).

14 'Housing in London 2023', Greater London Authority, October 2023 [Online]. https://www.london.gov.uk/sites/default/files/2023-10/Housing%20in%20London%202023.pdf (accessed 11 March 2025).

15 Geraghty, L., 'UK housing crisis is so bad that some people waiting 55 years for a social home: "We need change"', *Big Issue*, 21 April 2024 [Online]. https://www.bigissue.com/news/housing/social-housing-crisis-london-england-waiting-list/ (accessed 11 March 2025).

16 Swindells, K., 'On the waiting list: why the UK needs to Build Social', 10 October 2023 [Online]. https://www.insidehousing.co.uk/insight/on-the-waiting-list-why-the-uk-needs-to-build-social-82966 (accessed 11 March 2025).

17 'Housing in London 2024', Greater London Authority, November 2024, p. 56 [Online]. https://data.london.gov.uk/housing/housing-in-london/ (accessed 11 March 2025).

18 Swindells, 'On the waiting list'.

19 'London's housing crisis "threatens to break boroughs" amid £700m funding shortfall', London Councils, 12 September 2024 [Online]. https://www.londoncouncils.gov.uk/news-and-press-releases/2024/londons-housing-crisis-threatens-break-borough-budgets-amid-ps700m (accessed 31 March 2025).

20 'Housing in London 2024', Greater, London Authority, p. 22.

21 Delahunty, S., 'Exclusive: end of convergence and rent caps risks making 300,000 social homes financially unsustainable', *Inside Housing*, 13 May 2024 [Online]. https://www.insidehousing.co.uk/news/news/exclusive-end-of-convergence-and-rent-caps-risks-making-300000-social-homes-financially-unsustainable-86462 (accessed 11 March 2025).

22 Riding, J., 'For-profit providers address concern highlighted by NHF over "wholesale privatisation" of sector idea', *Inside Housing*, 21 January 2025 [Online]. https://www.insidehousing.co.uk/news/for-profit-providers-address-concern-highlighted-by-nhf-over-wholesale-privatisation-of-sector-idea-90146 (accessed 11 March 2025).

23 Riding, J., 'For profit provider recruits new stock acquisition boss from Hyde', *Inside Housing*, 19 November 2024 [Online]. https://www.insidehousing.co.uk/news/for-profit-provider-recruits-new-stock-acquisition-boss-from-hyde-89463 (accessed 31 March 2025).

24 Messenger, J., 'Kent-based provider completes 180-home stock transfer with provider owned by Octopus Real Estate', *Inside Housing*, 30 May 2024 [Online]. https://www.insidehousing.co.uk/news/kent-based-provider-completes-180-home-stock-transfer-with-provider-owned-by-octopus-real-estate-86704 (accessed 31 March 2025).

25 Hilditch, M., 'Ian McDermott talks Peabody's big merger and the future of social housing', *Inside Housing*, 28 January 2025 [Online]. https://www.insidehousing.co.uk/insight/insight/ian-mcdermott-talks-peabodys-big-merger-and-the-future-of-social-housing-90054 (accessed 31 March 2025).

Private renting

1 Finnerty, C. and Bicocchi, R., 'Understanding Recent Rental Trends in London's Private Rented Market', Greater London Authority, June 2023 [Online]. https://data.london.gov.uk/housing/research-notes/hrn-09-2023-understanding-recent-rental-trends-in-londons-private-rental-market/ (accessed 11 March 2025).

2 'Private rented housing supply in London', London Councils, 17 October 2024 [Online]. https://www.londoncouncils.gov.uk/news-and-press-releases/2024/private-rented-housing-supply-london (accessed 11 March 2025).

3 Das, S., 'Bidding wars, cash up-front and "auditions" – inside Britain's broken renting market', *Guardian*, 28 August 2022 [Online]. https://theguardian.com/money/2022/aug/28/bidding-wars-cash-up-front-and-auditions-inside-britains-broken-renting-market (accessed 11 March 2025).

4 Freedom of Information request responses received by the author in February 2025.

5 Stewart, J. and Jeavons, C., 'Regulating the Privately Rented Sector: What Can Universities Offer to Support Local Authority Workforce Development?', *Compass: Journal of Learning and Teaching in Higher Education*, 16.2 (2023), pp. 42–6, doi:10.21100/compass.v16i2.1447.

6 'Record £1.5bn invested in UK rental market by private equity firms', Private Equity Insights, January 9 2025 [Online]. https://pe-insights.com/record-1-5bn-invested-in-uk-rental-market-by-private-equity-firms/ (accessed 31 March 2025).

7 Freedom of Information response sent by Brent Council on 21 February 2025.

8 Cosh, G., 'Short-term and Holiday Letting in London', Greater London Authority, February 2020 [Online]. https://s3-eu-west-1.amazonaws.com/airdrive-images/wp-content/uploads/sites/6/20200804092416/GLA-Housing-Research-Note-4-Short-term-and-holiday-letting-in-London.pdf (accessed 11 March 2025).

9 Cairnes, S., 'Half of short-term lets in London "illegal" reveals Savills', *Negotiator*, 24 February 2025 [Online]. https://thenegotiator.co.uk/news/rental-market/more-and-more-landlords-switching-to-holiday-lets/ (accessed 11 March 2025).

10 Ibid.

11 'Only 5% of London private rentals affordable to low-income households, research finds', London Councils, 17 October 2024 [Online]. https://www.londoncouncils.gov.uk/node/10947 (accessed 11 March 2025).

12 McDonald, B., 'The Latin Village', Latino Life [Online]. https://www.latinolife.co.uk/gallery/latin-village (accessed 11 March 2025).

Buying a home

1. 'Housing in London 2024', Greater London Authority, November 2024 [Online]. https://data.london.gov.uk/housing/housing-in-london/ (accessed 11 March 2025).
2. Ibid.
3. Marriage, M. and Hammond, G., '"We are trapped": residents hit with soaring charges at luxury London homes', *Financial Times*, 13 March 2021 [Online]. https://www.ft.com/content/b135b814-dc9e-4abc-bb64-f378d11179d8 (accessed 31 March 2025).
4. 'Global investors could spark UK housebuilding boom', *FT Lex*, 19 January 2024 [Online]. https://www.ft.com/content/6f6b22a3-927c-43e3-808e-49f02beaf705 (accessed 31 March 2025).
5. 'Reasons for International Migration, International Students Update: November 2024', Office of National Statistics, 28 November 2024, [Online]. https://www.ons.gov.uk/peoplepopulationandcommunity/populationandmigration/internationalmigration/articles/reasonforinternationalmigrationinternationalstudentsupdate/november2024 (accessed 31 March 2025).
6. 'Student accommodation construction sector sees growth in demand', *Education Property*, 22 August 2024 [Online]. https://education-property.com/news/student-accommodation-construction-sector-sees-growth-in-demand/ (accessed 31 March 2025).
7. Jack, P., 'Average student rent in London now above maximum maintenance loan', *Times Higher Education*, December 10 2024 [Online]. https://www.timeshighereducation.com/news/average-student-rent-london-now-above-maximum-maintenance-loan (accessed 31 March 2025).
8. 'London SMEs will be worst hit by coronavirus but capital is set to remain as hub for enterprise growth', Simply Business [Online]. https://www.simplybusiness.co.uk/about_us/press_releases/london-sme-worst-hit/ (accessed 11 March 2025).
9. 'World Ultra Wealth Report', Wealth-X, 11 June 2024 [Online]. https://wealthx.com/reports/world-ultra-wealth-report-2024; 'The Wealth Report 2025', Knight Frank [Online]. https://www.knightfrank.com/wealthreport (both accessed 31 March 2025).
10. Bill, T., 'After the pandemic: London super-prime market rebounds as country house demand cools', Knight Frank, 15 December 2023 [Online]. https://www.knightfrank.com/research/

article/2023-12-15-after-the-pandemic-london-superprime-market-rebounds-as-country-house-demand-cools (accessed 11 March 2025).

11. Sachs, R., 'The Roaring Twenties: Why London is in a "golden decade" for super-prime property', *Spear's*, 24 May 2024 [Online]. https://spearswms.com/property/the-roaring-twenties-why-london-is-in-a-golden-decade-for-super-prime-property/ (accessed 11 March 2025).

12. 'London Helicopter Crossing Statistics 2007 to 2023', Civil Aviation Authority [Online]. https://www.caa.co.uk/publication/download/15813 (accessed 11 March 2025).

13. Atkinson, R., *Alpha City: How London Was Captured by the Super-rich* (Verso, 2020), p. 118.

14. MacMahon, A., 'London loses its crown as the five-star hotel capital of the world to Macau in the 2023 Forbes Travel Guide ratings, with the Chinese city now boasting the most top-rated hotels', *Mail Online*, 15 February 2023 [Online]. https://www.dailymail.co.uk/travel/article-11753115/London-loses-crown-worlds-5-star-hotel-capital-2023-Forbes-Travel-Guide-ratings.html (accessed 11 March 2025).

15. Craddock, I., 'These cities have the most Michelin-starred restaurants', *N&F*, 27 September 2024 [Online]. https://nearfarmag.com/these-cities-have-the-most-michelin-starred-restaurants (accessed 18 March 2025).

Homelessness

1. 'Highest ever recorded rough sleeping numbers in London', Homeless Link, 27 June 2024 [Online]. https://homeless.org.uk/news/highest-ever-recorded-rough-sleeping-numbers-in-london (accessed 11 March 2025).

2. Riding, J., 'Rough sleeping: on the frontline with an outreach team', *Inside Housing*, 18 December 2023 [Online]. https://www.insidehousing.co.uk/insight/rough-sleeping-on-the-frontline-with-an-outreach-team-84310 (accessed 11 March 2025).

3. 'On the Streets: An Investigation into Rough Sleeping', Shelter, December 2018 [Online]. https://england.shelter.org.uk/professional_resources/policy_and_research/policy_library/research_on_the_streets_-_an_investigation_into_rough_sleeping.

4. 'London's Temporary Accommodation Emergency – Housing Committee', London Assembly, March 2024 [Online]. https://

www.london.gov.uk/sites/default/files/2024-03/Housing%20 Committee%20-%20Temporary%20Accommodation%20report.pdf (accessed 11 March 2025).

5 Swindells, K., 'How many toddlers and babies are living in temporary accommodation in the UK?', *Inside Housing*, 20 December 2024 [Online]. https://www.insidehousing.co.uk/insight/how-many-toddlers-and-babies-are-living-in-temporary-accommodation-in-the-uk-86337 (accessed 11 March 2025).

6 'London's Temporary Accommodation Emergency – Housing Committee', London Assembly.

7 Burn-Murdoch, J., 'Why Britain is the worst in the world on homelessness', *Financial Times*, 17 May 2024 [Online]. https://www.ft.com/content/24117a03-37c2-424a-97ed-6a5292f9e92e (accessed 1 April 2025).

8 Hewitt, D. and Cooper, M., 'Exclusive: 55 homeless children have died in Temporary Accommodation since 2019', Shared Health Foundation, 5 March 2024 [Online]. https://sharedhealthfoundation.org.uk/news/exclusive-55-homeless-children-have-died-in-temporary-accommodation-since-2019/ (accessed 11 March 2025).

Exodus

1 'London's Population', London Datastore [Online]. https://data.london.gov.uk/dataset/londons-population (accessed 12 March 2025).

2 Lange, M., 'Escape to the country? How Covid changed London's population', Centre for Cities, 18 March 2024, Section 4 [Online]. https://www.centreforcities.org/reader/escape-to-the-country/population-decline-was-driven-by-people-moving-out-of-london/ (accessed 12 March 2025).

3 Salisbury, J., 'London population at "new record high" amid migration and reversal of Covid "race for space"', *Standard*, 18 March 2024 [Online]. https://www.standard.co.uk/news/london/london-population-covid-migration-centre-for-cities-space-rural-covid-b1145932.html (accessed 12 March 2025).

4 Brown, R., ' London's population growth is recovering, up to a point', *On London*, 19 July 2024 [Online]. https://www.onlondon.co.uk/richard-brown-londons-population-growth-is-recovering-up-to-a-point/ (accessed 12 March 2025).

5 Burns-Murdoch, J., 'London's parasitical housing market is driving away young families', *Financial Times*, 21 April 2023 [Online]. https://www.ft.com/content/d6bc22ed-d6d8-464b-b706-b4d478c6baf1 (accessed 1 April 2025).
6 Lewis, N., 'London's high rents causing big problems for recruiters', *LandlordZone*, 7 August 2024 [Online]. https://www.landlordzone.co.uk/news/londons-high-rents-causing-big-problems-in-jobs-market.
7 Yousef, A., 'Housing Affordability and Public-sector Recruitment in London', London Datastore, 28 August 2023 [Online]. https://data.london.gov.uk/blog/housing-affordability-and-public-sector-recruitment-in-london/ (accessed 12 March 2025).
8 Ibid.
9 'Housing crisis exacerbating teacher recruitment problems', *FE News*, 13 September 2023 [Online]. https://www.fenews.co.uk/work-leadership/housing-crisis-exacerbating-teacher-recruitment-problems/ (accessed 12 March 2025).
10 NHS Homes Alliance [Online]. https://www.nhshomesalliance.co.uk/ (accessed 12 March 2025).
11 Ibid.
12 Ward, J. and others, 'Key Worker Housing', Savills, 29 July 2024 [Online]. https://www.savills.co.uk/research_articles/229130/364541-0 (accessed 12 March 2025).
13 'Cost of living drives London nurses away and temp costs up – RCN', BBC News, 6 December 2023 [Online]. https://www.bbc.co.uk/news/uk-england-london-67626758 (accessed 12 March 2025).
14 Skopeliti, C., '"I can't do another year like last year": nurses in England on cost of living crisis', *Guardian*, 22 March 2024 [Online]. https://www.theguardian.com/society/2024/mar/22/nurses-england-cost-of-living-crisis-nhs (accessed 12 March 2025).
15 Gardner, J., 'Hospitality: London's recruitment crisis causing mental health issues', BBC News, 23 April 2022 [Online]. https://www.bbc.co.uk/news/uk-england-london-61149218 (accessed 12 March 2025).
16 Iafrati, S. and Clare, N., 'Out of Area Placements: Where Do the Households Go?', University of Nottingham, November 2024
17 'Canterbury barracks to house 200 Redbridge families', BBC News, 24 May 2016 [Online]. https://www.bbc.co.uk/news/uk-england-36370956 (accessed 12 March 2025).

18 'Temporary accommodation types in London (2002–2024 Q2)', Trust for London [Online]. https://trustforlondon.org.uk/data/temporary-accommodation-over-time/ (accessed 12 March 2025).
19 Gecsoyler, S., 'Councils move hundreds of homeless families out of London with 24-hour ultimatums', *Guardian*, 10 June 2024 [Online]. https://www.theguardian.com/society/article/2024/jun/10/councils-move-hundreds-homeless-families-london-24-hour-ultimatums (accessed 12 March 2025).
20 'Hundreds told: "Out of London or onto the streets"', *Waltham Forest Echo*, 1 October 2021 [Online]. https://walthamforestecho.co.uk/2021/10/01/hundreds-told-out-of-london-or-onto-the-streets/ (accessed 12 March 2025).
21 'Testimonials', Reloc8 UK [Online]. https://www.reloc8uk.co.uk/testimonials/ (accessed 12 March 2025).
22 Munro, V., 'Struggling Waltham Forest residents still being told to leave London', *Waltham Forest Echo*, 4 April 2023 [Online]. https://walthamforestecho.co.uk/2023/04/04/struggling-waltham-forest-residents-still-being-told-to-leave-london (accessed 12 March 2025).
23 '2021 Census', London Datastore [Online]. https://data.london.gov.uk/census/ (accessed 12 March 2025).
24 'Continued drop in school demand creates impossible choices for London schools', London Councils, 18 February 2025 [Online]. https://www.londoncouncils.gov.uk/news-and-press-releases/2025/continued-drop-school-places-demand-creates-impossible-choices-london (accessed 1 April 2025).
25 Barker, N., 'Housing crisis could be stopping two million people from having children, warns Affordable Housing Commission', *Inside Housing*, 24 February 2020 [Online]. https://www.insidehousing.co.uk/news/housing-crisis-could-be-stopping-two-million-people-from-having-children-warns-affordable-housing-commission-65176 (accessed 12 March 2025).
26 Apps, P., 'There are simply not enough children: London's housing crisis and the end of the city', *Peter's Substack*, 15 December 2023 [Online]. https://peteapps.substack.com/p/there-are-simply-not-enough-children (accessed 12 March 2025).
27 'Continued drop in school demand creates impossible choices for London schools', London Councils.

28 'Four primary schools in Hackney will close next September due to the ongoing decrease in the number of school-aged children', Hackney Council, 12 December 2023 [Online]. https://news.hackney.gov.uk/four-primary-schools-in-hackney-will-close-next-september-due-to-the-ongoing-decrease-in-the-number-of-school-aged-children/ (accessed 12 March 2025).

Generation rent growing old

1 Case studies taken from 'Hidden Renters: The Unseen Faces of the Rising Older Rental Wave', Independent Age, September 2023 [Online]. https://www.independentage.org/sites/default/files/2024-01/Hidden_renters_report_by_Independent_Age.pdf and 'Why Older Private Renters Need More Security', Age UK, January 2020 [Online]. https://www.ageuk.org.uk/siteassets/documents/reports-and-publications/reports-and-briefings/home-truths/home-truths---why-older-renters-need-more-security.pdf (both accessed 12 March 2025).

2 English Housing Survey 2012/13, Table 1 [Online]. https://www.gov.uk/government/statistics/english-housing-survey-2012-to-2013-headline-report (accessed 12 March 2025); English Housing Survey 2022/23, Annex Table 1.3 [Online]. https://www.gov.uk/government/statistics/annex-tables-for-english-housing-survey-headline-report-2022-to-2023 (accessed 11 March 2025).

3 '"Living in Fear": Experiences of Older Private-Renters in London', Age UK London [Online]. https://www.ageuk.org.uk/bp-assets/globalassets/london/documents/older-private-renters/living-in-fear.pdf (accessed 12 March 2025).

4 Montgomerie, J., 'Housing-based welfare strategies do not work and will not work', *British Politics and Policy at LSE* (blog), 30 January 2015 [Online]. https://blogs.lse.ac.uk/politicsandpolicy/homeownership-and-the-failures-of-asset-based-welfare/ (accessed 12 March 2025).

5 Interview with author, 14 March 2024.

6 'Two in five older private renters struggle to afford food, heating or clothes', National Housing Federation, 29 November 2023 [Online]. https://www.housing.org.uk/news-and-blogs/news/two-in-five-older-private-renters-struggle-to-afford-food-heating-or-clothes/ (accessed 12 March 2025).

7   Beveridge, A., 'An upsurge in older renters', Hamptons, July 2023 [Online]. https://www.hamptons.co.uk/articles/june-2023-lettings-index#/ (accessed 12 March 2025).
8   'Living pensions: An assessment of whether workers' pension saving meets a "living pension" benchmark', Resolution Foundation, 28 July 2022 [Online]. https://www.resolutionfoundation.org/publications/living-pensions/ (accessed 12 March 2025).
9   Crawford, R. and Karjalainen, H., 'Retirement saving of the self-employed', Institute for Fiscal Studies, 16 October 2020 [Online]. https://ifs.org.uk/publications/retirement-saving-self-employed (accessed 12 March 2025).
10 '2022 Retirement Report', Scottish Widows, June 2022 [Online]. https://adviser.scottishwidows.co.uk/assets/literature/docs/60677.pdf (accessed 12 March 2025).
11 Barnard, H., 'How do we defuse the pensioner poverty time bomb?', Joseph Rowntree Foundation, 2 March 2023 [Online]. https://www.jrf.org.uk/savings-debt-and-assets/how-do-we-defuse-the-pensioner-poverty-time-bomb (accessed 12 March 2025).
12 '"Will we ever summit the Pension Mountain?" – new analysis from Royal London', Royal London, 16 May 2018 [Online]. https://www.royallondon.com/about-us/media/media-centre/press-releases/archive/skyrocketing-cost-of-retiring-for-young/ (accessed 12 March 2025).
13 Barnard, 'How do we defuse the pensioner poverty time bomb?'
14 'Hidden Renters', Independent Age.
15 'Two in five older private renters struggle to afford food, heating or clothes', National Housing Federation.
16 'Households Below Average Income (HBAI) Statistics', Department for Work and Pensions, 23 March 2023, see https://www.gov.uk/government/collections/householdsbelow-average-income-hbai--2 (accessed 12 March 2025).
17 '"Living in Fear"', Age UK London.
18 Author interview.
19 English Housing Survey 2022/23.
20 'Older renters forced out of homes and communities by high costs, new report finds', Independent Age, 22 January 2024 [Online]. https://www.independentage.org/news-media/press-releases/older-renters-forced-out-of-homes-and-communities-by-high-costs-new (accessed 12 March 2025).

21 'New government data reveals accessible homes crisis for disabled people', Habinteg, 10 July 2020 [Online]. https://www.habinteg.org.uk/latest-news/new-government-data-reveals-accessible-homes-crisis-for-disabled-people-1557 (accessed 12 March 2025).
22 'Forecast for Accessible Homes 2020', Habinteg, January 2021 [Online]. https://www.habinteg.org.uk/download/forecast-for-accessible-homes-2020-finalpdf.pdf?ver=3581&doc=docm93jijm4n2829 (accessed 12 March 2025).
23 Belcher, E., Harding, C. and Quarshie, N., 'The Need and the Opportunity for Older People's Housing in London', in 'Third Age City: Housing for Older Londoners' [Online]. https://centreforlondon.org/reader/third-age-city/#the-need-and-the-opportunity-for-older-people8217s-housing-in-london (accessed 12 March 2025).
24 Brown, R., 'What has the 2021 census told us about London so far?', *On London*, 16 August 2022 [Online]. https://www.onlondon.co.uk/richard-brown-what-has-the-2021-census-told-us-about-london-so-far (accessed 12 March 2025).
25 Wills, J. and Belcher, E., 'London: A Place for Older People to Call Home', Centre for London [Online]. https://centreforlondon.org/reader/older-londoners-housing (accessed 12 March 2025).
26 'Passing on the Pounds: The Rise of the UK's Inheritance Economy', Kings Court Trust, February 2017 [Online]. Available at https://app-na1.hubspotdocuments.com/documents/2632673/view/49286495?accessId=f4570a (accessed 12 March 2025).
27 Hinsliff, G., 'Why inheritance is the dirty secret of the middle classes – harder to talk about than sex', *Guardian*, 3 December 2022 [Online]. https://www.theguardian.com/money/2022/dec/03/why-inheritance-is-the-dirty-secret-of-the-middle-classes-harder-to-talk-about-than-sex (accessed 12 March 2025).
28 Levitz, E., 'Will "the Great Wealth Transfer" trigger a millennial Civil War?', *Intelligencer*, 18 July 2021 [Online]. https://nymag.com/intelligencer/2021/07/will-the-great-wealth-transfer-spark-a-millennial-civil-war.html (accessed 12 March 2025).
29 'Sexual Orientation, England and Wales: Census 2021', Office for National Statistics [Online]. https://www.ons.gov.uk/peoplepopulationandcommunity/culturalidentity/sexuality/bulletins/sexualorientationenglandandwales/census2021 (accessed 12 March 2025).

Housing in the Anthropocene

1. 'Surface Water Flooding', Mayor of London [Online]. https://www.london.gov.uk/programmes-strategies/environment-and-climate-change/climate-change/climate-adaptation/surface-water-flooding (accessed 12 March 2025).
2. JBA Event Response, 'A retrospective look at summer 2021 London flash floods', JBA Risk Management, 15 September 2021 [Online]. https://www.jbarisk.com/products-services/event-response/a-retrospective-look-at-summer-2021-london-flash-floods/ (accessed 12 March 2025).
3. 'Surface Water Flooding in London: Roundtable Progress Report', Greater London Authority, March 2022, p. 28 [Online]. https://www.london.gov.uk/sites/default/files/flooding_progress_report_final_1.pdf (accessed 1 April 2025)
4. 'Half of renters have no home insurance in place, despite average £25k value of contents', Nationwide, 22 March 2021 [Online]. https://www.nationwidemediacentre.co.uk/news/half-of-renters-have-no-home-insurance-in-place-despite-average-gbp-25k-value-of-contents (accessed 12 March 2025).
5. Apps, P., 'Why are we building homes in high risk flood zones?', *Developer*, 14 November 2023 [Online]. https://thedeveloper.live/opinion/why-is-it-legal-to-build-homes-in-high-risk-flood-zones (accessed 12 March 2025).
6. 'London Sustainable Drainage Action Plan', Mayor of London [Online]. https://www.london.gov.uk/programmes-and-strategies/environment-and-climate-change/climate-change/surface-water/london-sustainable-drainage-action-plan (accessed 12 March 2025)
7. Hastings, R., 'Flash floods could cause disasters in UK cities – it's time for a drainage revolution', *i*, 20 August 2022 [Online]. https://inews.co.uk/news/environment/flash-floods-uk-cities-disasters-revolution-drainage-defences-1804627 (accessed 12 March 2025).
8. Milne, A., *London's Drowning* (Thames Methuen, 1982).
9. Ibid.
10. 'Thames Barrier closures', in 'The Thames Barrier', Environment Agency [Online]. https://www.gov.uk/guidance/the-thames-barrier#thames-barrier-closures (accessed 13 March 2025).
11. 'Thames Estuary 2100', Department for Environment, Food and Rural Affairs and Environment Agency [Online]. https://www.

gov.uk/government/collections/thames-estuary-2100-te2100 (accessed 13 March 2025).
12 McVeigh, K., 'Before the flood: how much longer will the Thames Barrier protect London?', *Guardian*, 30 June 2023 [Online]. https://www.theguardian.com/environment/2023/jun/30/before-the-flood-how-much-longer-will-the-thames-barrier-protect-london (accessed 13 March 2025).
13 White, A., '"London will flood and when it happens, it will be dramatic"', *Developer*, 24 October 2019 [Online]. https://www.thedeveloper.live/opinion/opinion/london-will-flood-and-when-it-happens-it-will-be-dramatic (accessed 13 March 2025).
14 'Major updates to Thames Estuary 2100 from 2012 to 2023', Department for Environment, Food and Rural Affairs and Environment Agency, 19 April 2023 [Online]. https://www.gov.uk/guidance/major-updates-to-thames-estuary-2100-from-2012-to-2023 (accessed 13 March 2025).
15 'Flood Risks in London: Summary of Findings', London Assembly Environment Committee, April 2014 [Online]. https://www.london.gov.uk/sites/default/files/gla_migrate_files_destination/14-04-07-Flood%20risk%20slide%20pack%20-%20FINAL_0.pdf (accessed 1 April 2025).
16 Lomas, K. and others, 'Dwelling and Household Characteristics' Influence on Reported and Measured Summertime Overheating: A Glimpse of a Mild Climate in the 2050's', *Building and Environment* 201 (2021), 107986, doi:10.1016/j.buildenv.2021.107986.
17 'Addressing Overheating Risk in Existing UK Homes', Arup [Online]. https://www.theccc.org.uk/wp-content/uploads/2022/10/Addressing-overheating-risk-in-existing-UK-homes-Arup.pdf (accessed 13 March 2025).
18 Lomas and others, 'Dwelling and Household Characteristics' Influence on Reported and Measured Summertime Overheating'.
19 'Addressing Overheating Risk in Existing UK Homes', Arup.
20 Weiss, S., 'New reservoirs could help battle droughts, but at what cost?', *Wired*, 12 September 2022 [Online]. https://www.wired.com/story/new-water-reservoirs (accessed 13 March 2025).
21 Sawer, P., 'Wennington fire: compost blaze that devastated village started just yards from fire station', *Telegraph*, 20 July 2022 [Online]. https://www.telegraph.co.uk/news/2022/07/20/

wennington-fire-compost-blaze-devastated-village-started-just/ (accessed 13 March 2025).
22. Lynch, B., 'Wennington fire: government support sought as council continues to work with residents'. *Romford Recorder*, 4 August 2022 [Online]. https://www.romfordrecorder.co.uk/news/20677199. wennington-fire-government-support-sought-council-continues-work-residents/ (accessed 13 March 2025).
23. Topping, A., 'Heatwave led to London firefighters' busiest day since Second World War', *Guardian*, 20 July 2022 [Online]. https://www.theguardian.com/uk-news/2022/jul/20/heatwave-led-to-london-firefighters-busiest-day-since-second-world-war (accessed 13 March 2025).
24. Stedman, H., 'Wennington resident fears "another accident" year on from fire', *Independent*, 18 July 2023 [Online]. https://www.independent.co.uk/climate-change/news/london-fire-brigade-havering-london-upminster-b2377010.html (accessed 13 March 2025).
25. Shennan, R., 'UK fires: map of wildfires and house fires caused by heatwave 2022 – from London to Dartford and Norfolk', *National World*, 20 July 2022 [Online]. https://www.nationalworld.com/news/weather/uk-fires-map-wildfires-house-heatwave-2022-london-dartford-norfolk-3775433 (accessed 13 March 2025).
26. Brignal, M., 'How climate change is pushing up the cost of your home insurance', *Telegraph*, 11 October 2023 [Online]. https://www.telegraph.co.uk/money/bills/insurance/climate-change-increasing-cost-home-insurance/ (accessed 13 March 2025).

Another way

1. Mason, C., 'The amateur landlord dream is dying – here are the numbers that show it', *i Paper*, 12 March 2025 [Online]. https://inews.co.uk/inews-lifestyle/money/property-and-mortgages/amateur-landlord-dream-dying-numbers-3580230 (accessed 2 April 2025).
2. Butler, P. and Rushe, D., 'UN accuses Blackstone Group of contributing to global housing crisis', *Guardian*, 26 March 2019 [Online]. https://www.theguardian.com/us-news/2019/mar/26/blackstone-group-accused-global-housing-crisis-un (accessed 13 March 2025).
3. O'Halloran, B., 'Ryanair buys most of the homes in new Dublin estate to rent to cabin crew', *Irish Times*, 25 January 2024 [Online]. https://www.irishtimes.com/business/2024/01/25/

ryanair-buys-25-homes-in-north-dublin-estate-to-rent-to-cabin-crew/ (accessed 13 March 2025).
4. Hale, T. and Wang X., 'China's migrant dorm entrepeneur bets on demand for cheaper housing', *Financial Times*, 2 February 2025 [Online]. https://www.ft.com/content/47b4e2af-e1f9-442c-b811-937446231602 (accessed 2 April 2025).
5. 'Germany has the highest proportion of rental tenants in the EU', Destatis [Online] https://www.destatis.de/Europa/EN/Topic/Population-Labour-Social-Issues/Social-issues-living-conditions/RentedAccommodation.html (accessed 13 March 2025).
6. 'Germany: 13.0% living in households overburdened by housing costs', Destatis [Online]. https://www.destatis.de/Europa/EN/Topic/Population-Labour-Social-Issues/Social-issues-living-conditions/HousingCosts.html (accessed 13 March 2025).
7. Stole, B., 'The tension is building: How Berlin lost its affordable housing crown', *Berliner*, 19 November 2024 [Online]. https://www.the-berliner.com/politics/berlin-affordable-housing-apartment-shortage-crisis-construction-rent-real-estate/ (accessed 13 March 2025).
8. As quoted in Glass, R., 'Housing in Camden', *The Town Planning Review*, Vol. 41, No. 1 (January 1970), pp. 15–40 (Liverpool University Press).
9. Hansard, HC Deb., vol. 884, col. 2070, 23 January 1975.
10. Ellis, D., 'After Grenfell, what can we learn from the housing policies of the 1970s?', History & Policy [Online]. https://www.historyandpolicy.org/opinion-articles/articles/after-grenfell-what-can-we-learn-from-the-housing-policies-of-the-1970s (accessed 13 March 2025).
11. Delahunty, S., 'Burnham unveils new powers for councils to buy up poor-quality homes and let to social housing tenants', *Inside Housing*, 27 June 2023 [Online]. https://www.insidehousing.co.uk/news/news/burnham-unveils-new-powers-for-councils-to-buy-up-poor-quality-homes-and-let-to-social-housing-tenants-82102 (accessed 13 March 2025).
12. Wilmore, J., 'Khan unveils plan for councils to buy 10,000 private homes', *Inside Housing*, 20 November 2023 [Online]. https://www.insidehousing.co.uk/news/khan-unveils-plan-for-councils-to-buy-10000-private-homes-83963 (accessed 13 March 2025).
13. Gayne, D., 'Financing affordable housing impossible in London, says CEO of homelessness non-profit forced to close', *Housing Today*,

10 April 2025 [Online]. https://www.housingtoday.co.uk/news/financing-affordable-housing-impossible-in-london-says-ceo-of-homelessness-non-profit-forced-to-close/5135470.article (accessed 25 July 2025).

14 Riding, J., 'Major house builder sells 102 homes built for market sale to east London council for social housing', *Inside Housing*, 28 June 2023 [Online]. https://www.insidehousing.co.uk/news/major-house-builder-sells-102-homes-built-for-market-sale-to-east-london-council-for-social-housing-82104 (accessed 13 March 2025).

15 Lydall, R., 'Affordable housing in London: councils and housing associations call for £5bn to buy unsold private homes', *Standard*, 7 July 2020 [Online]. https://www.standard.co.uk/homesandproperty/property-news/affordable-housing-london-unsold-private-homes-councils-a139171.html (accessed 13 March 2025).

16 Apps, P., 'The enduring economic case for Build Social', *Inside Housing*, 14 November 2023 [Online]. https://www.insidehousing.co.uk/insight/the-enduring-economic-case-for-build-social-83454 (accessed 13 March 2025).

17 Salas-Rojo, P., 'The trap of the "tenant generation": the case of Spain', *LSE Inequalities* (blog), 5 March 2024 [Online]. https://blogs.lse.ac.uk/inequalities/2024/03/05/the-trap-of-the-tenant-generation/ (accessed 13 March 2025).

18 Martínez, M. and Gil, J., 'The Struggle against Home Evictions in Spain through Documentary Films', *International Journal of Housing Policy* 22.3 (2022), 371–94, doi:10.1080/19491247.2021.1947124.

19 'Missions in Action: MOIN Casebook 2024', Institute for Innovation and Public Purpose, November 2024 [Online]. https://www.ucl.ac.uk/bartlett/public-purpose/sites/bartlett_public_purpose/files/moin_2024_casebook_-_missions_in_action.pdf (accessed 13 March 2025).

20 *Housing Barcelona: Barcelona 2015–2023*, Barcelona City Council, April 2023 [Online]. https://bcnroc.ajuntament.barcelona.cat/jspui/bitstream/11703/130616/7/HOUSING.pdf (accessed 13 March 2025).

21 Jofre-Monseny, J., Martínez-Mazza, R. and Segú, M., 'Effectiveness and Supply Effects of High-Coverage Rent Control Policies', *Regional Science and Urban Economics* 101 (2023), 103916, doi:10.1016/j.regsciurbeco.2023.103916.

22 Garcia Montalvo, J., Monras., J. and Raya, J., 'Los efectos de la limitación de precios de los alquileres en Cataluña', *Esade EcPol*

Insight 44 (2023) [Online]. https://www.esade.edu/ecpol/en/publicaciones/los-efectos-de-la-limitacion-de-precios-de-los-alquileres-en-cataluna/ (accessed 4 April 2025).

23 Whitehead, C. and Williams, P., 'Assessing the Evidence on Rent Control from an International Perspective', LSE London, October 2018 [Online]. https://www.lse.ac.uk/business/consulting/assets/documents/assessing-the-evidence-on-rent-control-from-an-international-perspective.pdf (accessed 7 March 2025).

24 Godard, N., 'Calculating the mixed impact of rent controls on French cities', *Le Monde*, 19 April 2024 [Online]. https://www.lemonde.fr/en/money-investments/article/2024/04/19/calculating-the-mixed-impact-of-rent-controls-on-french-cities_6668876_102.html?random=20825769 (accessed 7 March 2025).

25 'Rent restrictions impeding housing supply', Housing Ireland [Online]. https://housingireland.ie/rent-restrictions-impeding-housing-supply/ (accessed 7 March 2025).

26 Dickens, R., 'Gaining consensus for the Minimum Wage', University of Sussex [Online]. https://www.sussex.ac.uk/research/explore-our-research/business-and-economics/minimum-rage (Accessed 7 March 2025).

27 'Celebrating 70 Years of the New Towns Act', Town & Country Planning Association, 2017 [Online]. https://www.tcpa.org.uk/wp-content/uploads/2021/11/TCPA_TSP19_FINAL_VERSION.pdf (accessed 7 March 2025).

28 Apps, P., 'Oliver asks for more: a look at the Letwin Review', *Inside Housing*, 1 November 2018 [Online]. https://www.insidehousing.co.uk/insight/oliver-asks-for-more-a-look-at-the-letwin-review-58836 (accessed 7 March 2025).

29 Royal Institute of British Architects (RIBA), 'Foundations for the Future: a new delivery model for social housing' (February 2025), https://www.architecture.com/about/policy/social-housing-report-in-full (accessed on 11 June 2025).

30 Barker, N., 'Just 2.6% of homes built on public land will be for social rent, says thinktank', *Inside Housing*, 18 February 2020 [Online]. https://www.insidehousing.co.uk/news/just-26-of-homes-built-on-public-land-will-be-for-social-rent-says-thinktank-65104 (accessed 7 March 2025).

31 'Foundations for the Future: a new delivery model for social housing – an explainer', *RIBA*, 23 September 2024 [Online].

https://www.architecture.com/knowledge-and-resources/knowledge-landing-page/foundations-for-the-future-a-new-delivery-model-for-social-housing-an-explainer (accessed 7 March 2025).
32 'Kes: Citizen's House', London CLT [Online]. https://www.londonclt.org/kes (accessed 2 April 2025).
33 Maaoui, M., 'Social contract: Parisian social housing', *Architectural Review*, 30 June 2022 [Online]. https://www.architectural-review.com/buildings/housing/social-contract-parisian-social-housing (accessed 7 March 2025).
34 'Housing: one year after the "Kasbarian 1" law, outcry against "Kasbarian 2"', Batinfo, 4 June 2024 [Online]. https://batinfo.com/en/actuality/housing-one-year-after-the-Kasbarian-law-1-outcry-against-Kasbarian-2_28642 (accessed 7 March 2025).
35 Interview with Zoe Kenan.
36 Frearson, A., 'Tour Bois-le-Prêtre by Frédéric Druot, Anne Lacaton and Jean-Philippe Vassal', *dezeen*, 16 April 2013 [Online]. https://www.dezeen.com/2013/04/16/tour-bois-le-pretre-by-frederic-druot-anne-lacaton-and-jean-philippe-vassal/ (accessed 7 March 2025).
37 Wainwright, O., '"Sometimes the answer is to do nothing": unflashy French duo take architecture's top prize', *Guardian*, 16 March 2021 [Online]. https://www.theguardian.com/artanddesign/2021/mar/16/lacaton-vassal-unflashy-french-architectures-pritzker-prize (accessed 7 March 2025).
38 Messenger, J., 'RSH Global Accounts: spend on repairs and maintenance reaches "record" £8.8bn', *Inside Housing*, 9 January 2025 [Online]. https://www.insidehousing.co.uk/news/rsh-global-accounts-spend-on-repairs-and-maintenance-reaches-record-88bn-89975 (accessed 7 March 2025).
39 '2024 Global Accounts of private registered providers', Regulator of Social Housing, 9 January 2025 [Online]. https://www.gov.uk/government/publications/2024-global-accounts-of-private-registered-providers (accessed 7 March 2025).

Index

2012 Olympics 74, 93–4, 105–6, 121–2

ACORN 300
affordable housing
  in the 2000s 99–100
  in the 2010s 108–10, 128, 130, 137
  2012 Olympics 74, 122
  in the 2020s 154
  contemporary trends 212–13
affordable rents 129–30, 152
air pollution 52–3
Airbnb 165, 266
the Anthropocene 233–6
Apak, Meric 137
arm's-length management organisation (ALMO) 79, 80–1, 141–2
austerity, public spending in the 2010s 103, 125
Austria, social housing in 282–3

banlieues 286–7
Barratt 86, 262
bedroom tax 130
belonging, sense of 7–8
Bellamy, Jessica 274–5
benefits cap 129–30
Berlin, rental sector in 256–9, 300
bike hire scheme, London 104
Binfield, Michelle 93, 125, 180
black-cab drivers 104
black mould
  2010s housing 127–8
  2020s housing 2, 113, 150, 151, 166
  health impacts 182–4, 185, 215
  new technologies 295
Black people
  in the 1980s 41–2
  in the 2010s 203
  housing in the US 274–5
  racist policing 17
Blackstone 155, 174, 175, 252
Blair, Tony 71–2, 73, 98
boom and bust 65, 96–7
Brexit 139
Brown, Gordon 98, 102, 278
Brussels, community land trust (CLT) 283–4
building *see* house-building market
bust *see* boom and bust
buying a home 171–8
buy-to-let mortgages 61–2, 118–19

Callaghan, Pat 136
Cameron, David 108–9, 128, 136, 138–9
care home availability 225
Carlyle 174
Cave, Martin 132
change of use 281, 282
Chartered Institute of Housing 57
child mortality 186
cities, increasing population in 9–11
Citra 174
climate change 248–50
  extreme weather events in the 2000s 74–5
  flood risk 74–5, 233–40
  heatwaves 240–3
  wildfire risk 243–8

Index

CLT *see* community land trust (CLT) model
coffee shops 105
Cohen, Geoff 8
community land trust (CLT) model 283–5
Competition and Markets Authority 280
consumer-focused lifestyles 147
cost-based rents 294, 295
Council Homes Acquisition Programme 260
council housing *see* social housing
Covid-19 lockdowns 162, 173
credit ratings 297–8
crisis of belonging 7–8

debt, UK national debt 297–9
Decent Homes Programme 79, 141–2
Defend Council Housing 80
deindustrialisation 15–16
delivery drivers 104
demolition, vs. refurbishment 86–7, 289–94
Denmark, cost-based rents 295
deregulation
 banking and housing rules 47–9
 planning policy 108–11
 private landlords 37–9, 90–1
devolution 73
dockyards area of London 99–100
Douglas, Steve 129

Ebbsfleet development 278–9
Edwards, Michael 251
emmigrating out *see* migration out of London
enforcement of housing standards
 future policy recommendations 271–2, 285
 in light of austerity 152
 Renters Rights Bill 273

situation as of 2025 164–5
English Housing Survey 151
environmental health officers 164–5
estate regeneration 83–8
ethnic minorities
 in the 1980s 41–7
 in the 1990s 50, 53–6, 67–8
 in the 2000s 76
 in the 2010s 203
 changes in the 1990s 50–1
 housing in the US 274–5
 racist policing 17
Expropriate Deutsche Wohnen and Co.! 257

Facebook 101
far right 8–9, 288
financial crisis (2008) 101, 106–7
fire and rescue service 103–4
fire incidents
 Grenfell Tower 118, 143
 temporary accommodation 184
 wildfire risk 243–8
flood risk 74–5, 233–40
France
 rental sector 269–70
 social housing 286–90

Genesis (housing association) 133
gentrification, origin of term 259
George, Henry 9
Germany
 major cities 286
 rental sector in 256–9
gig economy 1–3, 104, 120, 218
gilt market 298
global financial crisis (2008) 101, 106–7
global warming *see* climate change
Greater London Authority (GLA) 24, 30, 73, 165, 197
 see also London County Council (LCC)

green belt, around London 281–2
Grenfell Tower fire 118, 143, 171–2
Hadden, Neil 133
health and safety *see* environmental health officers; fire incidents
health implications of living in poor housing 183–5, 186, 215
heatwaves 74–5, 240–3
Heidegger, Martin 8
Help to Buy 114–17
HMOs *see* houses in multiple occupation
holiday lets 165
'home' as concept
  crisis of belonging 7–8
  definitions 6–7
  home vs. investment 5–6, 111
home ownership
  in the 1980s 31, 41–9
  in the 1990s 65–6
  in the 2010s 114–15, 129–30
  in the 2020s 172–8
  comparison of UK with other European nations 256–9, 264, 266
  inheritance economy 227–8
  leasehold 100–1
  as policy goal 296
Homebuy scheme 96–8
homelessness
  current scale and international comparison 186
  due to unaffordable housing 125, 180
  leading up to London Olympics 93–4
  recent trends 179–86
house prices
  in the 1990s 63, 65–70
  in the 2000s 96–8
  in the 2010s 107, 115, 130
  in the 2020s 197–9

inheritance economy 227–9
  and interest rates 253
  since 1980s 3–6
house-building market
  in the 1970s 259
  in the 2000s 98–9
  barriers to prompt building 279–81
  care home availability 225
  community land trust model 283–5
  demolition vs. refurbishment 86–7, 289–94
  impact of Help to Buy 116–17
  in Spain 264
  trend towards smaller homes 99–100
house-price-to-income ratio 96
houses in multiple occupation (HMOs)
  in the 2000s 92–3, 96
  in the 2010s 119–20
Houses of Parliament, Westminster 286
Housing Act 1988 30
housing associations
  in the 2010s 132–5
  lack of action 150
  for profit 154–7
housing benefit
  in the 1980s 38
  in the 1990s 60–3
  in the 2000s 92
  in the 2010s 121, 123
housing conditions
  2010s housing 127–8
  in the 2020s 2, 113, 150, 151, 166–7
  health impacts 182–4, 185, 215
  new technologies 295
  see also enforcement
housing movements 299–300

immigration *see* migration to London
informal economy *see* gig economy
inheritance economy 227–9
interest rates 253
interest-only repayments 61
international finance 297–9
international purchase of London property 111
investment, property as
  in the 1990s 61, 62, 63
  in the 2000s 91–2, 95
  in the 2010s 125–6
  in the 2020s 165
  as deliberate policy change 5–6
  international purchase of London property 111
iPhone 101
Ireland, David 282, 284
Ireland, rental sector 269–70
IV One (GP) LLP 165

John, Peter 137–8
Johnson, Boris 104, 109

Labour Party
  in the 1970s 260
  in control of London County Council 24, 258
  election of Tony Blair 71–2
  growth areas 98–9
Lacaton, Anne 290, 292, 301
land prices
  in the 2010s 120–1
  change of use 281
  community land trust model 283–4
  international wealth 111
  RIBA report on public land 280–1
  rising with house prices 251
  Who Owns England project 285
leaks in rental properties 63–4, 81, 86, 150, 169
leasehold 100–1, 173–4
Legal and General Affordable Homes 155
Lendlease 137–8
Letwin, Oliver 279–80
Livingstone, Ken 30, 73
local housing allowance (LHA) 92, 123–4
Lock, Katy 278
London
  gig economy 1–3
  increasing urbanisation 9–11
  as our country's capital of everything 285–6
London County Council (LCC) 22, 24, 85, 258
  see also Greater London Authority (GLA)
London Renters Union 300
Louisville, Kentucky 273–5, 300
luxury rentals 120

macroeconomics
  house price rises 69–70
  uniqueness of housing and land 270–1
Macron, Emmanuel 288
maintenance, of social housing 289–95
  see also housing conditions
malnutrition 184
May, Theresa 139
mental health 112
migration out of London
  in the 2000s 76–7
  in the 2020s 189–213
migration to London
  in the 1970s-80s 25, 34, 42–7
  in the 1990s 50, 53–4
  in the 2000s 75–6
  in the 2010s 127
  post-war 41–2

mortgages
　buy-to-let 61–2, 118–19
　defaults on 101
　house price rises during 1990s 69–70
　increasing size of 96–8
　link between earnings and house prices 65–6
　link between interest rates and house prices 253
　negative equity 66
mould
　2010s housing 127–8
　2020s housing 2, 113, 150, 151, 166
　health impacts 182–4, 185, 215
　new technologies 295
Mulheirn, Ian 253–4, 298
multi-occupational tenancies
　in the 2000s 92–3, 96
　in the 2010s 119–20
municipalisation 256–63

national debt 297–9
nationalisation of housing 257–63
negative equity 66
the Netherlands 282
New Towns Act 277
new-towns, renewal of 278–9
no-fault evictions 252

Octopus Real Estate 155
off plan sales 107–8
Olympics, hosted in London (2012) 74, 93–4, 105–6, 121–2
Osborne, George 128, 288
overcrowding 153, 166–7

parental help to buy a house 227–9
Paris
　rental sector 269–70
　social housing 286–90
Peabody 30, 151–2, 155, 226

Peaker, Giles 137
pension plans, using property as security 63, 91–2, 95
pensioners, affordability of housing 122–3, 142, 157, 214–32
pests, in social housing 150, 183–4
planning policy, deregulation 108–11
police stations, sale of 104
political centrality of London 285–6
pollution 52–3
population
　in the 2010s 119
　changes in the 1990s 50–1
　increasing urbanisation 9–11
poverty
　in the 1990s 51–2
　in the 2010s 103
　in present-day London 147
Power, Anne 84, 88
Pritzker Prize 290, 292–3
private finance initiative (PFI) 79, 80
private landlords
　in the 1980s 33–9
　in the 1990s 60–3
　in the 2000s 77, 79–81, 91
　in the 2010s 118–19
　in the 2020s 157–70
　deregulation 37–9, 90–1
　home vs. investment 5–6
public services, austerity in the 2010s 103

quantitative easing 106–7

race
　in the 1980s 41–7
　in the 1990s 53–6, 67–8
　in the 2000s 76
　in the 2010s 203
　changes in the 1990s 50–1

Index   343

housing in the US 274–5
racist policing 17
Realstar Group 165
refurbishment, vs. demolition 86–7, 289–94
regeneration, of council estates 83–8
rent controls 268–73
rental sector
   in the 1980s 33–9
   in the 1990s 60–3
   in the 2000s 77, 79–81, 91
   in the 2010s 118–21
   in the 2020s 157–70
   ageing and insecurity 214–32
   deregulation 37–9, 90–1
   in France 269–70
   in Germany 256–9
   in Ireland 269–70
   luxury developments 120
   predicting the future 252–6
   recent reduction of number of homes 162–3
   in Spain 263–8
   UK compared to other countries 268–9
Right to Buy
   in the 1980s 27–8, 38
   in the 1990s 57, 65, 70–1, 82
   in the 2010s 136
   Council Homes Acquisition Programme 260
   homes then being let again 136
   leading to reduction of council housing stock 259, 278
rough-sleeping, efforts to reduce 93–4
Royal Institute of British Architects (RIBA) 280–1

Sage 155
Savills 154–5, 200
Segal, Walter 284

shared ownership 130
Sheffield, Park Hill flats 292–3
short-term rentals 165, 266
skyline of London 73–4, 104, 116–17
smog 52–3
social housing
   in the 1980s 26–31
   in the 1990s 53–4, 57–60, 62–3
   in the 2000s 79–85, 102
   in the 2010s 123, 128–37, 138–9, 141–3
   in the 2020s 149–51, 152–5
   estate regeneration 83–8
   in France 286–90
   in Germany 257
   options to build more 281–5
   tenancy availability 152–3
Spain
   left-wing populism 299–300
   rental sector in 263–8
speculative development 108
standard of housing *see* housing conditions
Starmer, Keir 278
Sterling Prize 293
Stratford, Beth 270, 271
student housing 120–1
subprime mortgages 101
surface water flooding 234, 237–8

tax
   on developers 281–2
   on landlords 271–3
taxi drivers 104
technological change 295
temperatures, increasing due to climate change 74–5, 240–3
temporary accommodation, council-funded 123–5, 183–6
Tenant Services Authority 132
terrorism, in the 1990s 52–3
Thames Gateway 99–100

Thatcher, Margaret 9, 57–60, 90–1, 279–80
transport in London 104
Tweneboa, Kwajo 153, 294, 300

Uber 104
United States
  homelessness rate 186
  Louisville, Kentucky 273–6
urbanisation as population trend 9–11

Vassal, Jean-Phillipe 289, 290, 292, 301
Vienna, social housing in 282–3

water, access to 184

Who Owns England project 285
wildfire risk 243–8
working class
  in the 1980s 17, 20–3
  in the 1990s 50–1, 53–4
  in the 2000s 85–7, 141–2
  in the 2010s 104–6
  deindustrialisation 15–16
  gig economy 1–3
  inheritance economy 228–9
  migration out of London 201–2
World War II 299

YouTube 101
Žižek, Slavoj 301

zoning laws 282

housing in the US 274–5
racist policing 17
Realstar Group 165
refurbishment, vs. demolition 86–7, 289–94
regeneration, of council estates 83–8
rent controls 268–73
rental sector
  in the 1980s 33–9
  in the 1990s 60–3
  in the 2000s 77, 79–81, 91
  in the 2010s 118–21
  in the 2020s 157–70
  ageing and insecurity 214–32
  deregulation 37–9, 90–1
  in France 269–70
  in Germany 256–9
  in Ireland 269–70
  luxury developments 120
  predicting the future 252–6
  recent reduction of number of homes 162–3
  in Spain 263–8
  UK compared to other countries 268–9
Right to Buy
  in the 1980s 27–8, 38
  in the 1990s 57, 65, 70–1, 82
  in the 2010s 136
  Council Homes Acquisition Programme 260
  homes then being let again 136
  leading to reduction of council housing stock 259, 278
rough-sleeping, efforts to reduce 93–4
Royal Institute of British Architects (RIBA) 280–1

Sage 155
Savills 154–5, 200
Segal, Walter 284

shared ownership 130
Sheffield, Park Hill flats 292–3
short-term rentals 165, 266
skyline of London 73–4, 104, 116–17
smog 52–3
social housing
  in the 1980s 26–31
  in the 1990s 53–4, 57–60, 62–3
  in the 2000s 79–85, 102
  in the 2010s 123, 128–37, 138–9, 141–3
  in the 2020s 149–51, 152–5
  estate regeneration 83–8
  in France 286–90
  in Germany 257
  options to build more 281–5
  tenancy availability 152–3
Spain
  left-wing populism 299–300
  rental sector in 263–8
speculative development 108
standard of housing *see* housing conditions
Starmer, Keir 278
Sterling Prize 293
Stratford, Beth 270, 271
student housing 120–1
subprime mortgages 101
surface water flooding 234, 237–8

tax
  on developers 281–2
  on landlords 271–3
taxi drivers 104
technological change 295
temperatures, increasing due to climate change 74–5, 240–3
temporary accommodation, council-funded 123–5, 183–6
Tenant Services Authority 132
terrorism, in the 1990s 52–3
Thames Gateway 99–100

Thatcher, Margaret 9, 57–60, 90–1,
    279–80
transport in London 104
Tweneboa, Kwajo 153, 294, 300

Uber 104
United States
    homelessness rate 186
    Louisville, Kentucky 273–6
    urbanisation as population trend
    9–11
Vassal, Jean-Phillipe 289, 290, 292,
    301
Vienna, social housing in 282–3

water, access to 184

Who Owns England project 285
wildfire risk 243–8
working class
    in the 1980s 17, 20–3
    in the 1990s 50–1, 53–4
    in the 2000s 85–7, 141–2
    in the 2010s 104–6
    deindustrialisation 15–16
    gig economy 1–3
    inheritance economy 228–9
    migration out of London 201–2
World War II 299

YouTube 101
Žižek, Slavoj 301

zoning laws 282